"So the Witch Won't Eat Me"

*Fantasy and the
Child's Fear of Infanticide*

"So the Witch Won't Eat Me"

*Fantasy and the
Child's Fear of Infanticide*

Dorothy Bloch

Houghton Mifflin Company Boston   1978

Library of Congress Cataloging in Publication Data

Bloch, Dorothy.
  "So the witch won't eat me."

  Includes bibliographical references.
  1. Child analysis. 2. Psychoanalysis.
3. Fear in children. 4. Fantasy in children.
5. Infanticide. 6. Fear of death. I. Title.
RJ504.2.B57   618.9'28'522   78-13115
ISBN 0-395-26290-9

Printed in the United States of America

V 10 9 8 7 6 5 4 3 2 1

This book is dedicated to my patients,
a constant source of insight
and inspiration

PREFACE

ALTHOUGH THIS BOOK is a departure from — I would prefer to call it an extension of — Freud's thinking, I would like to express my indebtedness to him for the inspiration of his extraordinary contribution. No matter how far we may deviate from his theories, his concepts frequently provide the impetus and serve as a springboard for the explorations of whatever fresh areas we may enter. In pursuing his theories further, using the tools he has bequeathed to us, we merely follow the example he so admirably set in his brilliant efforts to understand the human psyche.

My own search for a cohesive theory of what we have called emotional "illness," and a growing sense of the role of violence in its causation, suddenly became focused some fifteen years ago when Dr. Hyman Spotnitz called my attention to Freud's omission from his theory of the Oedipus complex of the parents' attempt to kill Oedipus. I am indebted to Dr. Spotnitz for the intellectual commotion that followed and for his continuing interest and encouragement. His own departure from Freud's theory of treatment stresses the primary importance of eliciting the patient's aggressive feelings, which has made possible the successful treatment of schizophrenic patients and has been of inestimable value to me in treating my patients. I am also indebted to him for his assistance in formulating the difference between homosexual fantasy and homosexual identity in Chapter 3, for reading this manuscript, and for the insistence that resulted in the writing of Chapter 13 and in the elaboration of the dynamics of several of the fantasies. Responsibility for the concepts that have finally resulted in this book, however, is entirely mine.

I would like to thank the *Psychoanalytic Review* for permission to reprint substantial sections of several chapters, which originally appeared in that journal, and *Modern Psychoanalysis* for permission to reprint Chapter 7. My thanks also go to Marie Coleman Nelson, editor, and to Murray H. Sherman, coeditor, of the *Psychoanalytic Review* for reading and commenting on this manuscript.

I am also grateful to Mary Wolman, a child psychologist and a friend, on whom I could always rely for her sensitive response and her never-failing interest in my concepts as they evolved; to Frances Tenenbaum, who facilitated the journey of the manuscript; to all those friends whose enthusiastic support has been an ever-present resource; and to Yuri Suhl, in particular, for his kind and generous help.

And, last, to my editor, David Harris, whose suggestions have enhanced this work and whose enthusiasm and appreciation have helped ease that last effort required to transform a manuscript into a book.

DOROTHY BLOCH

New York City
April 1978

CONTENTS

Introduction

Fantasy and the Child's
Fear of Infanticide

IF ANYONE HAD suggested, when I started my psychoanalytic practice some twenty-five years ago, that my patients would fear that I — or their parents — might kill them, I think I might have responded with shock. I might even have rejected it as somebody's nightmare. That the fear of infanticide might be their central preoccupation? Absurd.

As one child after another admitted me to his world of fantasy, however, I witnessed a terror of being killed that varied only in its intensity. Although frequently it was deeply buried in the unconscious of my adult patients, I discovered that in children it was usually right on the surface. Almost invariably they informed me, very often during their first session, of what they experienced as the precariousness of their lives. One four-and-a-half-year-old, whose terror I came to know in much greater detail, solemnly announced that her drawings were entitled "Danger City" and "Danger Sky." A six-year-old was too preoccupied with watching the clouds in fear of their "crashing" to engage in play. Another five-year-old, white-faced and unsmiling, confided that he had two pencils in his eyes that, whenever needed, could come out and shoot. When I casually commented to another six-year-old that I had noticed he always made sure we were seated at the table, but on opposite sides, he responded with a hysterical laugh, "So the witch won't eat me!"

Until I started treating children, my understanding of fantasy did not go much beyond its wish-fulfilling aspects. Usually we think of fantasy as an indulgence of the imagination. The mere mention of the term frequently conjures up recollected pleasures or anticipated delights. To transcend the boredom of the moment and enter a world of voluptuous enchantment, to shed our limitations and put on a mantle of infinite power — all this we familiarly associate with fantasy. Our concept coincides with Freud's characterization of it as "imaginary gratifications of ambitious, grandiose erotic wishes," a kind of "nature-park" where "everything may grow and spread as it pleases."[1]

The "nature-park" I encountered in my treatment of the children whom I discuss in the following chapters had little to do with either "erotic wishes" or pleasure. It abounded in beasts of terrifying mien, in cruel witches and monsters who pursued their victims with unrelenting savagery. In those preserves the air continually vibrated to the rat-a-tat-tat of machine guns, corpses hung from trees, and streams ran red with blood. "Do you want to help me run? The monster is after us," was the way three-and-a-half-year-old Ellie introduced a fantasy that lasted more than a year. A four-and-a-half-year-old continually informed me that "the robber is trying to knock over the Empire State Building." I was instructed by a five-year-old in the slaughter of multitudes by a carefully worked out routine that inevitably ended with our dumping the imaginary corpses over the roof and then brushing "the blood and dirt off our hands." I have spent many a session being shot to death and then revived only so that I might be shot again.

In almost every instance the fantasy represented the child's attempt to defend himself against the early terror of being killed. Perhaps no one has described more graphically the terror that invests children's fantasies than Melanie Klein, one of the first child analysts, who wrote: "We get to look upon the child's fear of being devoured, or cut up, or torn to pieces, or its terror of being surrounded and pursued by menacing figures as a regular component of its mental life . . ."

She was also clear about the source of that terror and went on to say: "I have no doubt from my own analytic observations that the identities behind these imaginary, terrifying figures are the child's own parents, and that those dreadful shapes in some way or other reflect the features of its father and mother, however distorted and fantastic the resemblance may be . . ."

The implications of the terror in those fantasies were apparently as difficult for her to confront and to define in explicit terms in the thirties as they have continued to be, with only slight modification, in our own time. The question that followed her description still reverberates: "How does it come about that the child creates such a fantastic image of its parents — an image so far removed from reality?"[2]

When I first tackled that question, like many beginning analysts, I focused on the parents. What kind of monsters were they? Although I came to understand the tensions and the pressures that very often determined their emotional state, it was only when I shifted my focus to the child himself that I found the answer. The first break came in response to two patients who were convinced, not only that their parents wanted to kill them, but that they actually would. When I examined the factors that produced such an impression, I discovered that in both instances they had been exposed to more than the usual degree of threat. Nevertheless, it was clear they were in no danger. Their unshakable belief that their lives were at stake, however, led me to study the range of fear that children expressed in their fantasies and to weigh the reasons that might account for the differences. I concluded that children are universally predisposed to the fear of infanticide by both their physical and their psychological stage of development, and that the intensity of that fear depends on the incidence of traumatic events and on the degree of violence and of love they have experienced.

Once I arrived at that concept, nothing could have seemed more obvious. Why hadn't it occurred to me sooner? When I suggested it to other adults, they also expressed surprise but immediate acceptance. Why shouldn't children be afraid of being killed? To begin with, consider their size. Is there anyone more "killable"? To be born tiny and defenseless in a world where even a mouse has the advantage of mobility is surely to find oneself at the mercy of every living being. That adults seem to have banished from consciousness the thought that children know this, and are often preoccupied by their fears, may simply reflect their need for a continuing state of amnesia concerning their own childhood. Otherwise they could not escape the conclusion, readily derived from even cursory observation, that children are soon aware of their vulnerability and their dependence on the good will of their parents for their very lives. That their resulting terror may become a central factor in the defenses they design in order to achieve a feeling of safety emerges with startling clarity from an investigation of those defenses.

The child's size not only exposes him to attack, however; it also determines what he is capable of absorbing from the outside world. Although by now we have a more or less accurate picture of a child's physical requirements, we are less knowledgeable when it comes to his emotional capacity. Contrary to the claims of those who defend the current programming on television, whether the child is the recipient or merely a witness, he has a limited ability to accommodate violence or violent feelings.

An equally serious liability is the kind of thinking with which the child emerges from infancy. The term "magical" has been used to describe it and reflects the child's impression that his thoughts, wishes, and feelings are endowed with a mysterious power. Since as an infant he apparently activates the seeming giants of his environment without the use of speech, how else explain the remarkable — and frequently unsolicited — accommodation of his needs? The concept that he equates thoughts, wishes, and feelings with deeds is corroborated, not only by the functioning of the young children whom I have treated, but by the always startling assumption of many of my adult patients that I know their thoughts and wishes without their having to verbalize them.

In those instances where the illusion of magical powers is naturally dissipated by reality and by experiences involving a normal setting of limits, and where his world remains relatively stable, unmarred by traumatic events or by excessive frustrations or quantities of rage, he may escape comparatively unharmed. Unfortunately, that is rarely the case. His feelings of omnipotence may be reinforced both by a failure to set limits or by inordinate repression and by an imbalance in the familial relationships. Where the parent of the same sex is frequently or permanently absent, and where the child feels preferred by one parent to the other siblings, he may develop a distorted concept of his powers and of his relationship to the world.

It would be difficult to measure the dangerous consequences of the child's resulting confusion. His feelings of omnipotence may lead him to expect deeds to materialize effortlessly, or he may inhibit activity in order to avoid exposing his limitations and risking failure. He may also renounce realistic goals for grandiose schemes that may unconsciously be designed to establish his absolute control. The inevitable disappointments may produce profound dissatisfaction with the self and stifle creativity or involve him in ever-expanding achievement that rarely satisfies his unconscious objectives.

With his concept of the magical nature of his thoughts, wishes, and feelings, he may also assume responsibility for an extraordinary range of unhappy events. Is there a death in the family? — he's a murderer. An accident? — he's the secret perpetrator. An illness? — he's the agent. His "badness" causes his mother to leave him for a job, or even to want another child, and drives his father to absent himself on business trips. The child may automatically feel he is the subject of every quarrel and the author of every disaster, whether it is estrangement of the parents or separation or divorce.

The igniting element in his hazardous predisposition for guilt, with its accompanying expectation of punishment, appears to be the child's own feelings of rage. His aggressive feelings are forbidden not only because his parents may condemn them, but because of the devastating power with which the child invests them. If to think and to feel and to wish is also to act, the child may understandably measure the magnitude of the threat he thinks he represents by the intensity of the destructive character of his inner world. The angrier he is, the more dangerous he may think he is, and the greater may be his fear of retribution. He imputes such powers both to his own and his parents' feelings. Where the parents are persistently angry or where they act out their anger, he may fear the worst.

That feelings are the child's major concern follows from his infantile experience, when they are the primary mode of communication. When words become the medium of exchange, it

is reasonable to assume that, for him, their essential function
may continue to be the transmission of feelings. The child
listens to words as much to gauge their emotional as their
informational content. In an ongoing process that involves the
weighing of words and even deeds against the perception of
feelings, it is frequently the perception that wins out, as adults
know only too well.

When we consider the child's vulnerability and the dangerous consequences of his magical thinking, it comes as no surprise that his greatest concern may be his life. A precocious
five-year-old put it very succinctly. Although it took a little
while to unravel his problem, he finally made it clear that
whenever his mother left him with a baby sitter, he became
"worried." When I suggested that he might be worried that
something might happen to his mother and she mightn't return, he assured me, "No, I'm worried for myself. What could
I do if something happened to the baby sitter?"

Whether the fear of infanticide dominated the child's life or
became a manageable element depended in large part, as I
suggested earlier, on the incidence of traumatic events and on
the degree of violence and of love he had absorbed from his
familial environment. Violence or the threat of violence confirmed his already well-established fears. Even concealed but
violent wishes, however, were sufficient for him to require a
specific set of defenses in order to protect himself. Were these
elements the only problem, the child's task would have been
comparatively simple. His need for defenses was compounded,
however, by his inevitably violent response to his parents'
violence or violent wishes and feelings.

For that response to take place, it did not appear necessary
for the child himself to be the target. With the children whom
I have treated, it was sufficient if the parents persistently
committed violent acts of any kind or were frequently violent,
not toward the child, but toward each other, or toward another
child or even toward an animal, or if they repeatedly permitted
one child to act violently toward a more defenseless one with
impunity. In some instances, violent and habitually attacking
older siblings were experienced as agents of the parents; where
the parents didn't intervene effectively to protect the child, he

assumed they wanted him killed. When he found the violence or the violent feelings he experienced within the family magnified, frequently beyond his wildest fears, on the television or the movie screen, or on the city streets, his terror became intensified.

The idea that children universally fear that their parents may kill them is a startling one; yet I have found that it is far more acceptable than the possibility that parents may actually have such a wish. Until recently the concept that parents may want to kill their children has been even more carefully buried than the thought that children may live in daily fear of it. Not only is the wish to kill one of the most deeply repressed feelings, but the general understanding of the nature of feelings is still the subject of considerable misconception. It is usually with a sense of shock and very often only after a period of agonizing denial that patients may gradually and reluctantly acknowledge that they not only hate, but that they want to kill those whom they hate. That such wishes are directed toward both the analyst and the people they love is an equally repugnant and frightening concept.

For some patients that fact is so loathsome that the discovery and identification of such wishes and feelings may precipitate suicidal thoughts. The prohibition that became a thundering commandment — "Thou shalt not kill!" — seems to have registered as "Thou shalt not want to kill!" or even "Thou shalt not feel like killing!" When we recognize that the magical thinking so characteristic of early childhood may persist into adulthood, it becomes evident that, for many, acknowledging a wish to kill is tantamount to killing. A complication arising from the repression of such feelings and wishes is the resulting belief that feelings exist in a pure form. It frequently comes as a surprise to patients that contradictory feelings can exist side by side. In any analysis, the startling recognition that love does not exclude hate, nor hate, love, is a milestone on the road to maturity.

When the question is not merely one of wanting to kill, but of wanting to kill one's child, however, we enter another dimension. The revulsion aroused by even the thought of such a possibility suggests the tragedy of parenthood. Most parents embark on their new role filled with love and high aspirations, inspired in many instances by a determination to correct their own parents' errors, to make up for their shortcomings. That their education has scarcely been designed to make the undertaking a success may partly explain the high incidence of failure. No matter how extensive their schooling, few people have received the tools for understanding either their own feelings or their children's. Their expectation that they will succeed where their parents failed is therefore frequently doomed to disappointment; further, their assumption of personal responsibility for what very often appears to be a mystifying transformation of love into hate compounds the problem by generating an almost intolerable burden of guilt.

Although many years have passed since Freud established the importance of infantile experience and its persistent influence on the adult personality, one of the most painful realizations to emerge in many analyses is the patient's recognition that, as much as he would like to disown it, he has been affected by his past and is a product of his upbringing. How damaging the denial of this truth may be is demonstrated by the frequent anticipation of parents that, no matter what traumas they may have lived through, they are expected — and they themselves expect — to raise perfect children. Few parents grant themselves the right to their own problems or forgive themselves for the feelings they have absorbed from their parents.

How difficult it has been to approach both the child's fear of infanticide and the parents' wish for it may be measured by Freud's avoidance of the issue. Although he left room for the possibility that his theory of the Oedipus complex might eventually be superseded, he himself never abandoned the concept that it was the central cause of emotional problems. To understand why, we have to look no further than the theory itself.

Many years ago Dr. Hyman Spotnitz called my attention to Freud's phenomenal omission of the first part of the myth of Oedipus in formulating his theory. The Greek legend commences with the conspiracy of the parents of Oedipus to do away with him in order to defeat the prophecy of the oracle that when he grows up, he will kill his father and marry his mother; it is their act of abandoning him on a hillside to die in order to circumvent the prediction that sets in motion the events that subsequently cause the prophecy's fulfillment.

In Freud's hands this story underwent a dramatic transformation. His theory omitted the murderous act of the parents and focused on the deeds of Oedipus. It treated the murder of his father and the marriage to his mother as universal drives, isolating them as inevitable stages in a child's development. Had Freud applied the same principle of inevitability to the entire myth, his theory would have established the link between cause and effect; the parents' wish to kill their child would then have been universalized as the inevitable first step in the Oedipus complex and as the precipitating factor in the child's preoccupation with incest and murder.

When I first recognized this distortion in Freud's treatment of the myth, I was astounded by its implications and immediately suspected that it might reflect a need on Freud's part to exclude parental influence as a factor in the genesis of emotional problems. Although we have come some distance since Freud formulated his theories, our understanding of psychological phenomena is still rooted in his extraordinary discoveries. It would nevertheless be as much an error to deny his limitations as to magnify them. Freud's method provided us with an effective tool for understanding the self, but, by the same token, underscored the difficulty of arriving at such knowledge alone. Only with the assistance and in the presence of another highly skilled individual who has undergone a similar process can the work be done.

In light of the concept that the child's central preoccupation may be his fear of infanticide, and his major investment in maintaining an idealized image of his parents, nothing could have been more predictable than that Freud should have ignored the role of the parents in the story of Oedipus. Although in his self-analysis he had the courage to confront the taboos of murder and incest and to expose himself for decades to the anathema that followed his theory that such wishes are universal, apparently the taboo of infanticide was too formidable for him to take on. We can assume he wore the same blinders most people use when they enter the labyrinth of emotional experience without the aid of a psychoanalyst and that, like them, he needed to draw a magic circle around parents. That he was unable to approach the wish for infanticide, or the child's fear of it, may therefore have been a natural consequence of his being the first psychoanalyst.

In spite of many people's rejection of Freud's theory that the Oedipus complex is the nuclear cause of all neuroses, his belief that there is a nuclear cause has continued to inspire investigators. For some time now the void left by the abandonment of his theory has been filled by the concept of the prime importance of the parent-child relationship in the genesis of emotional problems. It was after some years of working with this theory that I concluded that the child's fear of infanticide is a central factor in determining his need for defenses.

Although cases of actual infanticide are comparatively rare in our times, increasingly publicized accounts of child murder as well as growing information concerning instances of child abuse indicate the potential for parental violence. I have found no lack of evidence of the existence of the wish for infanticide. A mother who brought her twelve-year-old son for treatment had been helped over the acute phase of a postpartum psychosis and described her overpowering wish to kill him and herself during his first two years of life. Although she felt she had recovered, her communications established an intensely destructive attitude toward him. In another case, that of an adolescent boy who tried to commit suicide, the mother revealed that her first impulse after his birth was to "shove him back up." The mother of a four-and-a-half-year-old girl informed me in her third interview that she was constantly preoccupied with wanting to kill her daughter. She described an incident at swimming after which she reported the little girl had stated, "Mommy really loves me; she didn't try to drown me; it was an accident." One mother reported that her first impulse after she saw her newborn infant was to crush her to death. In still another instance a mother was brought out of a trancelike state by the frantic screams of her infant son, whom she found herself trying to drown in a basin. A mother whose behavior came to the attention of the city authorities left poison within reach of her young children; they ate it twice, but were revived. Another mother confessed in despair that when she felt hopeless and depressed and her five-year-old came at her with his demands, she wanted to kill him. At such times he responded by beating himself over the head.

When we consider both the child's physical and psychological vulnerability and the inevitably threatening character of his outer world, we may well marvel how he manages to survive. That, despite his terror, he does survive, except in rare instances, is a tribute to the psyche's resourcefulness as well as to the predominantly positive character of parental care. It is a rare parent whose wish for the child to die is not balanced or outweighed by the wish for him to live. The child may respond to the varying intensity of the hostile wish and its expression, however, by developing a system of defenses that we call emotional illness. In all the instances I have encountered, his refuge from his fear of infanticide appeared to be his parents' love. The hope of eventually winning it, therefore, became the foundation of the psychic structure he designed from his earliest years and, judging from its continuing role with considerably older patients, might frequently maintain until death.

The confusion that has most often assailed observers of psychological phenomena has stemmed in large part from the complex nature of that psychic structure. Self-deception appeared to be its primary component and identity the focus of its design. Patient after patient idealized his parents' image and devalued his own in a process that, paradoxical as it may seem, I gradually learned was intended to lay the groundwork for eventually being loved. In most instances, the patient convinced himself that his parents wanted to and were capable of loving him, but that it was his worthlessness that made them hate and even want to destroy him. The investment in this distortion seemed universal and reflected in the range of its expression the degree of terror experienced by the child and of the hope that as soon as he became worthy he would be loved.

A serious casualty of this defensive system was the patient's identity. When the ancients admonished "Know thyself," they could have had no illusion about the formidable nature of that undertaking. With the need to establish a sense of worthlessness in order to meet the unconscious requirements for eventually being loved, and, as the child concluded in many instances, to camouflage identity in order to avoid being killed, it became an almost impossible task for anyone to arrive at an accurate self-concept.

It would be difficult to measure the pain of the consequent loneliness or the feelings of confusion and bewilderment whenever any attempt at self-definition was made. In such an endeavor, the quality of intelligence appeared irrelevant. No matter how brilliant the individual or how profound his understanding or even his delineation of the most subtle relationships, when he trained his scrutiny upon himself, he became lost in a maze that apparently had no exit.

In almost all my patients, the primary instrument for maintaining the self-deception and defense against the fear of infanticide was fantasy. Although at first I was struck by what appeared to be the antithetical character of child and adult fantasies, it soon became apparent that they served an identical function. Children's fantasies appeared to concentrate on the fear of being killed, but the displacement of terror onto monsters and imaginary creatures was obviously designed to preserve an idealized image of their parents, from whom it was therefore possible to receive the love so essential for survival. The tenacity of my adult patients' dedication to a fantasy that appeared to focus on winning their parents' love, on the other hand, repeatedly concealed an unconscious fear of being killed by them.

A child frequently revealed his central fantasy as soon as he felt safe in the treatment situation. My acceptance was crucial to its further development, which might then proceed through several stages over a period that could last a year or more until the terror was resolved. In instances where fantasy dominated the lives of children or where they actually adopted a fantasied identity, it very often became apparent that the terror of being killed had reached unusual dimensions. Severely traumatized children frequently inhibited all fantasy.

My adult patients were rarely aware of the fantasies that

very often controlled the direction of their lives. Without understanding either the origin or the function of their depreciated self-image, they usually pursued a style of life that resulted in self-defeat and failure or allowed only very limited success. Praise or appreciation was very often discounted and could precipitate such severe anxiety that great caution had to be used. Only after they had achieved sufficient ego strength could they confront the terror that had dictated from its hidden vantage point the self-destructive pattern of their lives. It then became apparent that the self-deception that had begun in early childhood was still operating and that the investment in establishing their worthlessness was still designed to preserve an idealized parental image that would defend them against their fear of being killed. In isolated instances, where adults came into treatment with their early childhood fantasies still intact and operative on a conscious level, their analysis revealed that the degree of terror that had given rise to them was undiminished.

When I initially decided to write this book, I thought of it as a book about the children I had analyzed. As I examined my treatment of one child after another, however, I soon realized that I was actually writing about fantasy. Once I began to probe the function of children's fantasies, it became apparent that they were a means of survival and defended the children against their fear of infanticide. It was when I recognized that my discussion would have to include the fantasy in homosexuality that I began to understand and became interested in investigating the relationship between the defensive fantasies of children and of adults.

That what emerged is a single theme with variations has been as much of a surprise to me as it may be to the reader. The discovery that the fear of infanticide may be dominant in early childhood and may remain constant throughout life, although on a diminished and unconscious plane, started as a suspicion and took many years and exposure to many patients before it became what I now consider it: a fact. That there is also a continuity between the defensive fantasies of children and of adults follows automatically from their function as a defense against that fear.

I have divided this book into two sections, "Childhood" and "The Later Years." In each chapter I have dealt with a different aspect of fantasy and the specific fear that required it, and have illustrated it with the case that in many instances taught me the most about it. I hope that an understanding of children's preoccupations and the meaning of their communications may improve the relationship between children and their parents and enable those children, when they become parents, to function more happily. I also hope the views expressed here may be of some service to professional therapists.

PART I

Childhood

"I Don't Like to Think of Myself as a Giraffe": The Fantasy of a Three-Year-Old Girl

ANY DOUBT we may have entertained concerning the extraordinary reliability of psychic processes dissolves as soon as we begin to investigate the methods a child devises to insure his survival. Up to the moment he enters the analyst's office, the child is likely to have been more active than anyone else in providing a psychological framework to defend him against terror. The most dramatic instance I have encountered of a child's response, not merely to the parents' concealed wish for, but to what she experienced as an actual threat of, infanticide, occurred in the case of three-and-a-half-year-old Ellie. She was not only afraid that her father wanted to kill her, but had no doubt that he actually would. She sought refuge in two defensive fantasies. In one she perpetually had to flee a continually pursuing monster. In the other, as a baby or bratty child, she demonstrated repeatedly that she didn't deserve love, and finally, when all hope of winning it appeared lost, she sought death. Through the early intervention of psychoanalytic treatment, she succeeded in resolving these fantasies by the age of five.

When Ellie's parents first applied for psychoanalytic help, their major preoccupation was how to survive the next twenty-four hours under the scourge of her unpredictable behavior. She was their second daughter, the first having died in infancy, and her birth had ushered in three and a half years of nightmare. All thought of having another child had been abandoned as well as most other plans and hopes. By the time they made their first appointment, they had reached the end of their tether.

It took three sessions for them to lay before me the details of their anguish and its history. They described themselves as prisoners in their own home, victims of screaming tantrums by night as well as by day. According to the father, if Ellie was balked, "all hell broke loose." The mother's attempts to sew or write or read made her the target for any object Ellie had in hand. If the mother threatened to leave, Ellie responded by clinging and crying. She held on to infancy and insisted on being called "Baby." Her pacifier was a permanent fixture and its recurring misplacement a major source of hysterics.

It was during the night that disaster really struck. The initial phase of Ellie's sleep problem had been mastered by means of an alarm clock. When it went off, she accepted its signal and trotted off to bed without demurral. Her father then read her one of Grimm's fairy tales, and although at first they upset her, "she gradually got used to them." Then, clutching her security blanket, her pacifier firmly in place, she could be counted on to withdraw into sleep for about two hours. Almost invariably she then awoke screaming and frequently kept it up for two or more hours. The routine was then repeated. The neighbors of course were constantly disturbed. But "it didn't matter how many times Ellie was smacked"; she still kept it up. She also wet her bed constantly; any attempt to awaken her in time inevitably met with more screaming. In addition, she frequently interrupted her parents' sleep with a demand to be fed. Her mother reported that she jumped violently and talked in her sleep and had nightmares. During the parents' first interview, the mother broke down and wept at the misery that had befallen them with Ellie's birth.

The father presented this catastrophic situation with the kind of mystification that in the Middle Ages might have sought explanations in demonology or the science of the occult. He now came to psychoanalysis not out of any conviction of its healing powers but simply out of despair. He was a short, stocky man in his middle twenties, with thick black wavy hair and dark eyes. He was originally from Louisiana but, like his wife, had grown up in Detroit. He now lived on Long Island, where he was employed by a sales corporation with an international structure. He radiated intelligence and vitality, but his frequent smile underscored the tension that seemed to inform every nerve and muscle. He acknowledged being abrupt with Ellie and in general having extreme responses. He was always on edge and sometimes the slightest thing could set him off. He was convinced that Ellie detested him and reported that as soon as he arrived home she "started" on him. She tugged at his clothes, sometimes until they tore, pulled his hair, pinched his behind, and refused to allow him to sit down. He generally responded by finally "lamming her," which resulted in her bursting into tears, stretching out on the floor, and sobbing her heart out.

His involvement in Ellie's routine had started the moment she arrived home from the hospital. The mother was indisposed after the birth and found it difficult to function. Her severe ovarian difficulties continued to the present and frequently kept her in bed. She took a variety of painkillers, which very often produced a state of apathy and made starting the day a formidable problem. She was unusually attractive, dark-haired and dark-eyed like her husband, and capable of looking very beautiful. Her appearance, however, was usually a barometer of her state of feeling. Just a casual glance at her hair or her choice of costume was enough to establish whether she was in or out of a depression or just how deep it was. Despite Ellie's intolerable behavior with her parents, the mother described her as very adult, outgoing, sweet, generous, very good with other children, and beautifully behaved with strangers.

Because of the mother's frequent indisposition, the father had continued to take over and to assume responsibility for Ellie's care. His role still included dressing and feeding her in the morning, feeding, bathing, and getting her to bed at night, and all the emergencies that invariably followed. The full impact of this arrangement on Ellie cannot be accurately assessed, however, without taking into account the interruptions caused by the father's frequent absences. His work could take him away from home for anywhere from a day to several weeks. His leaving always precipitated a depression in his wife, who then packed herself and Ellie off to her family, consisting of her father, mother, and two aunts. After his return, Ellie and her mother moved back home and he resumed his duties.

This constant shift in handling would have presented any child with a formidable task. With Ellie's particular situation, however, it guaranteed disaster. If one were to scour the globe, one could not find two more antithetical personalities than those of her father and mother. Where he was tense, she was relaxed; where he was abrupt, she was gentle. His compulsiveness was matched by her permissiveness, his aggression by her passivity. The realm of feeling was unexplored terrain for him, whereas for her it was home. The grandmother also lived in terror of the possibly crippling effects of restraint and indulged Ellie's every whim. The contrast between Ellie's treatment in her father's absence and in his presence could therefore not have been greater.

A regular devastating feature of Ellie's relationship with her father was the character of their reunion upon his return from a trip. Since he was always anxious to get back as soon as possible, he traveled at night, often arriving in the small hours of the morning. He then tiptoed into Ellie's room, usually left a present on her table, and then tiptoed out. He had no sooner fallen asleep, however, than he was shocked into wakefulness by her screaming for him. He invariably shot out like a bolt of lightning and let her have it, but "much good did that do"; his rest was completely ruined. Between Ellie's screaming and all his wife's troubles, he was really fed up.

Although each parent blamed the other for the difficulties with Ellie, it had occurred to neither of them that the father's absences affected her in any way. His conviction that she detested him left no room for the possibility that she missed him or that she might interpret his leaving as a sign of rejection and the nature of his return as further proof he did not love her. When I mentioned this possibility to him during his second session, it reduced him to speechlessness. He had also failed to draw any connection between his arrival home and his brief appearance in Ellie's room with her waking, although he had noted it happened every time; he marveled that she could feel his presence in her sleep. When it became clear that the hard time she gave him was nothing compared to the hard time he and his wife gave her, he was quite overwhelmed. His own childhood had been so deprived that he had never guessed his love could be a central issue for Ellie.

After my preliminary interviews with Ellie's parents, I realized there would be nothing routine in my treatment of her, but I was unprepared for the dimensions of the drama that unfolded. I have come to recognize the importance of learning every possible detail of the history of the patient, particularly in work with children, if one is to comprehend the meaning of their verbalizations, their fantasies, and their play. The child unconsciously designs his communications so that they may not be understood. His fear of infanticide is apparently so intolerable to him, and his need to feel loved by his parents so overriding, that he devises whatever means he can to defend himself against his perception of their hostile and rejecting feelings and their power and that of his own helplessness. Not only does "the fantastic image" to which Klein refers seem to be very much a part of the child's emotional reality and "a regular component of its mental life," but his use of a vast range of "menacing figures" reveals the child's profound investment in displacing his fear from his parents, in concealing and camouflaging their identity, and in hiding his perceptions. The closest analogy to the process of his thinking is the work of the dreamer, who is also concerned with concealing meaning and to that end employs allusion, analogy, and symbolic representation. He condenses images and displaces references, devices also commonly used by the child.

In a letter written as early as 1897 to his friend Fliess,[1] Freud presented a definition of what he considered to be the defensive function of fantasy. "Fantasies arise," he wrote, "from an unconscious combination of things experienced and heard, constructed for particular purposes. These purposes aim at making inaccessible the memory from which symptoms have been generated or may be generated." If we add "perception" and "feeling" to "memory," we have a working definition of the defensive function of fantasy that accommodates the child's fear of infanticide.

Where fantasy flows freely and if one is correctly oriented, there is little difficulty in understanding the communication. A basic premise is that fantasy is never "divorced from reality." The important frame of reference in any fantasy is the particular world of the particular child. Out of this raw material will be woven the child's perception of his parents' feelings and his response to them, and his struggle to deal with these two components. Armed with the knowledge of the child's real world and his history, the analyst is able to enter this region of no dimension.

Although the fantasies I have encountered are as varied as the specific worlds that produced them, I have found that they fall into recognizable categories that appear to reflect the intensity of the danger to which the child feels exposed. Until I am admitted, there are frequently two major elements, the child and "the world." "The world" might be an abstraction of overwhelming power, danger, cruelty, insanity, or whatever quality represents the child's perception of his reality. Or it might be the opposite; the child might initially supply in fantasy all that is lacking in the real world and devote himself to a continuous idyll. In extreme instances, he may create a utopian world that becomes his adopted home. "Candyland," "Teddybearland," and "Mouseland" are a few whose geography I have come to know.

A second important variable in his fantasy is his own identity. In varying degrees, depending on the intensity of the danger the child has experienced, he frequently transforms himself. He creates the illusion that he is shadowy or invisible, or he acts out his fantasy and assumes an identity that endows him with superpowers or a different sex. One five-and-a-half-year-old sought refuge in the fantasy of a "germ," microscopic but deadly. He inhabited an invisible empire that, he explained, was small enough to fit into the setting of his ring. Another child, who appeared overwhelmed by his own murderous responses, established a sense of safety by depersonalizing himself and endowing objects with his feelings. Some children created another identity inside themselves or peopled the world with allied "spirits" who could be summoned by imaginary "telephones" whenever danger became too threatening.

After my sessions with Ellie's parents, I was so familiar with the material of her life that I had the startling sensation as I listened to her communications of having broken the sound barrier. Her thinking became so crystal clear that I felt as though I heard her through a system of simultaneous translation. In the course of one and a half years she was able to resolve her fantasy and to progress to direct verbalization, which culminated in a session of confrontation that was quite extraordinary for a five-year-old.

After my first encounter with her, I remember thinking of her as a cherub with a very deep voice. She was dark-haired, with dark, mischievous eyes and an all-over roundness that immediately called to mind the paintings of Renaissance babies. After her parents' description, I was thoroughly surprised not only by her angelic appearance but by the seeming directness with which she related to all the objects of the playroom. Everything delighted her, and one by one she carted off puppets and animals to her mother in the waiting room, exclaiming, "Look, Mommy, a monkey" or "Look at the sweet pussycat," until she had run through all of them.

Despite her seemingly normal appearance and behavior, however, I did have the immediate impression of a greater than usual pathology. Perhaps it was a kind of weariness that showed, despite her impish smiles, or the quality of her voice, unusually full-throated and at the same time fogged over as though it came from a great distance. Its huskiness seemed not quite natural, the result of an effort perhaps to be other than a little girl.

The other arresting communication was verbal. After she had finished with the toys, she averted her face and stated very matter-of-factly, "I don't like to think of myself as a giraffe." That first simple flat statement immediately mobilized all my attention, partly because of the tragic absurdity of such a preoccupation in an extraordinarily charming little girl, and partly because it corroborated my observation that children are quite ready and capable of verbalizing to any adult who will listen the major problem of their lives. This had happened in so many other instances that when I heard Ellie's statement, I received it as though I had expected it. Its form, however, was startling, and it took three sessions to understand it.

"Why not?" I responded.

"Because I don't like to," came the reply.

My momentary hesitation was cut into by her insistent repetition: "I don't like to think of myself as a giraffe."

I fumbled with it to no avail. By the second session, my pursuit of this theme elicited only the further information that her friend Mary thought of her as a giraffe and, more important, that "giraffes don't bite." It was not until the following session, which took place on a Monday, that a light began to dawn. Ellie gaily announced as she entered, "I don't think of myself as a giraffe today." Acting on a hunch, I stated, "Your daddy was home yesterday." Ellie's beaming face confirmed the hunch and encouraged me to follow it up with: "You feel happy when your daddy is home." Another beaming assent and further daring: "When you feel happy, you don't think of yourself as a giraffe." Broad agreement and the next step: "You think of yourself as a giraffe when you are angry," and finally: "You don't like it when you're angry."

Although that was the last reference to the giraffe, it did not leave a vacuum. Soon after, while we were exploring the terrace, Ellie stopped before a few bricks that were lying loose on the ground. Pointing to a whole brick, she stated, "That's a mean monster." Then, turning to a half-brick, she added, "That's a baby monster." A short time later, she confronted me directly in the playroom with the same insistence that had introduced the giraffe. "Do you think I'm a monster?" she demanded, thrusting her tongue out as far as it would go, drawing the corners of her mouth down and screwing up her eyes. Then, more emphatically, "*Do* you?" It may be that my simple denial satisfied Ellie, but, in any case, that ended any further mention of the monster identity.

At three and a half, Ellie was already acutely aware of her fear of being killed and of killing and of her need to feel loved in order to survive, and she had found the exact identities that defended her against her fears and laid the groundwork for eventually being loved. For her purposes she had initially chosen an animal from the Central Park Zoo that appeared huge enough to stand up to someone as imposing as her father and that, she had been told, "didn't bite." Like the baby monster fantasy that followed, the fantasy of the giraffe reflected the depreciated self-image that explained and justified her father's violence and hatred and held out the possibility of being loved as soon as she changed. In addition, the choice of a giraffe fulfilled the dual role of protecting her against her father's violence and her father against the rage that his violence had evoked in her.

In its tonal quality, the question about whether she was a monster now brings to mind another question that Ellie asked of her mother some months later. A nagging problem in Ellie's treatment that remained unresolved was her mother's presence in the waiting room throughout her sessions. At first I ascribed it entirely to the mother's need and Ellie's identification with it. At the beginning of treatment, no matter how carefully I had instructed the mother during my session with her, there was a later slip-up that resulted in her having to remain in the waiting room. Either she informed Ellie that she would be leaving in a tone of voice that was calculated to inspire anxiety or she slammed the door when she went out so that there was no ignoring either her message or her departure. It became clear, however, when the mother's reluctance to separate from Ellie became modified, that Ellie's alarm had its own foundations, which she explained very simply in response to my questioning during one session.

"Why don't you want your mother to leave and pick you up later?" I asked.

"I'm afraid she won't come back," she stated matter-of-factly.

"Doesn't she want you?" I asked.

"No, she doesn't," Ellie answered with conviction.

"Would she be happy without you?" I pursued.

"Yes," Ellie replied, and no amount of talking could change her position.

As she was leaving, she asked her mother with the same insistence that had attempted to establish if she were a monster, but without the grimace, "Do you like me?"

The mother was astounded. "Why, of course, darling. I love you," she assured Ellie. But it was some time before Ellie's behavior permitted that to be the mother's prevailing feeling and before Ellie was convinced that it was.

Our activity throughout the major part of Ellie's treatment was concerned with two dominant themes. In the first, Ellie was a baby or bratty child — in the beginning a very bad, baby-talking, crawling-on-all-fours brat of a baby — and I was the all-suffering, helpless mother who was completely at her mercy. In the second, we fled the pursuing monster. Although he clearly represented her father, the disguise provided by her fantasy allowed Ellie to discuss him freely in her father's presence. I took to inquiring about him as one would about a member of the family and elicited the information that usually he was mean, but occasionally he could be friendly or even "nice and cuddly this morning." The themes of baby or bratty child and monster might be played in the course of the same session, or one might be granted dominance for one or more sessions and then be dropped briefly, only to be resumed once more, sometimes on a different level. Both themes developed in the course of the next year and a half, and each had its own resolution.

The pattern of the monster theme was first introduced by Ellie's sudden gleeful announcement: "The monster is after us! Come on, we have to run! He's after us!" And we ran, over the terrace, into the playroom, up and down the hall, dodging, hiding, stopping, perpetually pursued. Frequently, on arriving for her session, Ellie asked, "Do you want to play with me?" My assent was then followed by: "Will you help me run? The monster is after us." Or we might be engaged in another game, "shopping." For that purpose, Ellie carried a small basket that contained a collection of necessary objects, which were checked over each time. There was play money, a few small toys, and inevitably a gun. Although our peaceful activity might continue for some time, eventually Ellie's cry: "He's after us! Come quick! We have to run!" would send us scurrying. Ellie's radiant smiles and squeals of laughter at first created the impression that we were engaged in a delightful game, and it took some time to adjust to the beguiling façade that she had found most effective in dealing with her world. Occasionally, however, when the effort of flight caused her to drop her guard, I caught glimpses of such driving terror as to leave no doubt about the deadly seriousness of our occupation.

My reading of its meaning was also double-checked by the communications of the baby theme. This commenced with such directions as: "You put me in the playpen and I crawl out and you put me back" — da capo, and da capo, and da capo. Or else: "I cry for my bottle and you give me my bottle and I throw it on the floor. Then I cry again and you give it to me again and I throw it on the floor." All of this activity could be subsumed under the heading of "Driving the Mother Crazy" or "Being a Bad Baby" and was apparently designed to justify the mother's negative feelings. Ellie tackled it with relish. Sometimes she started the session on this theme and crawled down the hallway on all fours into the playroom, making appropriate gurgling baby noises. "Well, I see the baby is here today," I exclaimed with unconcealed delight. After a momentary response to my greeting, Ellie started on her antics, always within the context of the game. This continued for many weeks and paralleled the game of fleeing the monster. Then a sudden change in the content of the baby game alerted me to what appeared to be a dangerous development in Ellie's situation and set off an alarm that caused me to alter the pattern of our monster game. In her usual gleeful manner, Ellie announced, "The baby's getting into the washing machine! Come on, we have to pull her out! Pull! Pull! Pull!" she cried gaily. And then: "She's getting in it again! We have to pull her out!"

It has occurred to me since that there could be several interpretations to such a fantasy. I responded to it, however, as though I had received a suicide note attached to a time bomb. There was no doubt in my mind that we were on a rescue mission that had nothing to do with naughtiness. Underneath the laughter there was no mistaking a desperate cry for help. My surmise proved to be correct; this marked the beginning of Ellie's death fantasies. The sense of urgency it communicated caused me to reexamine and to alter the direction of the monster game. I felt it was no longer enough simply to flee from him; we had to challenge and to conquer him.

"I'm sick and tired of running away from that monster," I suddenly announced soon after, in the midst of flight. "It's time we stopped him!" I insisted. "We're not letting him get away with it anymore!" Ellie looked at me in great bewilderment, greater skepticism, and with just a hint of a suspicion that I had gone out of my mind. Nevertheless she followed my lead as I reversed our direction and began to chase the monster. "You get out of here!" I shouted. "We've had enough of you!" Although I had to take the lead in our resistance for a while, it wasn't too long before Ellie took over and echoed my words with relish. "He's not getting away with it, right?" she cried. And sometimes she turned the hose on him.

He was not so easily routed, however, as I was to discover again and again for many months. No sooner had we driven him off in one direction than up he popped from another. He also engaged in a complete change of tactic. From having always pursued us at a distance, he suddenly started to attack Ellie directly. "He's on my back!" she yelled. "He's choking me!"

I quickly turned on him. "Get off her back!" I shouted, tugging at him. "Get out of here!" And after an appropriate time I exclaimed with relief, "There! That took care of him!" But I spoke too soon.

"He's biting my shoulder! He's breaking my arm!" rang out, and once more I came to the rescue. At times his power seemed so overwhelming that there was nothing for it but magic.

"I have a magic powder," I declared. "When this touches him, he's going to disappear. There!" I cried, throwing my hands around. "That will show him!" The magic impressed Ellie for a while, but inevitably the battle was renewed.

The increasing desperation of Ellie's fantasies and the parents' report of her regression, a few months after a dramatic improvement in her behavior, sent me on a search for clarity that led directly to an investigation of the parental environment. I had already noted in Ellie's actual appearance the signs of deteriorating care. She sometimes looked unwashed, and her clothing was somewhat bizarrely put together and completely out of touch with the season. Although she started wearing her snowsuit as it grew colder, she was frequently dressed in the lightest summer things underneath. She also had a bad cold during this period. My research into the causes of the reversal uncovered a number of traumatic factors. From the very beginning I had urged that Ellie attend a nursery school so that for several hours a day, at least, she would not be exposed to her mother's depression. There had been a waiting list. Just prior to the change in Ellie's fantasy, however, the mother had been informed of an opening and had responded with severe despondency and confided to Ellie what a sad thing it was for mothers when their children had to leave home. She also offered as a solution the possibility of having another baby. In addition, the father was away a great deal during this time. He was also deeply concerned about finances and had insisted just prior to leaving that therapy either be cut down or terminated. The effect of all these factors on the mother was reflected both in her appearance and Ellie's and in the mounting despair of Ellie's fantasies.

"The baby is dead!" she proclaimed with pleased surprise soon after these discoveries. I felt somewhat stunned by the news, but all the information I could elicit was that it had happened "on the highway, near the beach." Following this development, our play dealt with one hopeless situation after another. Most immediately, Ellie declared, "It's raining. We have to run." Every suggestion of refuge, however, was negated.

"Let's go indoors," I offered.

"It's raining indoors," she countered.

"How about the closet? It looks nice and dry in there."

"It's raining in the closet," she persisted. And in truth, there was no place on earth where it wasn't raining. There was no shelter anywhere in the world.

Not much later, Ellie's news became even more alarming. "I'm disappearing!" she blithely announced one day with the same undertone of desperate emergency that accompanied the washing machine fantasy. And not only Ellie, but many other things were disappearing. I listened at first, somewhat nonplussed by this development, and asked some questions that later seemed completely nonsensical to me. Then I realized that all that was required was action.

"I'm not letting you disappear," I asserted, grabbing hold of her from behind. She strained against my grasp as though she were being pulled in the other direction by a thousand demons. "I'm not letting you go," I affirmed and continued to reaffirm intermittently, for the next two months, every time this theme recurred. Confirmation of Ellie's approval of my handling of it was clearly expressed. "Help! I'm disappearing! Hold on to me!" became the amended signal that energized me.

It did not arrest the downward thrust of Ellie's despair, however. "I'm in the bottom of a well and I'm dead," she announced one day, falling limply onto the couch.

"I'm not leaving you in the bottom of a well!" I responded, "and I'm not allowing you to be dead!" I rushed over, seized Ellie, and, half-carrying, half-dragging her considerable weight, I got her to "safety," which was the floor space about ten feet away. "There!" I cried, depositing her. As I continued to reiterate my determination that she "shall not die," she gradually began to come back to life.

"Where am I?" she exclaimed. No sooner had she fully revived, however, than back she went to the couch. "I'm dead and I'm at the bottom of a well." The rescue operation had to be repeated again and again. Both Ellie and I were impressed by my efforts, and quite possibly there was something in their tirelessness that finally caused a breakthrough. Ellie began to look at me in a wondering kind of way. In subsequent sessions, "I'm dead and I'm at the bottom of a well and you rescue me" became the corrected version of the fantasy and marked a turning point in Ellie's treatment.

The monster game also registered the change. Ellie was no longer attacked by a huge creature who could destroy her. Sometimes he was still referred to in the singular, but more often he assumed a multiple character, all on a diminished plane, however, very much like a swarm of insects or of tiny animals. We now tiptoed around, hiding from them, and spoke in whispers. Sometimes Ellie delicately pointed to all the places where they were biting her and I drove them off.

"They're biting my neck," she softly confided, or "They're on my arm," or "my feet," or "my cheek," or "my elbow," or "your feet," or "your arm." With a sweeping gesture, I brushed them away. Sometimes, however, they alternated with a friendly monster who didn't mean to hurt. At the end of one session, Ellie announced, "Next time the monster will only be friendly and he will lick us." During this period, Ellie was still occasionally disappearing, but with the final demand: "Hold on to me!" The monster could also still be very menacing, but he had definitely been brought into contact with the law. I was a cop whom Ellie summoned by telephone each time her house — a corner of the room behind the puppet stage — was invaded by monsters. I arrived, listened to her complaints, drove the monsters out, and put them in jail. During the era that coincided with the rain, I was as ineffectual as a law enforcement officer as I had been at providing shelter. No sooner had I locked the monster up than Ellie exclaimed, "He has the key!" or "He's breaking through the window!" or "He's coming out the side!"

It was not a losing fight, however, as my efforts with the well had revealed. There was finally one session when, for the first time, Ellie allowed herself to play with the blocks while she directed me to keep the monster locked up. While she busied herself building a road, she instructed me to admonish the monster: "You can't get out of jail. You stay in jail. You're never getting out." She kept me on my toes, interrupting from time to time: "I can hear; he's trying to get out." I periodically issued threats to the monster and repeatedly demonstrated that the door to the jail was securely bolted. Apparently under those conditions it was possible for Ellie to feel free enough to engage in conventional play.

It was almost a year and a half after Ellie's treatment had introduced the monster when I became aware that several weeks had gone by without any reference to him.

"The monster doesn't seem to bother us anymore," I commented.

"No, he's gone to another country," Ellie replied. Nevertheless, continuing for some time after that, a mean spider perpetually peered through a window in Ellie's drawings.

The mother theme had several variants. In a frequent one, Ellie went shopping with her basket and with her baby, the doll Cathy, and I simply accompanied them. At a certain point, Cathy became ill and a doctor was needed. Usually I was instructed to be the doctor. Sometimes, however, the doctor's kit was too attractive to pass up, so Ellie chose that role and relegated the mother's to me. During the period when there was no shelter from the rain and when the monster had the key, however, my suggestion that the doctor could be called for Cathy's illness was met with: "The doctor is sick."

Another favorite variation was for Ellie to be the mother and I either the baby or the bratty child. The impressive element in this fantasy was the extraordinary patience of this mother. She was absolutely the most forbearing of parents. In one version Ellie directed me to cry and to demand soup even while she was in the process of making some. "I want soup!" I demanded, banging on the table. "And I don't wanna wait!" At first she answered me quietly and with a patience that surely would have melted the most incorrigible heart: "I am making soup and it will soon be ready." As I followed her directions and kept up the din, however, her anger began to rise until finally it exploded in a roar. Sometimes, after the soup was finished, I was instructed to change my mind. "I don't want any!" I yelled. At times, perhaps most often, her response would continue to be remarkably patient, but at others we engaged in a yelling match. Wanting soup alternated with getting hungry at night or early in the morning. "I'm hungry!" I shouted. "I want something to eat!" And again the mother, drooping with fatigue and half-asleep, patiently went to the refrigerator. "All right, darling, I'll get you something to eat," she reiterated in very gentle tones. "You don't have to shout."

Ellie's awareness of her inner problems was most clearly revealed in this theme. Her need to oppose was so troublesome to her, however, that frequently she tackled it directly. One day, for instance, on her way to the bathroom, she instructed me, "Say, 'Don't go to the bathroom.'" I complied, and she went freely.

One day, while toasting a slice of bread at her request, I

reminded her, "You know, Ellie, children often tell me their problems and I help them."

"I know," said Ellie. "I have two problems: I want to be a baby and I wet my bed."

Although Ellie did not have much more to say about either of them at the time, enough was apparently established so that when her mother once more raised the question of the bed-wetting, Ellie informed her, "I'm discussing that problem with Miss Bloch."

The key disclosure for which I had been waiting came only a short time later.

As I opened the door to the waiting room to greet Ellie, I was met with: "Close your eyes and I will guide you to the playroom." I waited until her hand found mine and led me down the long hallway. When we reached the room she let go and allowed me to find my way to the chair I usually sat in. "Don't open them until I say," she directed, and after a few moments she added, "First feel this."

I allowed my hands to wander over an object that she had brought with her and had placed on the table. "Something feels very furry," I said. After a few moments, she commanded, "Open them," without asking me to guess its identity. "It's an Eskimo doll. My daddy went to Chicago and he came home last night and he brought her."

I made some comment to the effect that she liked her daddy to bring her presents, to which she assented with enthusiasm. Then suddenly she asked, "Where's the cat?" referring to a rag doll that she had played with in the previous session. I indicated the closet and she found it, along with a small Japanese rattle that immediately inspired her.

"Would you like to see me dance?" she asked. Shaking the rattle as though it were castanets, she danced in circles with a great deal of verve.

"A dance of happiness," I commented as she finished.

She looked at me somewhat strangely and said, "I can also do a dance of sadness." Half-closing her eyes and with an expression of deep and moving sorrow, she slowly turned.

"That is a dance of sadness," I agreed as she came to a stop.

"If I wanted, the dance of sadness could go on until the next patient came and until tomorrow and next week."

"You feel very sad," I replied, moved beyond belief by this first direct disclosure by Ellie of her real feelings.

"Yes, my friend died," she stated so simply that for a moment I wondered if it were true.

"How did she die?" I asked.

"She was killed. A character with a gun shot her. It was thirty years ago."

My queries about details drew a very confused statement that nevertheless established among other things that "a character," according to Ellie's description, was either a drunk or a derelict, and that as her friend was walking in the park he hit her. At first she ran away, but then she returned and hit him back, and that was when he shot her. Not being sure where this was tending, I marveled at her bravery, stating, "Usually a little girl would run and tell her mother or call a policeman. She was very brave to run back and hit him."

"Do you believe me?" she suddenly asked.

"Shouldn't I?" I asked.

"I don't know, but do you?"

"I'm not sure," I answered.

"It's a story," Ellie confessed. "You know what I mean. It's not real."

"You made it up," I added. She nodded. I had been waiting for this moment ever since Ellie had announced a year and a half before: "I don't like to think of myself as a giraffe." Now I said, "I think you're very upset about your father." She readily agreed. "Children very often tell me what upsets them and why they're sad and I can help them," I added.

"My father wants to kill me," she stated very simply, "and I don't know why."

"What makes you think he wants to kill you?" I asked.

"I know he does," she assured me.

"Do you think he really will?" I asked.

"Yes, I think he will."

"But how will he kill you?"

"With his gun. He has a gun from the war. It's in the desk. He told me he threw the bullets away."

"If he threw the bullets away," I asked, "then how can he kill you with the gun?"

"He can buy more."

"I don't know if you'll believe me, but I know that your father will never kill you," I assured her.

"I know, but I can't believe it. I asked him and he said he wouldn't, but I keep on believing he will."

In my further effort to disabuse her of this conviction, I summoned up the image of the law and the jail that would inevitably be her father's lot if he killed her. I succeeded, however, only in alarming Ellie.

"Couldn't he come out?" she asked worriedly. "Could I go where he is and kiss him?"

For the past minutes I had been casting about for an effective approach and I finally decided that only a direct confrontation might help.

"Ellie," I said, "I've been wondering how I could help you. Would you like me to talk to your father about it?"

She agreed eagerly and immediately added, "Can I be there?"

The request was unexpected, but I agreed and asked, "Should I telephone this evening to arrange it?" Ellie was very willing. At the end of the session, she went to meet her mother in the waiting room, and I heard her explaining, "Miss Bloch is going to call Daddy to talk about why he wants to kill me." At that point I asked Ellie's permission to explain it further to her mother and stated, "Ellie can't stop believing that her father will kill her and wants me to talk to him. We agreed that I will telephone this evening. What do you think is a good time?"

The mother's face was a study in shock and consternation. She accepted very readily, however, a situation that I had actually discussed with her innumerable times. "Well, I think seven-thirty would be a good time to call," she quietly said.

When I phoned that evening, her husband answered.

"Has Ellie told you the reason for my call?" I asked.

"I heard the words," he replied. We agreed that Ellie's next session would be the best arrangement. I then suggested that he check first with Ellie before we made it final. He returned, spluttering with a mixture of indignation and amusement and at bottom amazement that his five-year-old daughter was to be taken seriously.

"I can't get over her casualness," he reported. "When I told her you were on the phone, she said, as cool as a cucumber, 'I know. I asked her to call.'"

Five minutes after I had hung up, my phone rang. It was Ellie.

"I wanted to ask Mommy too," she said.

"That would be fine," I agreed.

"Could we all go into the playroom first and then you come in?" she inquired.

"Why do you want to do that?" I asked.

"It would be goodly," she assured me. "Me and my mommy and my daddy would be there and then you come in."

I readily agreed, assuring her it would be exactly as she wanted it.

Never before in my career had a five-year-old asked for such a confrontation and for such a reason. In anticipation of the meeting, I speculated about the course it might take and the consequences. Nothing that I thought of, however, prepared me for its utter simplicity, or for its effectiveness. The family arrived and, as Ellie had requested, seated themselves in the playroom, Ellie in her usual chair at the little corner table, her parents at a distance so that she had to turn slightly away from the table in order to face them. I entered and also sat in my usual child's chair at the table with Ellie. Everyone seemed quite subdued. I looked at Ellie's slightly flushed, slightly smiling face and asked, "Do you want to begin, Ellie?"

She shyly looked at her father, whose face had turned a dull red, and stated, "I think you want to kill me. Do you?"

"No," her father stated flatly and without any show of emotion. "I don't want to kill you."

"Then why do you keep a gun in your drawer?" Ellie pursued.

"It's a souvenir from the war," he stated. "It doesn't have any bullets."

"But you could buy some more."

"I won't," her father stated. "I won't ever use it."

"I think it's the gun that makes it hard for Ellie to believe that you won't kill her," I intervened. "Can anything be done about it?"

"I don't really need the gun," said her father. "I can get rid of it."

"Do you think that would make you stop believing that your father will kill you?" I asked.

"Yes," Ellie agreed. And there seemed nothing else that anybody wanted to say. Ellie turned to her play, in which she at first tried to involve her parents, but I felt awkwardly and with some strain.

"Would you like your parents to wait for you now in the waiting room?" I asked. That seemed to meet with everybody's approval and they left.

That was the last session before the summer vacation. Although, as I learned later, the gun was seemingly too essential to the father's feeling of security for him to keep his promise, Ellie's direct confrontation with him in my presence was apparently sufficiently reassuring to liberate her from the intensity of the fear that he would kill her. After her return, she was free of her previous preoccupations and appeared to be very much in the real world. Ellie's interest in "wee-wees" had first been expressed in relation to the family of dolls with sex characteristics that occupy a shelf in the playroom. She had appeared quite entranced by the sight of them and expressed her interest freely. Now she reported to me with exaggerated indignation, "There's a very bad boy at school and he showed me his wee-wee."

I contemplated her frowning self-righteousness for a moment and then I said, "I have a feeling that you like wee-wees."

"I love them," she admitted, all smiles.

There were also certain words that she similarly reported to me one day were very bad and she would never say them. "Especially," she declared, "the one that rhymes with 'duck.'"

"Oh, you mean 'fuck,'" I asserted with an air of discovery.

"You embarrass me when you say that," she declared. "That's a bad word and I don't want to hear it. My mother says I must never say it."

"Oh, well," I answered, "she didn't mean here. Here we say anything; you know that."

But Ellie's alarm and her fear of having her defense against such words undermined were very real. After I had clarified with her mother a healthier approach to the problem, Ellie arrived at her session with the statement: "You know about the word that rhymes with 'duck.' Well, it's all right if I say it sometimes. I say all the bad words together. Do you want to hear me?" My assent set off: "Fuck, shit, hell, and damn." On another occasion, as we were playing on the terrace, Ellie warned, "I'm going to say all the bad words," and out they came.

During the final period of her treatment, Ellie's father was at home only on weekends. At the beginning of one session during this time, Ellie announced, "I have a problem. Can you help me?" And then she went on to explain, "Whenever I want something and I can't have it, I cry. And I just cry and cry and cry and my daddy gets mad. I want to stop it. Do you know how I can?"

I thought for a moment and then asked, "What happens when you cry and cry and cry?"

"I get what I want," Ellie promptly answered.

"Well, I think I know how you can stop," I replied, "but it isn't easy. You have to tell your mother not to give you what you want when you cry. If you know she won't give it to you, you'll stop crying."

Ellie looked incredulous. "Do you mean," she asked, "that I have to tell my mother not to give me what I want?"

"That's right," I assured her. "And then you'll stop crying."

And as I learned from her mother soon after, Ellie actually carried out my recommendation. Unfortunately, there is little more to tell of Ellie's development. Shortly after, at a point where Ellie was just beginning to feel safe enough to release her aggressive feelings in relation to me, the family returned to Detroit and removed her from treatment.

If we follow the evolution of Ellie's fantasies to their remarkable culmination, we are in a position to understand their function as a defense against her fear of infanticide and to learn something of the child's vulnerability and her way of perceiving the world. The particular purposes of her fantasies were to make inaccessible her terror of being killed by her parents and her perception of their hating and violently rejecting feelings and to preserve the possibility of eventually winning their love. Her magical concept of her own powers, which made her responsible for the unhappy developments in her life, reinforced the need to blame herself and helped to keep alive the hope that when she changed, so would her parents' feelings.

Her fantasy of a monster who perpetually pursued but never caught her not only permitted her to express and to master her terror, but, by transferring her father's murderous feelings to an imaginary figure, allowed her to maintain a loving image of him and to camouflage the real source of her fear. Her early fantasies of the giraffe and the baby monster were instruments of self-deception. Although when she emerged from her fantasy, she stated, "My father wants to kill me and I don't know why," these initial concepts of herself, which focused on her own murderous response, concealed the precipitating cause, her father's violence and his destructive feelings, yet justified it.

Similarly, the baby and bratty child fantasy defended her against her perception of her mother's rejecting feelings. The images of the incorrigible child and the perfect, all-suffering mother enabled her to deceive herself in fantasy, as she did in reality, into believing that she was to blame for her mother's feelings. Her mother's inevitable depressions following her father's necessary departures convinced Ellie that not only didn't her father love either of them, but that her mother didn't love her. That impression was further reinforced by her mother's frequent indispositions, which Ellie ascribed to her own misbehavior and her anger and interpreted as a measure of her mother's rejecting feelings. The dynamic relationship between Ellie's fantasies and her parental environment was demonstrated most clearly in this theme. The baby or bratty child fantasy, which started out as a way of justifying her mother's inability to meet Ellie's overriding need for her love, became increasingly suicidal in response to her mother's deepening depression and Ellie's growing hopelessness of ever securing that love.

The scale of her terror and of her suicidal despair was undoubtedly influenced by both her vulnerability as a child and her magical thinking. Her perception of her father's violent disposition, reinforced by the presence of his gun, and her own helplessness convinced her he would kill her. All she could do was run. Her child's appraisal of her relationship to her mother as well as her magical equation of wishes and deeds also persuaded her that if she let her mother out of her sight, she would never see her again.

Ellie's confrontation with her father was the culmination of a process that had extended over a period of a year and a half. The ego strength that allowed Ellie to request and to carry it through had built up very gradually as a result of her weekly sessions and of her parents' improved way of relating to her. Her behavior had begun to change almost immediately with the commencement of treatment and permitted her parents to feel more relaxed with her. The pacifier was soon relinquished, and the tantrums ceased as her parents learned how to handle them. The bed-wetting also stopped and the oppositional needs diminished. Once her mother understood the sources of Ellie's misbehavior, she was also able to modify her treatment sufficiently so that Ellie was able increasingly to believe in her love. Although her father was able to respond in a more limited way to Ellie's needs, he recognized that he played a role in her problems and agreed to leave discipline to his wife. Ellie's growing maturity and her developing understanding of her part in his violent outbursts also led her to change in her way of relating to him.

As psychoanalytic intervention modified her parents' attitudes and succeeded in reducing Ellie's terror, she was able to abandon the fantasies that had defended her against it. The gradual lessening of her fear, reflected in the modifications of her fantasies, entered a new phase with the departure of the monster for "another country." The "dance of sadness," her first undisguised revelation of her true feelings, followed soon after and led first to the disclosure of her central preoccupation, the verbalization that her father would actually kill her, and then to the confrontation.

We can only speculate about the course of Ellie's development had she been able to remain in treatment. The rage that hid beneath her suicidal depression was just beginning to find expression, as her need to "say the bad words" indicated. Releasing her aggression through verbal means would have been the next objective in her therapy.

Chapter 2

Mighty Mouse: The Birth and Death of a Defensive Fantasy

ALTHOUGH A CHILD may have previously created a fantasy in order to defend himself against the fear of being killed, a newly threatening incident in an already charged situation may render that defense ineffectual and call for a more drastic solution: the acting out of the fantasy, frequently of an assumed identity.

In the case of four-and-a-half-year-old Larry, the subject of this chapter, I was able to witness not only the moment when he recalled the exact experience of danger that had catapulted him into assuming a different identity, but also the precise instant at which he felt secure enough to abandon it and to become himself once more. Both represented points of culmination in a gradual process, the first of increasing terror, the second of its diminution and of the growing feeling of being loved. In both instances, the change occurred in response to incidents of heightened emotional intensity.

Larry was referred to me because for the previous months both his mother and his nursery school teacher noted that he had been withdrawing at an alarming rate, insisting in an all-encompassing way that he was Mighty Mouse. He was an only child whose parents had separated when he was three. They had lived in California during his first two years and then had moved east. Now he and his mother occupied a tiny apartment in Brooklyn that scarcely allowed him any space to play in.

His mother was an attractive if somewhat constricted woman of twenty-seven who related all of this in a hurried, matter-of-fact way as though her major objective was to get it over and done with so that we could both get on with our business, mine to help Larry get rid of his problem, and hers to get out of my office and on with her life. She had married a man fifteen years her senior, whose work took him away from home for long periods. She described him as violent and frequently morose. He spent a great deal of his leisure time staring at the TV and only very rarely paid attention to Larry. His violence culminated the night they separated in a scene in which he smashed the television, broke a vase, and hit her. Although Larry didn't see him at all for several months after that, for the past year he had been spending every other weekend with him.

When I first saw Larry I recalled his mother's last words. I had asked if he might object to leaving the aunt who would bring him and entering my office by himself, as his mother suggested, and she had answered without hesitation, as though there could be no alternative, "He won't like it, but he'll go." The world of feelings-ignored that her words called up declared itself in every aspect of Larry's being. I don't remember how long it was before I first saw him smile, but I shall never forget the sadness and desolation, the sense of a void, that his pale blue eyes and pasty look communicated, the clearly discernible evidence of a deep depression. He was diminutive even for four and a half, but perhaps one would not so immediately have noticed were it not for the air of bravado with which he attempted to carry it off. He strode as though he wore seven-league boots and carried himself in general as though he were a person of great importance.

His mother had been right, and he made no objection as the door closed on his aunt and he was left standing alone with me at the end of a long hallway. His feelings remained his secret as he led the way to the playroom.

"Mighty Mouse is my friend," he announced as he crossed the threshold. His voice simulated good cheer and fine spirits and was so curiously pitched that it struck me then that only terror could have pushed it so high up in his head. "He's very strong and he can do anything," he declared proudly. "Nothing can hurt him."

"He sounds like a pretty good friend to have," I said admiringly.

"He is," Larry agreed.

At the beginning of the next session, he immediately announced, "I brought Mighty Mouse with me today. He's sitting right here," he explained, indicating his right shoulder. "I want to tell you about him," he added, and then, "I hope you'll believe me." He then launched into a recital of all of Mighty Mouse's virtues.

"He wears a bulletproof vest," he asserted. "Nobody can shoot him. And he can fly. He can go anywhere he wants. And you know what," he added after a moment, as though conveying a matter of supreme significance, "he's not afraid of the cat."

Larry's enthusiasm mounted as his subject carried him on. Although his body movements seemed very restricted, at that point he adopted a fighting pose and began to make lunging gestures. "He likes action," he declared jubilantly.

I listened with great interest, and then finally I asked, "How old do you think he is?"

"He's four and a half," was the ready retort.

"Exactly your age," I responded with some surprise, only to realize that I had committed the cardinal sin in dealing with fantasy — getting too close to reality.

"I made a mistake," Larry said a little uncertainly. "He's really five and a half."

He also had two separate theories of Mighty Mouse's origin. "How did you get to know him?" I asked.

"One day we heard somebody knocking at the door and we opened it. And there he was. It was Mighty Mouse. And he was cold and hungry and we took him in. And that's how he came." Two and a half months later he had a significantly different explanation of Mighty Mouse's arrival.

His very first words had clearly established that the world of Mighty Mouse was his entire frame of reference. There was scarcely a subject that Larry did not find some way of bringing around to the mouse, very much as a lover finds a way to inject the name of his beloved. After the first few sessions he was also almost never seen without some insignia that established his adopted identity. Sometimes it was a cardboard vest that his aunt had helped him to construct, or a pair of goggles or a belt or a cape. On entering he lost no time in calling attention to this important item. He also asked me to look for games, toys, and books that had something to do with mice. Since Larry was a little ahead of the fad, I had some difficulty in finding what he wanted. I had managed to turn up a comic book and a coloring book, however, and finally one day while sauntering through a toy shop I discovered a basket of delightfully appealing little woolly mice, some white and some gray. I bought one of each and placed them on the table in anticipation of Larry's arrival. When he discovered the mice, his joy knew no bounds. "They're the cutest mice I ever saw," he exulted. Seizing one in each hand, he immediately announced, "The white one is Mighty Mouse and the gray one is Larry." He danced around the room bringing their noses together to the accompaniment of clucking noises. "They're kissing!" he exclaimed ecstatically. "They love each other!"

As I watched, it struck me that this may have been the first time that it occurred to Larry that Mighty Mouse — and he — were lovable. He stopped suddenly and declared, "Mighty Mouse needs a red cape." Since the Superman fantasy had already raged for many years, I was fully prepared for such an emergency. I quickly found the red cloth that had been left over from the last cape and asked, "Do you think this will be all right?"

"Oh, yes," he assured me. "That's just the right color."

I cut out a tiny square and proceeded to sew a cape for Mighty Mouse. While I was thus engaged, Larry scrutinized the contents of the playroom as though he were seeing them for the first time. He stopped before the family of dolls, which he had ignored until then, and holding the father in one hand and the mother in the other, he proceeded to bang their feet together.

"They're wicked!" he exclaimed. Then he picked up the boy doll. "They don't love their son!" he charged with mounting indignation. Finally, concentrating solely on the mother, he stated with deep feeling, "She wants her child to die!"

Following this confrontation, Larry approached me and spontaneously imparted the following confidence. "I remember the day that Mighty Mouse came," he offered. "I don't exactly remember what happened, but it was a terrible day. The man

was put in jail and they didn't give him any food and he died."
Then, with increasing intensity: "He was worse than a pirate!"
He studied my face for a moment, and added quickly, "It was
twenty years ago."

And that was Larry's first reference to the trauma of his
parents' violent battle a year and a half before, when he had
felt that only the magical powers of Mighty Mouse could save
his life. Mighty Mouse and Larry Mouse remained the focus
of his activity for the next few months. He created a hiding
place for them in the center of the building blocks and carefully
buried them at the end of each session in a fairly comfortable-
sized room with a secret door that led out into the playroom.
He frequently went directly there at the beginning of the
session and removed them with great pleasure. Sometimes he
busied himself with another favorite occupation, drawing or
painting or constructing Mighty Mouse figures.

Time and age were a very important second theme in Larry's
communications. "I'm four and a half," he had announced during his first session, "and four is my favorite number. On May
twenty-sixth I'm going to be five and then five will be my
favorite."

As that day approached, his excitement grew increasingly
intense. A week before, he asked if he could change his session
so that it would fall on his birthday. "And could you have
something special for Mighty Mouse on that day?" he requested. I sensed that he was living under the spell of some
fantasy concerning that day, perhaps one involving his father,
or perhaps even the mouse himself. Nothing elicited any clar-
ifying information, however. I searched the city and finally
found a large cuddly gray mouse the size of a small teddy bear
and placed it where Larry was bound to see it as he entered
the playroom but where he could also ignore it if he wanted
to.

Whatever magic he had associated with the day had already
fizzled before he arrived. He appeared quite depressed, his eyes
dark-circled and unsmiling, and he pretended not to see the
new mouse. It was only after several sessions had passed that
he called my attention to the fact that the new mouse had
neither a tail nor a red cape, both of which I promptly supplied.

During the week following his birthday, however, he spontaneously announced, "I'm going to see my father on Sunday" — his first reference to his father — as though this had been a regular topic of conversation.

During the ensuing weeks Larry's real situation improved markedly. A month and a half after his birthday, his mother moved from their tiny apartment to a considerably larger one where he had his own room and where he could play outdoors. She also changed her routine so that she could spend more time at home with him. The summer intervened, giving him a month at day camp and several weeks in the country. In addition, he had received a hamster as a present and welcomed him as another member of the rodent family. The hamster also appeared to have further expanded Larry's interest in such animals to include squirrels. When he returned to treatment after an absence of a month, the fantasy of Mighty Mouse appeared to have loosened its hold on him considerably.

"I have a golden hamster," he announced immediately on entering. "He lives in a cage and runs on a wheel and when he eats he stuffs his pouches and then he spits it all out. He's a rodent just like Mighty Mouse." He constructed a hamster out of some plastic construction material and then added a mother hamster and a father hamster and also a squirrel and built a nest for each one out of construction paper. During the following month he proceeded to construct what he called "the Rodent Apartments" to house them and the mice. He also became interested in guns for the first time and in playing "the bad guy" and in a new television character named Eighth Man, who appeared to Larry to have all the qualities of Superman.

A month after his return, toward the end of one session, he held up the gray mouse and asked, "Do you know how old Larry is?" He immediately followed with: "Five months — no, I mean, five weeks — five days — five minutes — he's just five seconds old!"

"He was just born!" I cried.

"Yes," he agreed jubilantly, "he was just born!" And he began to coo and to make clucking noises exactly as though he were holding a newborn infant.

"What a beautiful baby!" I exclaimed.

"Oh, yes, he's beautiful!" Larry agreed. He was ecstatic.

"It's almost time to leave," I reminded him. "What shall we do with Larry?"

"I have to make him a nest," he stated, and he spent the last few minutes bedding the mouse down. As soon as he arrived for his following session, three days later, he demanded, "Do you know how old Larry is today? He's exactly three days old," he announced, lifting him from his nest. "Coo, coo, coo," he cooed at the mouse, and "Cluck, cluck, cluck," and all the other sounds anyone has ever heard addressed to an infant.

"Oh," I exclaimed, "isn't he beautiful!"

His joy seemed boundless, and he turned first to the hamster baby and then to the squirrel and repeated his jubilating performance.

"What beautiful babies!" I repeated as he went from one to the other. It was a session of indescribable rapture.

This time he made a nest for each of them before departing and settled them in their beds. He bade me a joyous good-bye and walked down the long hallway to the door. As he was about to open it, however, he paused and turned toward me. His expression had changed to one of utter desolation.

"But I'm five and a half," he asserted in a voice filled with pain and protest. He then slowly opened the door and went out.

That moment marked the demise of the Mighty Mouse fantasy. The sense of danger that had precipitated its creation had finally been dispelled and the need to seek refuge in a magical identity dissolved. For the first time since the night of his parents' violence Larry did not require the illusion of supernatural powers in order to feel safe, and at last he returned to his own identity.

The process that brought this about is transparently clear. "I hope you'll believe me," was my first cue in Larry's treatment. My enthusiastic endorsement of his adopted identity liberated his energy and lifted him out of his depression; he had an ally. I also have to pay tribute to the extraordinary charm of the woolly mice, the good fortune that led me to them, and the intuitive sense that persuaded me to buy two for the speed with which I was able to get to the original trauma that required the Mighty Mouse defense. Nothing could make clearer the importance of feeling loved in reversing a pathological process than Larry's response to those mice. Their lovable character obviously took him by surprise and stirred up feelings that he could scarcely contain. "They love each other!" he exclaimed, and on the wave of the feeling that he also was loved he was able to revive and to confront for the first time the terrifying memory that had necessitated his magical defense. Still seeking refuge in fantasy, for the first time he was also freed to express, by way of the dolls, his indignation at both his parents for their rejection of him and to accuse his mother of wanting him dead.

The increased ego strength that led him first to the fantasy of being reborn and then to the acceptance of his own identity derived not only from his analytic sessions but also from the improvement in his environment. His mother was very responsive to my suggestions for building a feeling of security and providing more companionship, and she went to great lengths, including changing her abode, in order to meet his needs. As a result of both factors, the sense of danger that his father's violence had precipitated, and that his mother's feelings had reinforced, gradually diminished. When he felt sufficiently secure, he was able to discard his magical identity and accept his real one.

The concept that a defensive fantasy may be acted out at a specific moment when life is experienced as endangered, and then abandoned when the danger is experienced as past, is borne out by the events of Larry's treatment. We may, therefore, also assume that where the childhood fantasy continues to be acted out in adulthood, as in the assumption of a homosexual identity, the terror that precipitated it may still prevail.

Chapter 3

Four Children Who Insisted They Belonged to the Opposite Sex

AT A TIME OF SO MUCH confusion in many quarters concerning the origin and the meaning of homosexuality, I have found it increasingly illuminating to turn to my experience with four children — two boys and two girls — who were referred to me because they insisted they belonged to the opposite sex. Although homosexual feelings are universal, the persistent acting out of the fantasy of an assumed sexual identity appears to occur only under specific circumstances. That the dynamics are similar to those from which other defensive fantasies spring became clear to me when I explored the backgrounds of these four children.

As I had found in Larry's case, in each instance the child had commenced acting out the fantasy when a specific incident jeopardized his already precarious situation and convinced him that his life was endangered. That these children did not select Mighty Mouse or Superman or any other powerful identity but chose an opposite sexual identity appeared to be determined by a very particular and remarkably similar constellation of factors. In all instances, they had been exposed to the actual violence of one parent, so that they had to defend themselves, not merely against the fear, but against the threat of infanticide. In addition, the only refuge offered by the other parent against this danger was at most detachment and a seductive façade. The factors that appeared to determine the choice of a sexual fantasy, however, were related in all instances to the children's perception of the character of their parents' relationship. In all cases they were convinced, by the feelings and the behavior of the parents either toward each other or toward them, that the parents did not love each other and that the parent of the opposite sex preferred them. They therefore ascribed the other parent's violent rejecting character to jealousy and experienced themselves as the target of that parent's jealous retaliation. The children consequently concluded that the only way they could save their lives was to change their sex. By creating the fantasy that they really belonged to the sex that they felt was preferred by the threatening parent, they hoped not only to allay that parent's jealous fears, but to transform violence into love. The acted-out fantasy of a sexual reversal thus provided a refuge against the fear of being killed by supplying a framework within which it was possible to maintain the hope of eventually being loved.

With all four children it was possible to establish the event that created the immediate need for an acted-out opposite sexual identity. Although each child had found other means until then to protect himself against the parents' violence, the new and more formidable development rendered them ineffectual and required a more drastic defense. In three instances the birth of a sibling of the opposite sex or of one who resembled the parent of the opposite sex precipitated the acting out of the fantasy of a homosexual identity. In the fourth, it was the seductive exposure to the parent of the opposite sex that further jeopardized already perilous relationships with the violent familial members of the same sex.

Although homosexuality generally implies the satisfaction of instinctual needs by a partner of the same sex, the cases of these four children indicate that the actual transformation of sexual identity may occur well before the development of such needs. Perhaps a good part of the confusion that has surrounded the understanding of homosexuality stems from the concentration on physical behavior in relation to the sexual partner and the variety of its expression. When approached from the vantage point of childhood, however, the problem is remarkably simplified. Since the maturational level of the child usually precludes a need for instinctual gratification, physical acting out of sexual feelings has little relevance. It is nevertheless clear that the child has developed a homosexual defense and that its essential feature is the persistent acting out of a sexual reversal. With all four children the acting out was well established, but corresponded to their developmental stage and limited itself to assertion, appearance, and mannerism. Since in most instances psychoanalytic treatment resolves the child's need to adopt an opposite sexual identity, we can only conjecture that, without it, sexual maturation would also require sexual expression.

The seemingly bewildering symptomatology of homosexuality takes on a new meaning as soon as we recognize that the issue is frequently one of life or death. Any doubt about the function of the homosexual acting out may be clarified by Freud's explanation: "The greater the resistance the more extensively will expressing in acting (repetition) be substituted for recollecting."[1] Perhaps in no other fantasy is the scale of the repression so formidable. In the case of one adult patient, every experiencing of a forbidden feeling was followed by panic and the compulsion for homosexual contact. Frequently, however, the dimensions of the homosexual's resistance to recollecting are not adequately accommodated merely by the acting out. The denial in the acted-out fantasy of a homosexual identity is as striking as the repression that it serves. The homosexual's frequent insistence that his fantasy is real, that he actually does belong to the opposite sex or a third sex, that he is simply fulfilling his true nature, or that he was "born that way," is unquestionably a symptom in the service of his resistance to recollecting and may suggest both the unbearable dimensions of his memories of terror and his conviction that his life depends on preserving his assumed identity. His only hope of love, and thus of safety, appears to be sustained by it.

Because there is a wide range of dynamics that may also result in the persistent acting out of a homosexual identity, I shall confine my discussion to those I discovered in my treatment of the four children. Nevertheless, the unwavering intensity of the simple assertions of these children that they belonged to the opposite sex, and the familial conditions that necessitated it, have provided a reliable frame of reference in my effort to unravel the added complexities of similar phenomena at a later age.

In three of the cases, I shall limit myself to an examination of the dynamics. In the fourth, the actual psychological transformation from homosexual fantasy to homosexual identity and its dynamics are so clear that I shall present it at some length.

Rose was brought to see me at the age of four because her aggressive, provocative behavior had caused her expulsion from nursery school for the second time in little over a year and boded ill for the future. She insisted she was a boy, refused to wear dresses, and played only with boys. She also bit and threw things, took other children's toys, and was generally uncontrollable. The mother dated her insistence on a sexual reversal from the age of two, when her brother was born. Although the mother described the weaning process at three months as "no problem," Rose immediately after developed a coeliac condition that lasted until she was two. Exactly coincidental with that period, she also fainted whenever she received injections in the doctor's office, when she cried, and when she fell and hurt herself. Both conditions disappeared at the time of her brother's birth but were immediately replaced by her adoption of an opposite sexual identity.

Rose's parents, a very good-looking couple in their late twenties called Bobby and Robby, arrived for their first interview in identical sports attire. Although there was nothing masculine in the mother's manner, her clothes were clearly designed to correspond to her husband's. He seemed the more dominant of the two and appeared as aggressive and energetic as she seemed passive and detached. Their main interest was sports, and they devoted their leisure time, mainly Sunday, to its pursuit. The mother stated that Rose's birth had been planned and that she loved children. The father concurred in this feeling, but confessed that before Rose's birth he had been set on her being a boy. After the initial disappointment, however, he enjoyed her just as much, treated her no differently, and had already inducted her into the realm of sports. He became so fond of her, in fact, that he was not particularly eager to have a boy when his son was born. Since the birth of a third child, a girl, three months before, Rose had shared her room with her brother, but she had always been a poor sleeper and invariably came into her father's bed at three or four in the morning and finished the night with him. She actually saw little of him in her waking hours since he was home only on Saturdays, her contact being mainly a few minutes each morning and again at bedtime each evening. He was very strict with her and resorted to spanking as a way of dealing with problems. Her relationship with her mother was easier.

Rose's conflict was revealed dramatically during her first session when she took up her position in the public corridor outside my door, insisting she preferred it to my office. The elevator man who happened by was charmed by her appearance and innocently exclaimed, "What a pretty little girl!" She was immediately transformed into a pugnacious demon as she hurled back at him the most scathing epithet she could command, "I'm not a little girl, you kid!" Several sessions later, seated on my couch, she confided with inexpressible pleasure, "I have a penis and it's inside and it's a secret."

Rose's development suggests that just before the age of two she had faced the crisis created by the imminent birth of a sibling that was then exacerbated by the fact of his sex. Her fainting, which commenced at four months, had no organic cause according to her physician, who explained it as a "temper tantrum." It was possibly a response to terror, however, a hypothesis suggested by its occurrence following fear-instilling incidents. Although we don't know how the father's initial disappointment expressed itself, we are aware that he habitually used spanking as a means of punishment and, according to the mother, was "very strict." There is reason to believe, however, that Rose experienced both her father and her mother as sources of danger. From what we know of the effect on the child of a seductive relationship with the parent of the opposite sex, we can safely conjecture that her father's acceptance of her as a sleeping partner cast her mother in the role of vengeful rival. Nevertheless, of the two parents, the mother was clearly the more protective and more accepting. Her passivity and detachment offered some refuge and possibly came closest to Rose's experience of love. The imminent birth of a sibling, particularly of a male, who would gratify his father's wishes, therefore threatened Rose not only with complete abandonment on his part — and in Rose's terms, possibly death — but, even more, the loss of whatever protection her hope of her mother's love offered. Her previous somatic defenses were rendered ineffectual. In what may have been a desperate attempt, therefore, to save her life by winning love, Rose insisted that she herself was a boy.

The dynamics, which had to be arrived at partly by conjecture in Rose's case, emerge more clearly in the case of Richard. He was referred to me because at the age of six his insistence that he was a girl, which had started a year and a half before, had reached such proportions that life for him and his family was becoming unendurable. At school his preference for female attire and for playing with the girls and their dolls, his concentration on the female figure in his drawings, and his refusal to get undressed in public for swimming or gym made him the center of ridicule. At home he dressed in his mother's clothes, used her cosmetics at every opportunity, and stood in front of the mirror endlessly admiring his reflection. Since he didn't play well with other children, he was his mother's constant companion and concern. His resentment of his thirteen-month-old brother was another source of difficulty. He particularly objected to the injustice of the fate that had allowed his brother to have the same brown eyes and dark hair as his mother — that is, in his words, "to be a girl" — whereas he looked like his father and was therefore ugly. Possibly to deny this resemblance he fluttered his eyes when he talked, moved his body in an unmistakable imitation of a female manner, and endowed his speech with a rhythm and an inflection that he presumably borrowed from women. At six he was as convincing a male homosexual as his age allowed.

Richard's father was engaged in computer research but suffered from such severe depressions that recently he had scarcely been able to function. He had made one suicide attempt and had required hospitalization just a year prior to Richard's referral. Several times during the period of Richard's treatment, he appeared again to be close to breaking down. He was extremely withdrawn the few times I saw him and gave the impression of a man whose energy seemed concentrated on keeping feelings as far removed and as safe as possible. He had been totally uninterested in Richard's birth and ignored him during the first year of his life. By the time Richard entered treatment, his father's contact with him consisted in his lying next to him for a few minutes at Richard's bedtime and dutifully taking him on an occasional outing. Whenever he became aware of Richard's feminine proclivities, however, he exploded in rage. He also felt enormously guilty for his neglect of Richard and hopeless about ever changing.

Richard's mother was a small, good-looking, but passive woman who remained sympathetic but detached during the year and a half I knew her. Richard's perception of his parents' relationship had led him to conclude that he was his mother's preferred companion, a concept that expressed itself in fantasies of dating movie actresses. On his Rorschach, Richard revealed that he was afraid of "a madman" who "hides bombs in buildings," and he responded to the "mother" card, which usually elicits a human or animal response, as "a sunsuit or a dress."

Although the father was openly rejecting and violent from Richard's birth and his mother equally detached, it was from age four and a half that his mother dated his insistence that he was a girl, his adoption of feminine mannerisms, and an interest in feminine clothes and activities. At that time she was three months pregnant. As shadowy and shell-like as the "sunsuit or dress" image of his mother apparently was, as in the case of Rose, she was his only source of protection as well as his only experience of love. Faced with that loss at the imminent birth of a new sibling and, as he undoubtedly perceived it, abandoned to his father's murderous violence, he resorted to the only solution that could save his life, to be a girl. Once the baby was born, he also very possibly correctly perceived that his father's rejection of him was partly due to his son's resemblance to him and his easier acceptance of his baby brother to the baby's resemblance to the mother, that is, to his being "a girl." Richard's homosexual defense was obviously designed to protect him against the threat of being killed in an atmosphere that was charged with violence and insufficiently invested with genuine loving feelings. He was unfortunately removed from treatment when his father, emerging from a deep depression, suddenly realized that his son was being treated by a lay analyst, but not before Richard had triumphantly announced at the beginning of one session, "I know you won't believe me, but I'm joining the Cub Scouts."

Lorna, being a girl, was at the opposite end of the spectrum; her only recourse was to be a boy. Her switch in sexual identity also occurred at the same age as Richard's and also around the birth of a sibling, this one also a boy. The dynamics in Lorna's case, however, were somewhat more complex. Both parents were violent and engaged in physical combat. The father, however, used violence only against the mother. Although the mother never initiated violence against the father and merely defended herself, she used violence against Lorna. In addition, Lorna was caught in a psychological bind that robbed her further of any sense of safety. The father, a successful accountant who had married for the second time, had another child by his first wife. Although he was extremely self-absorbed and immersed himself in work to the exclusion of almost any other interest, he had assumed the authoritative role in relation to Lorna's care from her birth, constantly disparaging the mother and contradicting and correcting her handling of the baby. This continued as the baby emerged from infancy into childhood and assumed the character of an alliance against the mother. In addition, Lorna's needs and wishes became the father's commands, whereas the mother's were ignored. This elevation of the child's importance enraged the mother and filled the child with terror at the threat of her mother's retaliation. Since she actually saw little of her father, Lorna was caught between his seductiveness and neglect and her mother's greater care and rage. Of the two, the mother was apparently more reliable, although terrifying. With the birth of a brother, who escaped Lorna's fate and held little interest for the father, Lorna had to contend with a sibling whom the mother felt free to enjoy. To the terror of her father's seduction and apparent preference and her mother's violent rejection and rivalry was now added the evidence that being a boy not only provided greater protection but even evoked love. At that point, all safety was undermined and a masculine identity became the only solution.

When we turn to the case of five-and-a-half-year-old Danny, the relationship between suicidal fantasies and an opposite sexual identity emerges with some clarity. In that connection there comes to mind the comment of one patient when suicidal wishes had come to the fore. At that point she stated, "For someone like me, homosexuality is in the luxury class; staying alive is the issue."

Initially, Danny's fantasies defended him against suicide and the threat of being killed; only as these preoccupations subsided did his secret fantasy of a reversed sexual identity begin to emerge. The actual acting out of an opposite identity was then precipitated by a seductive exposure to his mother. This also yielded in response to an improved life situation but returned when extraordinary circumstances once more required it. Although he was referred to me by his protesting parents because his kindergarten teacher felt he was too immature to advance to first grade, it soon became clear that Danny was engaged in a life-or-death struggle. He himself could see only one end for it all — death by violence; whether by his own hand or another's seemed immaterial. His brother Joe, five years his senior and as big and bulky as Danny was diminutive, was a major source of his problem. Joe was a friendless and withdrawn boy who had clearly not welcomed Danny's birth. When Danny was old enough to play games with, Joe organized a class consisting of the cat, Jocko the monkey, Bozo the clown, and Danny. Unhappily for Danny, the star pupil was the cat, as her consistently higher grades demonstrated. This early "school" experience and Joe's constant reference to him as a "dope" undoubtedly played their role in convincing Danny, by the time he entered treatment, that every new experience was simply another opportunity for failure. In addition, Joe passed his door every night after Danny had fallen asleep and called in until he woke him up. He also confided to Danny periodically that he wanted him to die.

"He says he'd like me to be killed," Danny related some time later, "but I don't believe it. He'd really be sorry and cry over my grave." Nevertheless, Danny disclosed, "at night I think that someone is coming in the room to stab me — not Joe — someone from the alley. I can't think who, maybe a monster."

Monsters were a regular part of Danny's waking and sleeping life; he saw them on TV every day. "Someone took a picture of a ghost," he informed me. "Barbara saw it. When people die against their wishes, they return as a ghost." In reality, Danny's difficulty in identifying the monster may have stemmed from the fact that he had two choices. At another time, he described the image of his father "with a knife in his hand."

When Danny was tested prior to entering treatment, his feelings of hopelessness were revealed in his response to one of the pictures on the Children's Apperception Test. "A baby," he stated, "one night was sleeping in the crib and a robber smashed the window. Mother and Father came in and the father said, 'I'm going after the robber.' They took the baby to the hospital, but they couldn't make him better. They had to bury him. They were sad and that's the end of the story." The role of the parents in this tale was a very accurate presentation of what occurred in reality. "I'm going after the robber," the father said, but there was no indication of action. As Danny reported, he repeatedly complained about Joe, but his parents never did anything.

The parents' failure to protect Danny from his brother's murderous wishes was only one facet in a way of relating that produced in him an expectation and desire for death. He clearly felt, as he indicated in another test response, that his parents shared Joe's wishes. In a long story about a mother and father monkey who are "telling secrets" while the baby is with the grandmother, he stated, "They don't like the others and they're making a plan. They get a rifle and they kill the others. They don't like the baby and the grandmother."

Although his parents contributed in different ways to Danny's tentative hold on life, they both found it unnecessary to inform him about any plans they had for him, and they had both apparently felt it appropriate to keep him in a crib until he entered treatment. "My father's going to screw my new bed together tonight!" Danny announced exuberantly during one session. "That crib was too small! It made me feel like a baby. I kept telling my parents, but all they said was 'Soon. Soon.'"

That was the closest Danny came to criticizing his parents for several years. At another time, referring to a classmate whom he generally accepted as his authority, he did so merely by innuendo. "Ronnie says he likes his mother better," he announced one day with unconcealed surprise.

Danny's father was undoubtedly the more dependable parent at that time and continued to remain so. He woke Danny up every morning and got him his breakfast in a fairly reliable ritual. He was also the one to take him to the store to buy him whatever he needed. His father's way of relating to him unfortunately took the form of "kidding around," however; he apparently delighted in feeding Danny misinformation and then roared at the results. Danny consequently concluded that he must be a comedian. By five and a half he had come to recognize that he never knew when he was being taken and made it a rule always to be a little suspicious. There were always new traps, however. "My father is going to build a house this summer," he volunteered one day, "and he says I can help. I can hammer the nails." Danny's father was a building contractor, a tall, muscular man whose measured speech and mocking laughter suggested a controlled violence that never ceased to be a major preoccupation.

It was Danny's mother, however, who kept the ground shifting beneath his feet. She was a small attractive woman whose tenuous hold on reality extended to her perception of her children. Danny was never sure how real his existence was where she was concerned. When he returned from school, it was a toss-up whether he would find her or the housekeeper or just a message that she would be home "in ten minutes," a possible prelude to what seemed like endless waiting. He always ate alone with his brother and sometimes didn't see her for the entire evening. His anxiety about whether she would forget him altogether was a constant factor in his treatment until he was old enough to take care of himself. The school bus dropped him at my door, but his mother picked him up at the end of the session. She was usually late, but it wasn't until Danny actually saw her that he could be sure she would come at all. His fears were only too well grounded, as I discovered one afternoon when she phoned some time after the session to tell me that he had completely slipped her mind and would I put him in a cab.

Not until several years later did I learn of one particular fantasy with which Danny defended himself at that time. He stated, "Everybody was putting on a show for me. You weren't Dorothy Bloch. People were posing as my parents. They used to be there, but someone took them away. I still think so sometimes. They made themselves look like my parents, but they tied my real parents up. I guess my real parents would be nicer to me; they'd love me more. These other people I guess wouldn't really."

The more real aspect of Danny's world actually was "a show." Any exploration of the decisive elements in his life would be incomplete without taking into account the influence of television. He was set adrift in it without chart or compass and permitted to expose himself to its deadly rays for four or five hours a day during the week and apparently endless hours on weekends. The world of violence it projected became his continuing frame of reference. When he wasn't watching it, he was thinking about it. Where other children related their encounters in the real world, Danny spoke of the latest exploits of his favorite television characters. It was a mark of progress when he turned from his preoccupation with war to "The Jetsons," who lived in "A House of the Future" and became his model for family life. For him the new frontiers of science featured among other things hypodermic syringes that made it possible to melt down brains, invade minds, transform not only personalities but flesh and bone, and cause people to disappear. Atomic warfare became television-real, and invasion from outer space imminently threatening. "Do midgets have to go to war?" he inquired apprehensively, obviously referring to himself. The world was peopled with monsters, and the powers of evil flourished. Apparently, for Danny all of this was simply a corroboration and perhaps an elaboration in another dimension and on a vaster plane of his perceptions of the world of reality. The television screen also provided him with one helpful fantasy, however; he was Superman. Only occasionally did I get intimations of the dimensions of this secret involvement. He could repeat the opening lines of the program verbatim and from time to time for several years was preoccupied with the design and creation of an appropriate costume.

In my effort to understand the quality of the impact of this world of horror and monstrosity on Danny, I had the impression that it came in on him unfiltered. There appeared first of all to be no frame of reference that allowed him to sift and strain this material and to emerge with some sense of balance between the real and the unreal. Not only did he not enjoy the protection of a limited exposure, but he had little acquaintance with the kind of health that could have provided the necessary foil to the sick imaginings of the television screen. Quite on his own and without the intervention of outside forces, he could conjure out of the darkness of the night images of sufficiently blood-curdling terror. With the aid of modern technology, however, his own powers were expanded into infinity. As he related to me, "Since I saw *The Phantom of the Opera,* I never take my eyes off my room."

In addition, I had the impression of a decided failure in his "filtering system." The first outward sign that something was wrong with it was the fixed smile with which he attempted to barricade himself for lack of something better. His parents had concluded from it that he was "a happy, carefree child." When it began to dissolve in the course of therapy, exposing his sadness, they attacked the treatment.

The smile, however, was only one facet of Danny's armature. His inner world of thought and feeling was also vaulted and double-locked; Danny actually gave the impression that he thought the key was in everyone else's pocket. His rejection of all responsibility for what went on inside him gave rise to some strange phenomena. At one point, about two years after he started treatment, Danny began to complain that his eyes "watered." His parents responded after a while by taking him to an eye doctor, who could find nothing wrong with the ducts. Nevertheless, the "watering" persisted. Danny related to me that it could happen anywhere, sometimes without any warning in the midst of his lessons at school or on his way to my office or while he was just sitting doing nothing at home. The problem was clarified during one particular session when he described in some detail a televised ball game in which he had seen a baby in the audience.

"He didn't know what was going on," said Danny.

I looked at him for a moment and then commented, "I don't know if you remember when you were a baby."

He paused, then volunteered, "I sucked my mother's bosoms when I was a baby. I'm sorry I did it," he added. "I don't like warm milk."

"I guess there are some things you don't like about her," I ventured.

"That's true," he agreed for the first time.

"Especially when she leaves you alone."

"My eyes still water," he stated, as though we both understood the meaning of that term and its relation to what we were talking about.

"Do you think your eyes water when you feel sad?" I asked.

"I think so," Danny agreed.

"People frequently feel like crying when they're unhappy," I said. And with that, Danny granted himself the right to sadness and tears.

Danny maintained a similar relationship to his thought processes; they didn't belong to him. Some years later, when he was able to lay claim to himself, he marveled, "I can't get over it, that it's my mind and it does all these things, that it's mine." There had been intimations that he had not thought it was his from the very beginning.

During an early session, when he had been shooting darts against the wall, I observed, "You seem pretty angry to me."

"How do you know?" he asked. "Do I look it?"

"No," I said. "You generally smile. But underneath I think you're angry."

"What am I angry at?" he demanded. Danny's conviction that his thoughts could be read had already been established. As he explained some time later, he kept himself from thinking in order to avoid exposure. The revelation of the power he imputed to others always startled me, however.

"I think you're mad at me," I again commented one day.

He looked at me in evident surprise. "You mean you think when I'm walking down the hall behind you that I want to stick a knife in your back?"

Similarly, on another occasion I observed, "I notice that you don't like to tell me what happens in school."

"You mean about Ronnie?" he retorted. "That he wants to kill me? Well, I told him he'd be electrocuted."

When Danny began to take notice of his own inner workings, he at first approached them cautiously. After finishing an airplane model, he stated, "A thought went through my mind to break off all the propellers, but I think I won't." When he began to grasp the true dimensions of the swelling rage inside him, he felt impelled to define it in verbal terms. "An angry man could knock through a wall," he declared one day. "He could smash your desk. Even more. An angry boy could tear a mouth apart," he asserted, pulling his own mouth out of shape. "He could if he was angry. He could knock down a wall."

When his anger finally erupted, Danny found it overwhelming. I commented one day, "I think you're very worried. Maybe if you tell me about it, I can help you."

"You mean so that I won't be mad and scream all the time?"

Danny's fear of being murdered as well as his suicidal wishes were apparent in the fantasies that he revealed from the beginning of treatment. Initially he created a fantasy in which I was locked up at one end of the terrace while he reclined in a lounger at some distance. When I commented after some minutes that he must be tired, he stated, "My enemies are far away, and I'm resting." For weeks after that he occupied us with the murder and the disposal of multitudes or hand-to-hand combat with the enemy. His scathing comments about my poor performance and the ineffectual quality of my assistance left no doubt about both the formidable character of his enemies and the unreliability of help. When he turned to play with soldiers, the soldier who represented himself was inevitably destroyed.

At a later point, about two years after the beginning of his treatment, when he drew a "new style" airplane and announced that it exploded, I asked, "What happened to the pilot?"

"He parachuted," Danny replied, then, as an afterthought, "Only he forgets to pull the cord until he lands. Then he pulls it."

"He gets killed," I added, to Danny's assent.

During the same period he frequently confronted me with various types of suicidal riddles. "What would happen," he asked, "if a boy was put in a sack and thrown off the roof? What if he was tied up in a rug? What if it was made of iron, or lead?" "What would happen if a boy was on a roof and he sniffed glue until he went crazy and he didn't know what he was doing and he jumped off?"

Nevertheless, alternating with his suicidal fantasies, there gradually began to emerge fantasies in which all his soldiers were demolished but he alone made his getaway in a plane. It was following that time that the first intimations of a homosexual fantasy were revealed. His interest in "The Jetsons" had already displaced his preoccupation with war, and their house became the subject of his drawings. During one session he announced that he would draw anything I liked, and when I suggested, "A boy," like Richard, he quickly asserted, "I can't draw boys." He started a figure that looked like a capital M, apparently two legs and a penis, but he quickly turned the paper over in obvious dissatisfaction and drew a figure that consisted of two sticks with a double crosspiece on the top, capped it with a head and long hair and referred to it as "her." He next drew father and mother, the father simply being a larger version of "her" without the hair and the mother having enormous arms swinging upward. As an afterthought he added huge hands on line-arms on the father and outsize hands on "her."

Shortly afterward, Danny had an experience that apparently precipitated the transformation of his homosexual fantasy into a homosexual identity. Although he was still quite small for his age, at eight and a half he was a very handsome boy with a very pleasant, agreeable manner. For the first time his mother selected him as her sole companion on a week's vacation in California. He returned tense and anxious, however, with a new and embarrassing problem: he had a constant urge to urinate. His need to leave the room very frequently at school mortified him, but the real nightmare was the prospect of camp with such a condition.

From time to time I had proposed to Danny, with little success, that he use the couch, and now when he presented his predicament to me, I took the opportunity to suggest again that if he used the couch and simply talked, we might both begin to understand it. "You mean, before camp?" he demanded eagerly. On the couch, he initially spoke of his continuing difficulty in making friends and his brother's wish for him to die. By the third session, however, he reported a dream about a naked lady who was taking a bath in a sink in his room with her legs hanging over. After describing the dream, he stated that he "saw" a jet plane, a black one with a long point, hovering in the room. He confessed that he liked to think of naked women, and although he had seen his mother naked only once, when he was four, he frequently saw her in just her bra and pantyhose, only he couldn't see through them. It appears that he saw her a lot that way in California, although she always went into the bathroom to put her nightgown on and they slept in separate beds. He was continually preoccupied by sexual thoughts and stated several times that he couldn't wait to grow up "to do it." He also wanted to know about fucking and presented the concept that when a man fucks, he "makes" in a woman's vagina. As I corrected this concept, it became clear that his urge to urinate resulted from his overstimulation and his impression that the sex act involved urination. He happily devoted the next few sessions to his sexual fantasies about his mother. His urination problem disappeared and he went off to camp without this particular anxiety.

After that summer and for the next year and a half, however, Danny was obviously acting out a homosexual identity. Although he initially resumed playing, as his anxiety mounted, he decided to return to the couch. His first communication then related to his sex play with two boys in his class, one of whom ignored him after the experience. During the following months he also adopted unmistakable feminine mannerisms. The Beatles were the vogue at that time and long hair for males was just coming into fashion, and Danny let his hair grow. He also selected clothing with an unusual interest for his age in color, texture, and line. As he lay on the couch, he appeared constantly to be absorbed in admiring his legs; he also began to adopt what might be called a feminine walk. Although his exhibitionism provoked the children at school, Danny apparently preferred their attacks to what he had previously experienced as their rejection or indifference; he also appeared to derive satisfaction from their taunting him with being a girl. His father also reported during one session that at three different times during a week's trip, adults had pretended to mistake him for a girl, to Danny's delight. Danny's sessions during this period were also marked by frequent references to this confusion and his apparent enjoyment of it.

A development then occurred that might have led to the resolution of his problems. About a year before, Danny had persuaded his father to buy him a trumpet, and as a trumpeter he began to win the admiration of his classmates. He soon joined a combo that was deemed good enough to be hired for parties. His brother had also been in treatment for the past year, and both his life and his way of relating to Danny had improved. He took pride in Danny's accomplishments, and his friends now urged Danny to play with them. He accepted several invitations to perform at high school parties and was very successful. He had also begun to distinguish himself at school as an actor. It was the high point of his life. Contempt and ridicule became a thing of the past. For the first time, not only was he free of suicidal thoughts, but his acceptance by others, particularly by his brother, and his unprecedented feelings of worth led to a self-acceptance that appeared to make any reversal of identity unnecessary. He carried himself with a new dignity and seemed confident about making friends and organizing his life.

At that point his mother suddenly decided to leave the family and move to the West Coast. Danny's immediate response was to plunge into a relationship with a girl in his class that was much more intense than is usual in an eleven-year-old. It lasted for almost a year and ended in a shower of recriminations that he recognized were clearly related to his rage at his mother. His brother had also terminated treatment and reacted to his mother's abandonment with reawakened hostility toward Danny.

Although Danny did not reassume the outward symbols of his feminine identification, from time to time he betrayed the existence of his secret identity. Whenever I saw fit to make any generalization about boys, for instance, he invariably objected to the exclusiveness of my reference. Following the severance of his relationship with his girl, he returned to sex play with the same two boys and described the mutual masturbation that had taken place. In attempting to diminish any feelings of guilt that might have resulted, I commented, "Boys sometimes like to do that." He immediately protested with, "Why do you always say 'boys'? Why don't you say 'boys and girls'?" At another time during a discussion of his fantasy that I always emerged for his session after making love in the other room, I commented that maybe he had thoughts of making love to me, adding, "Boys very often can think of making love to women." I again drew the protest, "You know, it's very funny. You always say 'boys.' You never say 'girls.'"

During the period of his relationship with the girl, when he came to his session one day feeling very depressed, he reported that when he had called and asked her what she was doing, she had replied, "Shimmying on the door. It feels like fucking." At first Danny was shocked and then depressed. Acting on a hunch, I stated that the conversation made him realize that he and his girl were different — he could never feel the same way about a door. At that, he remembered wanting to know what it was like to menstruate, just once.

Following his father's remarriage, Danny's life situation continued to deteriorate. Until the termination of his treatment, his major preoccupation became acceptance by boys to the seeming exclusion of any interest in girls. Whether that was a passing phase or whether he later acted out his fantasy of a homosexual identity, I have no way of knowing.

When we compare Danny's fantasies with those of the children discussed earlier, we note a difference in their characters and, as we would expect, in the life situations that produced them. Of the four, Danny was the most threatened and the least protected. Not only did he feel that all the members of his family wanted him killed, but there was no one who offered him sufficient refuge for him to feel loved. His initial fantasies were therefore concerned with suicide and death. It is note-worthy that only when the treatment situation established enough security to allow him to turn from them to family life, via television, the first intimations of a fantasy of a feminine self emerged. Danny's acting out did not commence until after his vacation with his mother, however, because her seductive-ness and her preference for him over his father and brother increased the precariousness of his position by sharpening the already existing rivalry and by making him even more vul-nerable to attack. To protect himself against his fear of mur-derous retaliation by demonstrating his innocence in relation to his mother, and to secure the love that he felt was his only bulwark against annihilation, he adopted an opposite sexual identity. Following his initial desperate response to his mother's abandonment and his involvement with a girl, his inexpressible yearning for his father's and brother's love, with its promise of protection, also reasserted itself.

Among the children I have treated, those who acted out the fantasy of a different identity had all been exposed to an environment that offered little emotional security from per-sistent acted-out violence. Detachment was frequently the only refuge available. Although the child may have been nurturing a fantasy of a different identity for some time, its actual acting out in all instances was precipitated by a single event that intensified already existing terror and convinced him that his life was in imminent danger. At that point he decided that the only way to save himself was to be someone else — generally, someone who was invulnerable to attack.

In the cases of the four children who acted out the fantasy of a homosexual identity, each felt his life was threatened by the parent of the same sex. With all four, the feelings and the behavior of the parents toward each other and toward him convinced him that not only did they not love each other, but that the parent of the opposite sex preferred him to the other parent. His expectation of the latter's retaliation in an atmos-phere that was marked by violent acting out and a paucity of genuine loving feelings led him to conclude that only a change

of sex could secure the threatening parent's love and thus save
his life. In three instances the children sought this drastic
solution when an already charged situation was further exacerbated by the birth of a sibling of the opposite sex or of one
who resembled the parent of the opposite sex. In the fourth,
intimations of a reversal of sexual identity emerged with the
diminution of suicidal and death fantasies. When the mother
chose the child as her sole companion and exposed him to the
intimacy of a shared bedroom, his fear of retaliation from his
father and his father's violent surrogate, his brother, increased
his already considerable terror of being killed by them and
precipitated the acting out of the fantasy of an opposite sexual
identity.

In all instances, the child's magical thinking, which generally leads him to equate thoughts, wishes, and feelings with
deeds, further undermined his sense of safety when he was
confronted with actual violence and an inadequate supply of
love — he expected to be killed. In a desperate attempt to save
his life at a specific moment of what he experienced as acute
danger, he therefore transformed himself. In so doing he hoped
both to neutralize the violence of the threatening parent by
eliminating what he perceived as its cause and to secure the
love that would protect him against it.

Although not all instances of the persistent acting out of the
fantasy of a homosexual identity can be explained by the dynamics that prevailed in the cases of these four children, the
similarity of all four is very striking and suggests that those
dynamics may be present in a large number of cases. A great
deal can also be learned from them about the symptomatology
of adult homosexuality. The homosexual's frequent insistence
that his fantasy is real, that he actually does belong to the
opposite sex or a third sex, or that he was "born that way"
cannot help reminding us of the unwavering intensity of the
children's assertions. When we also recall that with all four
children the stake was life or death, we may be in a better
position to assess the meaning of the self-deception and denial
that are so essential in maintaining the adult fantasy.

Chapter 4

"I Didn't Come Out of My Mother's Stomach": A Fantasy That Took Three Years to Evolve

UNTIL A CHILD enters treatment, the extraordinary function of his fantasies rarely becomes evident. It is not unusual for a child to reveal during his first session a fantasy that he may then play out for the next two or three years. That he is involved in a question of life or death — and with the analyst's help is proceeding toward the resolution of the fantasy he has created in order to defend himself against his terror — may not emerge until the fantasy's actual dénouement. That the process may take years tells us something about the nature of feelings; once they are established, it is no easy matter to dislodge or to modify them.

In handling the fantasy in psychoanalytic treatment, the analyst takes his cues from the child. Since the child has created the fantasy in order to defend himself, it appears essential to respect his right of authorship and to leave the work in his hands. Unless he adopts a destructive course, I have found it most important to leave the initiative to him even when he insists that the analyst assume the lead. His proven reliability in creating a fantasy to meet his needs seems to indicate that if he is allowed to remain in charge of it, he may be able to resolve it with the analyst's help.

It is characteristic of work with children's fantasies that they may frequently appear to proceed without any discernible direction until their actual resolution reveals the master plan. Very often only in retrospect does the progress of the fantasy become clear. The climax itself may come as a surprise and may suddenly illuminate an activity that has extended over several years. Although the analyst may often feel at sea, if he simply takes the cues and adopts the lines offered by the child, he may later find that he has advanced the fantasy from one stage to the next. In instances where the child's ability to fantasize appears constricted for any reason, once the child has set the guidelines, the analyst may liberate and enrich the fantasy by simply elaborating on what the child has set forth, always mindful of not usurping the child's role. Where there is any doubt about the usefulness of the child's occupation, his functioning in reality is usually an excellent barometer of the validity of the analyst's handling of the treatment situation.

In the case of five-year-old José, the fantasy of a secret identity, which he revealed during his first session, reached its climax after three years of treatment. Although I had already had intimations of its presence, the dramatic session that finally proclaimed his true identity was impressive, not only because of the suddenness of the culmination of an extraordinarily slowly evolving fantasy, but because of the speed with which the revelation of his real self was followed by a rapprochement with the more threatening parent.

"I'm not an American," he volunteered at our first meeting. "I didn't come out of my mother's stomach like my sister, Mary."

"Where did you come from?" I asked.

José became vague and distracted. "Maybe from inside my aunt."

Although that information was to remain my frame of reference throughout José's treatment, I was not to learn its true meaning until the climax of his fantasy. The extraordinary scale of the feeling of rejection implied by the theory of his birth was immediately clear. It took almost three years, however, to discover that "I'm not an American" did not mean merely being different or alien. Since he was convinced his father wanted to kill him, he assumed he must belong to the group of people his father had killed in the war, the Germans. His fantasy of an assumed identity defended him against his fear of infanticide by explaining and justifying his father's murderous feelings toward him and providing the hope that when he changed and became an American his father would love him.

The process that led José to his true identity was as devious as one might expect of someone who had found himself living in the camp of the enemy almost from birth. Only after the battles he devised had culminated in the slaughter of the Americans did José feel strong enough to claim equal status with his father. The immediacy with which that assertion followed the resolution of the central theme of his fantasy was startling in itself and without precedent in my experience. Once again the unerring direction of a fantasy established the extraordinary reliability of the psyche in the fight for survival.

Although my psychoanalytic treatment of children had already led me to expect the disclosure of core problems, frequently during the first session, very little in my interview with José's parents had prepared me for his initial disclosure, and I was taken aback. In retrospect, I realized that his mother had certainly suggested the basis for his feeling that she preferred his sister, although not for its dimensions. Nothing in his father's communication, however, had given the slightest indication that José lived in daily fear of extermination by him.

My first interview with them had left me somewhat confused. I recall thinking afterward, Could it be that at last a child is being referred who doesn't need help? I had heard such a phenomenon reported by others but had never encountered it in my own practice; I had finally concluded that if a parent thinks a child needs help it's a safe assumption that he does. In this instance, however, I had some doubt and, to my credit, I felt that my very question suggested something suspicious in the situation.

It was mainly his father's exultant laughter as he spoke of José that kept me wondering. He was an extraordinarily charming man in his early thirties, tall and slender, with light brown hair and blue eyes, a former cabinetmaker who had become a successful manufacturer of furniture. He had come here from Argentina in late adolescence and had met and married his Spanish wife a few years later. He commenced by announcing he was merely indulging her by consenting to what he called "a preventive interview" and asserted with conviction that he had a very happy relationship with his son, whom he presented as a paragon.

At five, José had mastered all the skills that were expected of him and more. He was a leader among children and easily won their admiration. His creative gifts were a joy to both parents. José was an "artist" who was capable of losing himself in the contemplation of a cloud; was that neurotic?

The wife, somewhat rounder but as tall as her husband and with darker coloring, appeared tense and unsmiling and somewhat intimidated in his presence. She immediately conceded overconcern and perhaps mismanagement; nevertheless, it seemed to her there was something that merited attention. To begin with, José's "artistic" temperament was such a source of exasperation to her that it ruined their relationship. Just the night before, it had taken him two hours to get undressed, bathed, and ready for bed. The same difficulty occurred every morning in preparing for school or whenever there was a time deadline. She felt that it had all started with the birth of their infant daughter, Mary, toward whom José had a punitive attitude, although at times he also seemed affectionate. There had been a great deal of tension between her and her husband at the time of José's birth. It seemed to her now that she had been too strict with him, and she recognized how relaxed she felt with Mary, to whom both of them responded much more easily. And then there were certain peculiarities in José that she couldn't dismiss. After Mary's birth, he had started to suck his thumb almost constantly. That had lasted a month and had been followed in succession by masturbation, coughing, and finally by blinking. She also reported in an apologetic way, as though not quite sure of her ground, that José loved the feel of hair, that he was constantly touching it; it seemed exaggerated. There were also very occasional outbursts of rage, like a dam breaking. Her husband laughed at her presentation so that she faltered and seemed almost ready to erase it.

Only much later did I realize that her husband's performance was so convincing that it almost succeeded in blurring for me what I recognized as a familiar symptomatology. I had no difficulty in gauging the degree of terror that might be required for a child to adopt covert means to express opposition or to employ compulsive acts to repress rage. Only after I had grasped the scale of the deception employed by José's father, however, could I marvel at the skill that made me question for a moment the need for help established by his wife. As I discovered from subsequent sessions, José's father deceived not only me but himself. The "happy relationship" was obviously a myth or a fantasy that soon proved a formidable barrier to his continued involvement in his son's treatment.

As I became acquainted with his parents, I came to know that it was José's misfortune that he reminded not only his father of a hated younger brother, but also his mother of a hated older one. When José's mother arrived at the distressing discovery that she didn't enjoy José because she always expected him to defeat her, she was soon able to trace that feeling to her older brother, with whom she had been in constant conflict as a child. For José's father, however, that early relationship had been too traumatic to approach. His mother had died when he was quite young, and as he was approaching adolescence his father had married a woman who bore him another son. That son was adored, whereas he himself was ignored and made into a workhorse. He had left his father's house in rebellion and did not see his brother again for many years, and then only briefly, so that his memory of him remained fixed at just about José's age. José's birth had very likely revived that experience and made him the focus of the rivalry and the murderous hostility that belonged to the earlier relationship.

Although José's father never verbalized any hostile or competitive feelings toward him, his rivalry with his son led him into an unconscious analytic contest with him despite his intense opposition to analysis. Instead of focusing on his relationship with José, he soon launched into a description of his own life, of his early years and of the hardships he had had to overcome, in a manner that was unusual under those circumstances. His wife also reported with some embarrassment that at José's birthday party he had competed with the children and had tried to show them up. It was also from her that I learned of an incident that dramatized his impact on José.

José had spent an afternoon in the park with his father. When he returned and his mother asked him about the day, José had stated that it would have been better if he hadn't been so thirsty. She was puzzled, but asked if there wasn't any water in the park. José's expression was one of abject misery. It hadn't occurred to him that he might — or, as she implied, dared — ask his father if he could get a drink.

Although José's response to the violent feelings of both parents became the warp and the woof of his analysis, his ability to resolve the fantasy that dominated it for two years was a measure, not only of the growth of his ego strength and the improvement in his way of relating to them, but also of their ability to change. They had both been brought up in violent households and accepted violence as a method of control. It is therefore not surprising that the scale of the terror induced by José's perception of their feelings placed him outside his mother's womb and transformed him into an enemy alien. That they were also caring people, however, was clearly established by their concern and their willingness to respond to his newly defined needs.

For the first few minutes after I met José, I remembered his father's exulting laughter. José was a big fellow for his five years, a little heavy, but a delight to the eye. His extraordinary head, whose form was accentuated by its light brown, close-cropped hair, his serious face, so filled with intelligence and wonder, and a skin coloring that seemed to have been arrived at by mixing sunlight and golden sand brought to mind his mother's reports of strangers who were frequently moved to admire and caress him, much to José's annoyance. He was impressively self-sufficient. Ignoring me and immediately concentrating on the possibilities offered by the playroom, he set about creating one of the most beautiful collages out of shells and colored glitter I had seen there. In the process he spoke little. Finally he volunteered what I suspected was his central preoccupation, the mystery of his identity.

From the first, José struck me as a child whose only solution for such formidable enemies was to retreat and hide. Only

covert opposition was possible, only devious methods of warfare. He appeared to maintain a sense of safety and control
magically by excluding adults from his line of vision. For
months, as soon as I opened the door to let him in, he rushed
past me down the long hallway to the playroom, looking to
neither right nor left, greeting me either inaudibly or not at
all.

"You don't like to say 'Hello,'" I commented one day.

"I did say 'Hello,' but you didn't hear it," he replied
defensively.

"You don't have to if you don't want to," I assured him.

"But I did," he insisted.

José rarely laughed or smiled and for the most part maintained an expressionless mask. He spoke in low tones, sometimes measured, sometimes running together in a way that
made it difficult to understand. He moved very quietly and
appeared to avoid looking at me. This resulted in my looking
at him, and I wondered if that was also his intent.

During the first few weeks he continued to ignore me and
occupied himself mainly with drawing, making no attempt to
involve me in any way. Apart from his original disclosure, his
communication remained very guarded. The "dreaminess"
that repeatedly moved his mother to rage and that his father
ascribed to an artistic temperament appeared to be an inge-
nious defense, protecting him by its ambiguity. I suspected his
pretense of not noticing me was part of it, but it manifested
itself most clearly at the end of the session as a covert method
of control.

"It's time to stop," I announced, allowing several minutes'
leeway. But José seemed preoccupied and gave no sign of
having heard. When he finally arose from the table, he appeared absorbed in the contemplation of a drawing and then
began an intense examination of a toy that he had ignored
until then. "You find it very difficult to leave," I attempted
further, but with the same lack of success. Finally, by the
third or fourth session, I came up with: "I think we'll stop ten
minutes earlier so that you can take your time leaving." José
was impressed.

"Did you leave ten minutes today?" he asked innocently at the end of the next session, all the while maneuvering to make it fifteen. I decided there was nothing for it but a direct confrontation.

"I've been noticing what you do at the end of every session," I observed. "As soon as I say, 'It's time to stop,' you become very busy," I continued, imitating him. "You suddenly begin to study this and to study that; you're so absorbed that you don't know what's going on. That's what you'd like me to think. But you know very well what's going on; you just don't want to budge. You're just a big fake," I charged. At first José appeared to listen with deaf ears. Then a broad grin spread across his face until finally he let out a delighted laugh at the picture I drew, the first I had heard. It marked the beginning of a loosening up of his relationship to me and the first expression of a sense of humor that was increasingly liberated as his treatment progressed. The problem of his dilatory tactics was not wholly solved, however, but thereafter centered mainly on getting his coat on. His resourcefulness in dividing this seemingly simple operation into various stages — first assembling the garment in front of him, then treating each sleeve as a separate area of conquest — never failed to astound me.

"Let's have a race," I announced one day in desperation. "I bet you can't get your coat on before I straighten my desk." But he won, and that eventually ended that oppositional maneuver.

José's demeanor was unusually correct. Occasionally he inquired whether certain acts were permissible, but more often he acted as his own censor and rarely even expressed a wish to go beyond very decorous forms of conduct. He ignored all the toys, including the guns and soldiers, which might have encouraged some freedom of expression. Even his drawings were mainly static descriptions of buildings, bridges, and cars. When he wasn't drawing, he seemed at a loss for an activity. Once he brought some Silly Putty, which clearly challenged his controls. It gave him a great deal of pleasure, but only within the careful limits he permitted.

As far as I was aware, his "dreaminess" was the only conscious expression of his rebellion against the need for rigid compliance. In order to create a sense of safety, the dimensions of the rage engendered by the hostility of his environment appeared to require an additional, unconscious defense whose objective was the massive repression of feeling. His mother had referred briefly to earlier compulsions, but I soon discovered they were a constant element in his behavior. When he first came to see me, he repeatedly cleared his throat. After a while that stopped, only to be replaced by his smelling every object he used, sometimes shamefacedly, as though recognizing that there was something strange in it. The smelling then gave way to licking. His tongue had to make contact with every object he handled. He could no longer conceal at that point the discomfort of this activity nor the helplessness he experienced in the throes of it. By that time I had established enough of a relationship for him to be able to talk about it.

"Sometimes," I said, "you don't really want to lick, but you can't help yourself; you feel forced to do it."

He looked at me half-embarrassed, half-appealing. "My tongue feels sore," he admitted.

That was probably the most intense and uncomfortable compulsion he developed, and also the last one. As his feelings were liberated, he no longer required that defense.

Fantasy became the dominant instrument that led to its resolution. During the entire first year of treatment, however, he allowed it to surface only once and permitted me a glimpse of the inner world that dictated his need for the extraordinary repression he maintained by means of compulsive acts.

One lovely day in the late fall he allowed himself to yield to the temptations of the terrace for the first time. "Can we go outside?" he asked. He looked about him, wandered aimlessly, then spotted the hose. "Can I turn it on?" he inquired. He did so, full force, and proceeded after a few minutes to aim it with unusually concentrated attention at a circumscribed area of the quarried tile roof.

"It looks like a flood," I ventured, suspecting that murderous feelings were involved.

"It is a flood," he exulted.

"What's getting flooded?" I pursued.

"The whole city!" he cried on a note of triumph. Pointing to the cracks, he added, "Those are the streets."

"What streets are they?" I guessed they could not be too far from home.

"That's Eighth Avenue, and that's Twenty-second Street, and here's Broadway."

"Where's West End?" I asked, wondering where I was in the fantasy.

"That's way over. The flood hasn't reached it yet."

Then I mentioned his street. "Under water!" was the unhesitating reply.

"And what's happening to the people?"

"They're getting drowned!" he jubilated.

"The flood" remained a gratifying although occasional part of his activity. The theme of murder and annihilation was picked up in his drawings, which began to concern themselves exclusively with soldiers, guns, and warfare. It also gradually dominated his play, which was soon structured around soldiers and guns, and spilled over into his model-making, with its exclusive concentration on fighter planes, battleships, and tanks. Except for occasional excursions into board games and one domestic interlude, these activities lasted about two years and reflected in their development the various stages of his emotional growth and of the resolution of his fantasy of an assumed identity in response to his fear of infanticide.

The slowness with which this world unfolded confounds belief. In its almost imperceptible movement it suggested what one might imagine the waking process to be for someone who had slept for many years. Sometimes I was tempted to intervene with the hope of speeding things up, and sometimes I was successful. In general, however, José needed to take his own time, to be allowed to let the process flow without interference.

For some time his play appeared to be internalized. Its paucity of movement or sound created the impression that he was "thinking" most of it. Among his first tentative efforts was a game he devised with two little cars he brought from home. He transformed the tabletop into a street, using some jars of paint and a box of chalk as props. Taking one car and giving me the other, he proceeded to move it slowly across the surface, directing me to do the same with mine from the opposite direction. And that was it. There was no sound, no contact, only the unhurried motion of each car as it followed a path across the table. Its monotony was matched only by his contentment with it. As I watched his silent, seemingly uneventful play, I cast about for some way of bringing his feelings to the surface and welcomed the opportunity he provided when after several sessions he announced that his was a police car. I immediately became a reckless driver, disobeyed all the traffic rules and argued endlessly when he brought me to a halt. At first he found great difficulty in verbalizing his role and smiled self-consciously as he replied to my provocations, which frequently moved him to laughter, timidly imposing light fines and a very mild threat of jail if I didn't mend my ways. It took many weeks before he developed any assurance in this role. Whenever I dropped mine, however, the game again became seemingly dull and uneventful. The law, order, and discipline imposed by terror were deeply entrenched and too formidable for José to challenge at that point.

After some months in treatment, he also became interested in making models, a complicated activity for someone who did not yet know how to read, and at this stage he selected them indiscriminately. He studied the diagrams and the parts and did an amazing job of putting them together. There were moments, nevertheless, when he was clearly stuck. After watching him struggle silently for some minutes, I commented, "You don't like to ask for help." There was no response. After I tried several variations, including, "Sometimes when people ask me, I can help them," he finally acceded. Nothing had seemingly been established, however, and the next problem was tackled in the identical manner. This time, however, I tried another tack and asserted with some vigor, "You don't really expect any help from me." His unhesitating reply cleared up the mystery.

"Women don't know very much," he stated.

He had already made known his position on the relative virtues of the sexes when he presented an apparently indisputable argument: "If a family was in a boat, and one of them was a girl, it would probably sink." To his credit, be it said, his illustration was accompanied by laughter.

Now, following his game with the cars, he returned to making more complicated models, this time directing his choice at first to any fighter plane and then only to those of World War II. He also restricted himself to tanks and battleships of the same era. This occupation afforded me an opportunity to become his indispensable assistant. At first with an air of indulging me, he permitted me to read the directions step by step as he put the parts together. Sensing that he experienced help as an attempt to wipe him out, I was careful never to exceed the limits he assigned me and waited patiently for him to request aid when the task became too difficult. Gradually he experienced our cooperative effort as fun and delighted in asking me when he arrived, "Do you have your reading glasses on?"

Model-making continued for several months to the exclusion of all other activity and showed no signs of diminishing. When I began to feel that as much had been derived from it as could be expected in terms of the growth of our relationship, and when it seemed as though José was beginning to use it as a resistance to further development, I proposed that we limit it to once a month and find other things to do. He accepted this arrangement, but was left once more with the problem of an unstructured session. After a few sessions of board games, during which time, I soon learned, José had been giving some thought to his next activity, he introduced a game with soldiers, retaining the basic structure of our previous game with cars. Very gradually it had become apparent that he had one major preoccupation — war and destruction — to which he at first gave very quiet expression. His concentration on fighter plane models had already indicated this direction. Now the tabletop became a battlefield, and once more the paint jars, the box of chalk, and the crayons were the props — this time, fortifications. He divided the soldiers between us, each of us having a doctor and a plane and a soldier in whom our identities were vested. The importance he gave the doctor indicated José's profound fear of war, as did his selection for his identifying soldier — the only one who carried, not a gun, but a coffee mug. Just as in the traffic game, he encouraged me to talk to my men and relished my manner of speaking, moved to laughter by such terms as "bombardment." He himself spoke very softly, almost inaudibly, and once more gave me the impression that most of the game was occurring inside his head. He was also very surreptitious in the movement of his men, frequently using the word "sneak" to describe it. The next session, he came without his cars, announcing that we would each have a plane and instructing me to divide the soldiers so that he would have just a few men, leaving the bulk of them to me, and also giving me the jeep. "And talk the way you did last time," he directed.

After we had each selected the soldier who represented us he asserted, "I'm putting mine in a safe place." He removed the cover of a container of wooden beads and buried his soldier, leaving only the tip of the face showing. He then replaced the cover so the soldier was completely invisible. "It's an invincible tank," he commented.

"But how are you going to talk to your men?" I asked.

"By radio," was the immediate reply. And a more accurate symbol of José's way of relating to the world at that point would have been hard to find.

That was the beginning of a kind of play that eventually led José out of his hiding place to confront and conquer his enemies, freeing him finally to establish his identity in a more friendly world as an "American." He soon became more active in this war, constantly attacking my men, bombing them and wounding "me" seriously. He interspersed the war sessions with board games, which also became an instrument for the release of his aggression. He played with increasing spontaneity and real fun, pretending repeatedly to "kill" my token, at which time I exclaimed, to his delight, that I was being "murdered," "shot," "stabbed," and "slaughtered."

When we returned to the war game after a brief interval, it progressed on a new and expanded level. I had bought some new airplanes and thereby revolutionized our activity. Not only were we now impressively airborne, but we were involved in a new industry, the construction of hangars with building blocks. Our planes now took off on the tabletop and landed on the desk.

More significantly, however, we were no longer enemies, but allies. Our common foe, the Germans, were at first located on the desk. One day José related to me his new television experience, a war program that he recommended I watch. Later he added still another. Both of these became the models of our activity.

"Who do you want to be?" José inquired after the soldiers had been divided and the armies deployed.

"I haven't quite decided," I replied. "Who do you think I should be?"

"You can be anyone you want," he asserted with some impatience. "You be the leader."

"Well," I said, somewhat dismayed by this threat to the liberation of his fantasy, "I could be the leader, but why don't you be the leader?"

"No, I'm the lieutenant." There was no room for argument.

"This is me," he informed me, selecting the soldier with the coffee mug. "Which is you?"

"This is me." I selected one at random; then, each of us grasping our identifying soldier, we set forth for battle.

"You're supposed to give the orders," José reminded me.

"Oh," I responded as though it had slipped my mind. "What orders do you think I should give?"

José snorted. "Did you ever hear a leader ask the lieutenant what orders he should give?"

"Well, maybe you should be the leader."

"No, I'm the lieutenant. Give the order to go forward."

"Go forward, men," I complied weakly.

"That's not the way to do it," said José in disgust. "Here, you be the lieutenant," and he stepped in front of me in the position of leader. "Forward, men," he commanded. And from then on José directed our activity.

Thus began the new stage of our battle. Our field was now the entire room. One day I was momentarily surprised to see José toss his coat in the middle of the floor on arriving.

"This is the mountains where the Americans are hiding," he announced. The next ten minutes were spent in deploying the

soldiers in the gullies and caves and hilltops created by the
folds of his jacket. From the American encampment we moved
to the far reaches of the room, where among the cushions on
the couch we effectively laid out the German fortifications.
Always carrying our identifying soldier, usually isolated from
the main force and outnumbered, we frequently engaged in
stealthy reconnoitering missions, "sneaking" up on the German camp. Sometimes traveling on foot, sometimes in our
single fighter planes, we made forays into enemy territory;
occasionally one of us was captured, only to be rescued mirac-
ulously by the other, who brought up reinforcements.

There were some moments of comic relief. I had already
noted José's usually concealed but lively sense of humor, and
now I always insisted on a "literal" interpretation of army life.
As soon as we had settled into an area, I drew forth our
imaginary rations and ate with relish, identifying our victuals.

"That's a delicious egg sandwich," I commented very soberly.
And José went off into gales of laughter at what apparently
struck him as an incongruity. Another detail that never failed
to draw a comment from me was José's inevitable choice of his
favorite soldier. "Always taking a coffee break," I chided, with
predictably hilarious results.

And this play went on and on and on, stretching from weeks
into months. At a point where progress seemed to be at a
standstill, I added some new equipment to the playroom, a
puppet stage and some new hand puppets, mainly an alligator
with huge, sharp-toothed jaws and a crow with an enormous
beak. I had always had an assortment of puppets around, a
family and odd characters ranging from a witch to a clown,
but José had never evinced any interest in them. The alligator,
however, immediately intrigued him. He picked it up, studied
its jaws, and completely lost himself in staging a scene without
words in which the alligator avidly devoured every other character, one by one. When the last had been consumed and
thrown to the floor, José suddenly looked up at me a little
sheepishly, as though aware on some level of the significance
of his play, and proceeded to pummel the alligator. During the
next few sessions he ignored the puppets. When he returned
to them, however, it was evident that he had spent the interim

creating a structure for a new activity. He discarded the stage and concentrated on an open-roofed dollhouse to which he had heretofore paid only glancing attention, usually at the end of the session. Grinning broadly, he would announce that he wanted to "fix it up," a process that involved dumping the furniture topsy-turvy into the center of each of the five rooms. Now he selected for his purpose only two characters, the alligator, which he manipulated, and the crow, which he assigned to me.

"Well," he announced through the jaws of the alligator, "I guess I gotta fix up this room; I like it comfortable." The alligator then proceeded to knock everything over in the largest room, permitting only one tiny oasis for the bed, which was then extravagantly fitted with most of the little pillows and blankets of the entire household and equipped with a night table and an assortment of miniature books. The alligator lolled in this splendor with an indescribable *joie de vivre.* "Aren't you fixing up your room?" the alligator then inquired of the crow.

"Why, of course," said the crow, "I was just wondering which room I should take."

"Well, how about the room right next to mine?" suggested the alligator.

"That looks like a mighty fine one," responded the crow, "but I guess it needs some fixing up." The crow then proceeded to duplicate the alligator's actions, chaotically toppling chairs, tables, and cabinets, but again leaving a little clearing for the bed, with the further comment in imitation of José, which set him roaring with laughter, "There's nothing like a nice neat room."

The alligator and the crow thus lived together in what approximated connubial bliss, with the alligator assuming the responsibility for maintaining the household and the crow performing the domestic chores.

"I think I'm getting hungry," announced the alligator. "It's time to eat. Guess I'll go out and kill a couple of people."

"Come back soon," chimed the crow.

And out he went, returning soon with two corpses. "I'm pretty thirsty," he stated. "Gotta drain their blood for cocktails. Here, put the rest in the refrigerator," he directed, handing me an imaginary pitcher. He then served himself and the crow. "Here's blood on the rocks," he offered. Life for the alligator and the crow constantly bubbled with gore and mirth.

By this time, José's personality had undergone radical change. Compulsions were a thing of the past. As his puppet play indicated, his inhibitions had decreased and his behavior had become more spontaneous. He had also found his sense of humor, which was highly developed. His fears of his father had diminished to a point where he dared take him on in argument. At first his father attempted to meet this new assertiveness with stormy repression, but under my direction he finally acceded to the new order and allowed José to express himself.

In her monthly sessions with me, his mother had struggled for some understanding of her role in José's problems. Once I had grasped the underlying structure of his opposition, I was able to help her reduce the areas of friction between them by assisting her with such practical details as José's dressing and undressing. Since José loved school and would have hated to miss any of it, it was a simple enough matter to make him completely responsible for getting himself ready. The evening routine was somewhat more complicated, but also eventually yielded.

Initially she was somewhat taken aback by my description of José as an extraordinarily obedient child who never misbehaved. Although she had referred to her greater strictness with him, which she began to understand in terms of her relaxation with Mary, she had little awareness of the degree of repression that prevailed in her household and was reflected in José, even though she could acknowledge the severity of the home in which she herself was brought up. As José emerged from his withdrawal, he became a more enjoyable companion and now delighted both his parents. His silent subversion disappeared.

He had not yet become an "American," however. Although it was not until the resolution of his fantasy that I fully understood its direction, in retrospect it is now clear that he had already been leading up to it in his model-making and his drawings, which had remained a continuing focus of his interest throughout his treatment, concentrating exclusively on soldiers and war scenes. The first sign that he was preparing for the dénouement came with his selection of German planes and German submarines for his models. His drawings had also begun to concern themselves with German subjects — German guns and helmets and finally German soldiers. His drawings of battle scenes assumed a new character. Although he still concentrated on Americans in combat, they were invariably being bombarded or wiped out by the Germans, who at first remained outside the picture, only their bombs and missiles being represented. I had been struck from the very beginning by José's use of the term "German" rather than "Nazi." Each time I heard it, I had reacted with a question that only now began to define itself.

When he returned to the war game after the weeks of domesticity enjoyed by the alligator and the crow, he introduced a significant — and final — change in that activity. At first covertly, but then with increasing assertiveness, he began to reveal his conviction of German superiority and his unbounded admiration for their military know-how. There was no piece of equipment that did not establish it.

"Look at this powerful rifle," he said, admiring the imaginary weapon. "It's much better than the Americans'." And, "Do you know what kind of pistol this is? It's a Lüger; it's the best." After the opposing armies had been deployed, José would also scrutinize the American forces and state disparagingly, "Their matériel is not too good."

Clay now became a necessary feature of our activity. Using a liberal admixture of water, in a truly abandoned mood, José frequently turned the tabletop into the muddiest terrain imaginable, and he exultantly maneuvered the armies, flooding them and half-burying them in ditches, the Germans always seeming to get the better of it. When the conflict was restored to the larger battleground represented by the desk, the couch, and the floor, I began to notice a curious phenomenon. Just as the armies were getting ready for the assault, José would dart away from the Americans, whom we were both manipulating on the desk or the floor, and join the Germans on the couch.

After momentarily directing their side, imitating the sound of the machine guns that were trained on the Americans, he then slipped back to rejoin me as though nothing had happened.

"I see you're helping the Germans," I commented, deadpan, as he avoided my glance.

"Just for a minute," José stated casually.

It was only a matter of time, however, before the mounting scale of José's help resulted in an unabashed surrender of his role as an American in favor of the German side. At the end of one session he finally bombarded the American camp and triumphantly announced, "They're slaughtered."

Three years had passed since José had entered treatment. In all of that time, he had referred to his father only once and then very reluctantly in connection with putting decals on the models.

"It's very difficult to put the tiny pieces on," I had observed after watching him struggle with them. I heard a mumble that sounded like "Just like my father," which was followed after some urging with "My father yells at me sometimes when I lose the pieces."

Now, soon after having vanquished "the Americans" in battle, he arrived at his session one day proudly bearing American military insignia.

"My father gave them to me," he disclosed.

"Why, what are they?" I asked.

"My father's army insignia," he replied. "That's what he wore when he was a soldier in the U.S. Army. He was a lieutenant."

"When did he give them to you?" I pursued, quite stunned by a development that had followed so quickly the resolution of his fantasy.

"Oh," said José, "I asked him about his experiences in the war and he put his uniform on for me. He was in some pretty big battles."

"You're very proud of him," I commented.

"You ought to see his souvenirs. He keeps them in a chest, and he said I could have these. My mother's going to sew them on my jacket."

José never returned to the war games after this. Having

proven that he could vanquish the real enemy — the Americans — he appeared ready to abandon the role of German. His father's insignia from now on established his true identity.

His fantasy and its resolution represented the first stage of his struggle back to health. My major concentration during this period was the creation of an environment that would enable him to liberate his aggressive feelings via his fantasies. So severe were the repressions that almost a year went by before he dared expose them even once. The compulsions that had kept them in check were possibly a response to the repressive force exerted by both parents so that José had to control, not only forbidden feelings, but also forbidden impulses. The fantasy of the flood that drowned his parents almost took him by surprise, as did his initial play with the voracious, man-eating alligator.

Because of his extreme passivity, he had to be encouraged first of all to adopt an active role. To that end I tried never to intrude by assuming a dominating position, but always managed to leave the choices to him so that his fantasy could develop unimpeded. Until he advanced to an aggressive role by declaring that his was a police car, for instance, I maintained an equally passive position. Once he announced himself, however, I took his cue and proceeded to engage in behavior designed to encourage his aggression within the framework of the fantasy. Similarly I refused the role of leader, which would have placed me in the position of determining the direction of his fantasy, just as I waited for him to indicate my role as the crow. Because his sense of humor was so available to him, I stimulated it as a means of relaxing his repressions.

Since he had withdrawn to a point where he did not even allow me to enter his line of vision, in order to help him release his murderous fantasies my first task was to establish myself as a helpful and trustworthy ally. Starting very cautiously with the silent procession of the two cars, he at first assigned me the role of enemy. Only by dint of becoming his indispensable assistant, and by gradually letting it be known that I accepted and even enjoyed aggressive feelings, did I make it possible for him to transform both his fantasy and my role in it. I then became an ally, and we were Americans at war with a common enemy, the Germans. When the war fantasy was resumed after the interlude of the alligator and the crow, it was clear that my complete acceptance of his role as a marital killer-companion and my readiness to share the bloody spoils permitted him to take the next step and to expose his secret — that he was a German and the Americans were the enemy. He was then able to triumph over them, and by overcoming his terror, to establish his mastery and to claim his true status.

That his first act after his triumph over the Americans in fantasy was to invite his father to discuss his experiences in the war and then for him proudly to claim the insignia of an American soldier dramatically established the unconscious direction of his drive toward health from the very first session, when he revealed his central preoccupation with the disclosure, "I'm not an American." His fantasied adoption of the identity of an enemy alien had defended him against his fears of infanticide by explaining and justifying his father's murderous feelings toward him. Only when he had developed enough ego strength to establish his superiority and to defeat his enemy, the Americans, did his terror diminish sufficiently for him to resolve his fantasy and establish his true identity. He was then ready to verbalize directly the murderous and libidinal feelings that he had thus far expressed only in fantasy.

Chapter 5

The Fantasy of "A Dog That Didn't Deserve to Be a Child"

As soon as the child feels sufficiently secure and assured of acceptance, the fantasy, which may be a remarkable condensation of his perception of his central conflict, may begin to evolve until its resolution frees him to verbalize directly the perceptions and the feelings it had camouflaged. Whether or not the fantasy can successfully reach that point may depend on both the parents' capacity for change and the analyst's skill in handling the fantasy. Where there is little or no alleviation of the threat coming from the environment, the child's need for a defensive fantasy may not be entirely resolved.

The crucial issue in the handling of fantasy is, first of all, the meaning of the communication. As long as the method of child analysis was influenced by the concept that children's fantasies are "divorced from reality," a prime source of investigation was cut off. Although Melanie Klein's play technique provided an invaluable tool for understanding fantasy, her elimination of the parents' role in treating children limited its usefulness. Anna Freud's readier acceptance of the "objective world"[1] as an important factor in the child's mechanisms of defense prepared the way for our present understanding of the role of the parent-child relationship in the genesis of the child's emotional problems. That orientation and the recognition of the child's fear of infanticide provide the key to the meaning of his communication.

As established in the case of Ellie and of the other children discussed, the first task in understanding the child's fantasy is to amass as much data as possible on the history and the development of the child's life. Other procedures in the handling of fantasy are dictated by its dual function. Defensive fantasies are designed, not only to provide an outlet for the child's unbearable terror, but also, by projecting it onto imaginary creatures, to conceal its source, thus enabling him to preserve the idealized and potentially loving image of his parents that appears so fundamental to his feeling of security. It therefore follows that any exposure of the real basis for the child's fantasy or any attempt to reach beyond its framework with a suggestion of its true meaning may threaten the defense to such a degree as to put an end to the fantasy and disqualify the analyst as a trustworthy confidant. Such exposure may even endanger the child's life. This principle was dramatically demonstrated when a young colleague asked a child whom he was treating if he could identify the figures in his fantasy and the reply came: "If I knew who they were, I'd kill myself."

A very impressive aspect of the child's use of fantasy is its revelation of his frequently unerring sense of his psychological requirements in his struggle to stay alive. Since identity is a primary instrument in his defense and an essential element in his system of self-deception, as we have seen in the cases presented so far, it may become the focal point of his fantasy. In working out his fantasy, his identity and mine and our relationship to each other may be continually modified along with the situation and the setting, which may also change to accommodate his changing needs. A fantasy may progress through several stages over a number of years until its resolution brings the child to a point where he is ready to express directly the thoughts and feelings his fantasy had concealed. What may happen to children's fantasies when the child does not receive psychoanalytic help was revealed in my work with adult patients. In those instances where they were able to disinter them, the early fantasies appeared simply to have gone underground, and as part of their unconscious, they continued to exert a controlling influence on their lives.

In the case of Patty, an only child who was referred at the age of seven with a diagnosis of schizophrenia, the fantasy that she lightly introduced during her first session developed over a period of more than three years. Identity was her major concern. At the outset of her treatment, she was a "nonhuman," a lowly sexless creature who gradually became feminine. After a preliminary phase in which she assumed roles that would elicit praise, she adopted the identity first of a horse and then of "a dog that didn't deserve to be a child." Having been left to my own devices initially, I was also assigned an identity, first of a wicked and then of a good owner. Her ability to meet her emotional needs at each stage of her constantly evolving fantasy until she emerged from schizophrenia was a remarkable testament to the reliability of the psyche in the struggle to remain alive. All she seemed to require of me was acceptance and understanding and a willingness to assist her along whatever paths she followed. Although, as the process was unfolding, I was frequently at sea concerning her direction, Patty's steady progress verified its correctness. I had very little success with her parents, however. They remained unchanged in their feelings toward Patty and therefore, I surmised, prevented a resolution to her fantasy.

Although I have no firsthand knowledge of the violence to which Patty's parents had exposed or subjected her, both her symptoms and the nature of her fantasy suggested unusually cruel treatment. From their first interview her parents made very clear that Patty had been an unplanned and untimely interruption in their lives that they had never ceased to resent. Her father was a lawyer whose career had scarcely gotten under way when she was born; her mother had wanted to be a singer but abandoned her ambition with Patty's arrival. I had the impression that neither parent had received adequate mothering or had known anything but a hostile, ungiving environment. Patty's father was small and unsmiling, his aggression locked in and, like most of his feelings, unavailable. Her mother was slight, blond and blue-eyed, and moderately attractive. She appeared more open and less inhibited about expressing her destructive feelings or, as I learned, in acting on them.

They were both mortified by the impression Patty created in public. The incident that precipitated their bringing her to see me was a children's birthday party at which her bizarre behavior filled them with shame. She appeared unrelated to the others and off in a world of her own. Although she generally ignored other children, she was very ingratiating with adults and latched on to every visitor with a hunger they found embarrassing. She was friendless and withdrawn and usually cried herself to sleep at night. Both parents were united in their description of her uncooperative, negative, provocative character.

My first memory of Patty is indelible. I recall a curious sinking feeling as she first strutted stiffly past me, slapping her feet as she walked, robot fashion, unsmiling and apparently unseeing, down the long hallway to the playroom. She was small for her seven years and wore her red hair long, in unkempt masses that dramatized the delicacy of her face but also reinforced the general feeling of shabbiness that her drab shapeless dress conveyed. There was some conversation; I recall now that she started talking as soon as she entered.

"What a long hallway!" she exclaimed. "You have a lot of books, just like my father."

It was not the content of her communications, which continued in a steady stream of polite chatter for several minutes, but her voice that filled me with a sense of shock. It seemed to come from high up in her head, as though she were onstage in a performance where the director strove for the utmost sense of unreality. She seated herself at the little corner table in the playroom and lapsed into silence.

"Do you know why you've come to see me?" I asked after a few moments.

"There's one thing I know — you're nice," she replied, still not looking at me. Later she picked up a crayon and, her nose almost touching the paper, drew what looked like a blur.

"That looks very interesting," I said, "but I'm not quite sure I know what it is."

"It's an angel"; she paused. "She can turn bad people into good."

During her next session, Patty chalked her face and her arms. "I'm Clang, the clown," she asserted, and after a moment added, matter-of-factly, "There's a lion outside on the terrace."

"A lion!" I exclaimed, just an edge of alarm in my voice.

"You don't have to be scared," she assured me. "I'm also an animal trainer."

When we entered the roof terrace, however, we found not only a lion, but a hairy elephant, a fire-breathing dragon, a poisonous alligator, and a host of other deadly creatures.

"You live in a very dangerous world," I observed.

"I am brave," she stated very simply. "I have courage."

Except for a brief reference to her mother's unprovoked and inexplicable anger and Patty's equally mystifying friendlessness, this was the world we dwelled in for many weeks. Patty arranged two loungers side by side, and we reclined in them while the terrace vibrated to the tread of her monstrous beings. She felt right at home with them and tried to put me at my ease, always treating me like an honored guest who must never suffer a moment's discomfort.

"Don't worry," she assured me. "I know how to control them."

Happy, the dragon, spoke in sheets of flame and was the favorite. He was harnessed to provide chariot service for us. We mounted him and rode over the world. One day, far below us, Patty noted a circus tent and signaled Happy to descend. We hovered over it, watching the performers through a flap. They appeared to make a strong impression on Patty.

"I'm a bareback rider," she announced. "Happy, we're coming in for a landing."

We joined the circus. Since I was left to my own devices while Patty rode, I decided to assume the role of audience. As my enthusiastic applause rang out, Patty took her bows like an old trooper. She quickly added other acts to her routine.

"I'm a trapeze artist," she stated. And then, "I'm a Wonder Dog," and finally, "I'm a dancer."

As one round of applause followed another, the monsters vanished into thin air, never more to haunt my terrace or to inhabit Patty's world. The circus was installed and, since I continued to be left without direction, as the acts multiplied I decided there was room for a barker.

"Hear ye! Hear ye!" I cried. "See the world's greatest bareback rider, the one and only undefeated champion." Or, "Come one, come all! Don't miss the chance of a lifetime! The great ballet dancer performs tonight! Hurry! Hurry! Hurry!" Patty accepted these interventions with undisguised pleasure and acknowledged them with deep bows.

After several weeks Patty began to talk about a horse that lived in her garage. "He takes me to school every day," she informed me. "Sometimes he wears my clothes and sits next to me and gives me all the answers." She named the horse Tiger. "Tiger brought me today," she sometimes announced as she entered. Or, "Tiger's waiting outside for us." Tiger galloped over the terrace with an abandon that evoked only admiration.

"Bravo!" I cried. "Bravo! What a beautiful horse! What a gorgeous mane! What galloping! I don't think I've ever seen a more graceful creature." From time to time Tiger also escorted us to the circus and blended in with the performers.

One day Patty arrived at her session looking especially downcast. "Tiger and I ran away from my mother," she confided. "We found a water hole in the desert and we're going to stay there for the rest of our lives and live on camel's meat." Away they went over the terrace. When they returned, Tiger galloped straight into my arms. Looking directly into my eyes for the first time, Patty stated, "You're the first master that's been good to me. I had two others, but they were both mean. One gave me water, but no food; the other gave me food, but no water. They locked me up in the garage twice and planned to blow me up, but I fooled them. I escaped. That's when you found me. I'm very glad. You're the first master that treats me right and gives me the right food and the right bed — a human bed."

Soon after this, summer and vacation intervened. When Patty returned, Tiger alternated for a while with Wonder Dog, whom I was directed to train. During the previous period, the theme of a dog had come up intermittently. In addition to Wonder Dog, there had been the "fairy dog" whom Patty had brought with her occasionally. One time he had assumed the shape of her umbrella and had provided some comfort against her father's anger on their way to her session. At another, he was just a tiny ball that answered to the name of Tinkerbell. Early in her treatment she had also told me about the sad loss of her real dog, whom her mother had given away because he was bad. Now I was instructed to put Wonder Dog through increasingly difficult paces. He was made to jump over an imaginary rope that was continually raised higher and higher until it was obvious that only a Wonder Dog could meet such a challenge. Patty directed me to be harsh with him, to be constantly displeased with his efforts, to be threatening. Occasionally I had to crack a whip.

"Hop to it, now," I warned. "We're not tolerating any sloppy performances around here." Wonder Dog cringed. I had definitely developed a streak of meanness and Wonder Dog an attitude of martyrdom. By the time the cold drove us indoors to the playroom, Patty announced that she was "a dog that didn't deserve to be a child" and that I was her owner.

"The dog that didn't deserve to be a child" was called by a number of feminine names before she finally became "Priscilla." She was as bad as a dog could be. She disobeyed, pretended to bite and claw, to tear and smash the furniture, to run away. In this role, Patty used words only to give me directions; otherwise she remained in character and barked all her communications. She also used no props.

"You have to punish me," she directed. "You have to tell me how bad I am."

The routine usually started with my going shopping, leaving Priscilla home alone. When I returned, I found such disorder that I could only stand in the doorway stunned. When I caught my breath, I gave vent to dismay, disappointment, and rage. "Why, I thought I could trust you," I exploded. "And just look what you've done to this house — you've wrecked it! It seems as though I can't turn my back for a moment. You're just a bad dog and you're going to be punished."

"You have to beat me," Patty directed.

"There!" I cried, pretending to wield a strap. "That will teach you."

"Harder," Patty interposed. "Harder."

"You worthless dog!" I shouted, lashing about me. "That'll teach you to disobey me! Maybe next time you'll think twice before you tear up my couch!"

"Now you must lock me in a cage and starve me."

"There, that'll show you, you worthless creature! Into the cage with you and not a scrap to eat!"

And Patty crouched in a corner, pretending viciousness and occasionally snapping at the bars. There were many variations of this scene, all in a rising crescendo of provocation and punishment, and there were many, many repetitions of variations.

"You have to beat me until I bleed," Patty directed one day. And then, "Now you have to call the doctor."

The doctor was called and I arrived in my new role. "Well, who's sick around here?" I inquired with professional joviality. Then, as I took in the details of the sordid scene, I could scarcely repress my feelings of shock. "Well, what's happened here?" I inquired. "This looks pretty bad," I said, observing Priscilla's wounds. "I know it hurts," I added as I tenderly lifted first one limb and then the other, "but don't worry. This will take care of it. I'll have you fixed up in no time." I pretended to bind carefully the suffering Priscilla's wounds and then, as I was leaving, admonished the imaginary owner, "This dog needs plenty of rest and good food."

With the advent of the doctor, the fantasy assumed a new direction. There was no doubt that the doctor had reacted to what he considered an act of barbarous cruelty. The good but necessarily punitive owner had actually already undergone a transformation by this time that required only the kind doctor's tender ministrations to define. Almost inperceptibly, Priscilla had also evolved from a bad to a good dog that was abused by a wicked owner, who neither understood nor appreciated her. I was now directed to engage in unprovoked cruelty. Nothing that Priscilla did could please me. The mere sight of her was enough to stir me to rage. "You beast!" I shouted. "You miserable beast! Always doing everything wrong! Get out of my sight!"

Then a new element was introduced.

"There are two owners," Patty announced one day. "There's a bad one and a good one. The bad one gets disgusted and sells Priscilla to the good one."

And so the doctor underwent a metamorphosis. Now the session started with Priscilla's misbehavior and the bad owner's abuse and punishment. Then the sale took place and Priscilla entered her new home, where every effort to please found a reward.

"I've never seen such a good dog," the good owner marveled. "And smart. You only have to tell her something once, and she knows." Priscilla performed all the good traditional acts of good dogs. She brought me my slippers and my newspaper and snuggled quietly at my feet while I read. Gradually more and more time was given over to the good owner, the scene with the bad owner dwindling to merely a point of departure for the sale and then disappearing altogether. The entire session was now devoted to the idyllic relationship of a dog that wanted only to please and an owner whose response was to reward. The contents underwent constant elaboration. My adult consultation room became a pet shop where each time we purchased new clothing for Priscilla. From there we progressed to the waiting room, which became a license bureau. Each time, following the acquisition of a new wardrobe, which always included a collar and a leash, we applied at the bureau and received a license and proof of ownership. We then returned home, where Priscilla feasted on a fine steak and very special dog biscuits.

After many repetitions the inevitable change was introduced. "I don't listen to you and I run away and I have an accident and I'm brought home wounded and you call the doctor," was the first version of the new departure. After one or two tryouts this was amended to "I get hurt because I save somebody's life crossing the street." This then became "I save five people's lives and the newspapers call you to find out about it." When the telephone rang, I answered with great pride, "Yes, she did it all by herself. Yes. She's a very brave dog. No, I never have any trouble with her. She does everything right."

"They ask about a reward," interposed Patty.

"A reward?" I asked the reporter. "I certainly agree that she deserves one. You'll see about it? Well, thank you. Just let me know."

After a rerun, Patty had a further inspiration. "I save the whole city," she announced, "and the mayor hears about it and there's a reward and he gives it to me himself. And the news-papers keep telephoning."

While Priscilla lay recovering from her wounds in a state of transcendent bliss, I was kept busy dealing with the reporters and the mayor's office. Gradually plans for an award ceremony developed in which the mayor himself would make the presentation. This prospect apparently presented a serious challenge to Patty's fantasy.

"I can talk," she informed me one day. "You have magic powers and you make me talk."

Accompanying my incantations with the traditional mystical gestures, I cried, "Abra-ca-dabra-ca-dabra-ca-dum! You can talk!"

From then on, this ritual started each session. The barking disappeared and Priscilla was free to talk to the reporters herself and to respond to the mayor. She decided that the most appropriate place for the entire scene was the top of the large playroom desk. This gave the photographers an excellent vantage point for their picture-taking. Holding both my hands high over my head, I opened and closed them in a clicking motion, running around the desk in what appeared to be a thoroughly acceptable simulation of camera action as far as Patty was concerned. The height of the desk, however, also suggested other possibilities and a further extension of Priscilla's powers.

"Priscilla can dance," Patty stated one day. "She's a ballet dancer." And the program of the award ceremony was amended to include this extraordinary feature.

At this point countless gifts began to arrive from all parts of the country, and considerable time was devoted to the construction of warehouses large enough to accommodate them. Patty now seemed ready to end the fantasy.

"You marry the President and we move to the White House," she announced happily at the close of one session with an implied "and they lived happily ever after" feeling.

When she returned after another summer, she had apparently abandoned the fantasy and now briefly became absorbed in the problems of her actual relationships with parents and friends. She missed one month of treatment in the late fall, however, and when she resumed, still somewhat irregularly, her unkempt hair and artificial voice betrayed a partial state of regression. As she was leaving she commented, "It's a long time since we talked about Tiger and Priscilla." At her next session, she immediately asked, "Can we play the dog game?"

The fantasy was resumed, but with an altered cast and a completely different theme. The bad owner was reintroduced with the name of Meaninda. Several variations in which Priscilla was lost or abandoned in a basket outside my door were tried out, followed by other variations in which Meaninda first informed me that I could keep her dog if I found her and then, in a change of mind, attempted to buy her back. I was directed to conceal from Meaninda that Priscilla had the power of speech and to conduct the entire negotiation myself.

The session usually started with my finding Priscilla.

"What is this?" I exclaimed in delighted surprise as I discovered the basket on my doorstep. "What a beautiful dog! And right on my doorstep! I can't imagine who would want to leave such a lovely creature. You come right in here where it's warm and comfortable and I'll see about getting you some food."

"Thank you," said Priscilla.

"Why, you can talk!" I exclaimed in amazement.

"Yes, I have the power of speech," Priscilla stated modestly.

Priscilla was always fed and then, under my prompting, launched into her complaints about her owner.

"Now tell me what happened," was the usual opener, which was inevitably followed by a sad tale of mistreatment and cruelty. "But why is she so mean?" I asked. "What makes her so wicked?"

"She's a witch," replied Patty with passion, "because her mother was a witch, and now she's trying to do the same thing to me."

Following this introduction, there was a knock at the door, and Meaninda entered and engaged in casual conversation. At first she disparaged Priscilla, then expressed a rather ambivalent feeling of wanting her back, and finally offered to purchase her. At the mere mention of such a possibility, frightened barks were heard from Priscilla. She became extremely agitated and directed me to put Meaninda out.

"How dare you raise such a question?" I demanded. "Can't you see how upsetting it is to Priscilla? Don't ever mention such a subject again. I wouldn't part with Priscilla for all the money in the world. And now you'll have to go. I can't allow anyone to disturb Priscilla in this way."

This version of the fantasy lasted several months and eventually became the game of "jailing the witch," and with the intervention of another summer it was finally abandoned. That it could not be resolved was indicated by Patty's inability to achieve the status of "a child" throughout its duration. Although "the dog that didn't deserve to be a child" was permitted to evolve into an exemplary creature on whom the power of speech was repeatedly conferred and who also was permitted to dance, at no point did she become human. Patty's only solution to the persistent danger of her threatening environment and of her mother's uncompromising character of a "witch" was to move in with me. The fantasy of living with me, which frequently develops in response to the child's need for refuge, is usually abandoned as the child's health returns and the parental environment improves.

In Patty's case, the lack of any real change in her parents gave rise to a curious development about whose complete significance I can only speculate. Patty returned from her vacation with a persistent rage at me that was mainly expressed in silence. Although I did not have ample opportunity to explore it, I have the impression that with her improved sense of reality her recognition of my limited role in her life resulted in a feeling of betrayal. As in other rare instances where the parents remain unchanged, I can only guess that Patty turned her rage against me for having been a party to a fantasy, which, although it had led to her improved health, remained unresolved and incapable of realization.

It was also a measure of the success of her treatment that she reached the stage of a negative transference. Had her parents supported her analysis and allowed her to remain, Patty would have had an opportunity to vent her rage and to establish on a verbal level what she had achieved in fantasy.

As it is, with the development of her negative feelings, they terminated her sessions.

The fantasy that led Patty from schizophrenia into the world of reality progressed through three different phases and a coda, each one representing a step toward health and marked by evolving identities for both of us. When she initially delineated me as a "blur," an "angel who can turn bad people into good," she presented her central preoccupation with feelings of worthlessness and the ephemeral hope, epitomized by the unsubstantiality of her drawing, that I possessed supernatural powers that could transform her and so make her eligible for love. The first identity she assumed reinforced this impression; she was a clown, surely the lowliest creature, with a name that had no reference to anything human and no clearly defined sex. It took no more than my acceptance of her fantasy, however, for her to conjure up a lion on my terrace, and in response to my further acceptance, my expression of mild alarm, to advance to the role of animal trainer who proceeded not only to reveal the terror of her inner world but to protect me from it.

It was evident from the very first session that Patty's greatest need was approval. My unstinting praise and admiration were called forth by the structure of her fantasy and marked the first phase of her treatment. From my appreciation of the ease with which she controlled her monsters to my enthusiastic applause of her various circus roles to my proclamation of her virtues, I simply picked up her cues in a spiraling expression of need and response. Throughout this period of unalloyed praise, when Patty was essentially a performer of extraordinary merit and had no particular identity herself, she left me pretty much to my own devices and never defined my identity either.

The second phase of Patty's fantasy was foreshadowed by a transitional period that ended with her designation, for the first time, of a role for herself that allowed her to confront and express her unbearable feelings. It was not until her unconditional acceptance of me following her fantasied escape forever from parents who had twice attempted to "blow her up" that, as "the dog that didn't deserve to be a child," she finally

permitted herself to adopt a role in which she was unquali-
fiedly "bad." At the same time she assigned me a role that
enabled her to explore and to evaluate her relationship to her
mother and, finally, to modify to a large degree the horrible
self-image that defended her against her mother's hatred. The
first intimation that I was being transformed into a Simon
Legree and that she was also evolving into something other
than a magnificent performer came in relation to the training
of Wonder Dog. As she allowed herself to experience her "badness" to the full, she apparently also began to question the
validity not only of this concept of herself but of her concept
of the virtue of her "owner." This slowly led to the reversal of
roles and, finally, as her new need asserted itself, to the third
stage, the gradual abandonment of the enactment of viciousness and hatred and the institution of a joyous era where
virtue was rewarded and love reigned supreme.

Although I was frequently in the dark, particularly during
the early period, about where Patty's fantasy was leading, the
positive changes in her personality and her relationship to
reality were always reassuring. After about one year, her creativity burst forth with a flurry of drawings that gradually led
her to painting, music, and dancing, all of which continued
during the rest of her treatment. The classmates who had
previously ostracized her began to admire her, and their recognition and acceptance further motivated her tolerance of the
realistic demands of the school situation. Her bizarre and
seemingly myopic manner of reading, her strange way of slapping her feet when she walked, and the curiously artificial
pitch of her voice all disappeared. She now sought and received
approval.

As the coda to Patty's fantasy indicated, the one element
that remained relatively unchanged was the feeling her parents communicated and her response to them. Their attempt
to withdraw her from treatment was reenacted in the thinly
veiled fantasy in which I defeat Meaninda's efforts to "buy her
back." Patty's clearest statement about her mother was expressed in that connection: "She's a witch because her mother
was a witch, and now she's trying to do the same thing to
me." Although her fantasy contains only one reference to

her father, it is quite evident that she imputed to him the same murderous intention toward her that she ascribed to her mother — the twice-repeated attempt to "blow her up." He is also one of the two mean owners who gave her either food without water or water without food and treated her inhumanly.

Patty's all-absorbing preoccupation with feelings of worthlessness, not only reflected the intensity of her parents' hostile feelings and the absence of their love, but also served as a defense against her terror of being killed. We can measure the magnitude of that terror by the fact that Patty required the symptomatology of schizophrenia in order to deal with it. Her murderous response to her parents' murderous feelings was so intolerable to her that she had to wipe out all sense of her own identity and project her overwhelming rage onto monsters whom she could control.

Although she was finally able to express those feelings, her ability to do so only in fantasy suggests that the terror of her real world remained too threatening for her to confront directly. Transparent as her references to it were, she was some distance from being able to acknowledge the smallest part of what she conveyed in fantasy. Unlike Ellie, who moved quickly from "I don't like to think of myself as a giraffe" to "Do you think I'm a monster?" and then to her fear of being killed, which she dealt with first in fantasy and then in direct confrontation, Patty allowed her terror to surface only occasionally and only within the framework of her fantasy.

We can trace Ellie's ability to discard her unbearable self-images and then to work through her monster fantasy until she could abandon it and verbalize her terror directly to both her increased ego strength and the improved conditions of her objective reality. My efforts to make Ellie's responses understandable to her parents and to modify their manner of dealing with her had met with some success, particularly with her mother, whose depression had also decreased. Her mother's genuine appreciation and understanding of Ellie as well as her father's willingness to leave discipline to his wife were important factors leading to Ellie's improved health.

I had no such success with Patty's parents. Even though

psychoanalytic treatment had enabled Patty to emerge from schizophrenia through her use of fantasy, the unyielding character of her parents' hostility and their inability to meet Patty's need for love required a continuing defense that restricted to fantasy the expression of her perceptions of their feelings and of her response to them and prevented it from being resolved. Her treatment was terminated at a point where her rage was becoming available to her.

Chapter 6

The Inhibition of Fantasy and the Predisposition to Kill

ALTHOUGH MY PSYCHOANALYTIC treatment of children initially confronted me with the challenging task of unraveling the meaning of their fantasies, I soon became aware that the degree of the inhibition of fantasy, no less than the range of its expression, may be a measure of the child's defensive needs. My speculation about the dynamics of the inhibition ended when I turned to investigate the family backgrounds of those patients who revealed this incapacity. In those rare instances, despite the unquestionable existence of other causes of inhibition, I found that the fear of infanticide, which normally gives rise to children's fantasies, had been intensified by persistent violent abuse in a nonloving environment, which elicited not only a wish but an impulse to kill. In such cases the child responded by developing feelings of alienation and became consumed by a fear of losing control that caused him to inhibit all fantasy.

Perhaps no other single factor teaches us more about the central role of violence and the fear of violence in the psyche's defensive system than their impact on children's fantasies. Although fantasy normally defends the child against the fear of being killed, where he encounters actual violence or the threat of violence without the ameliorating influence of love, the fantasy itself may not suffice and he may be forced to act it out, frequently by assuming a "safer" identity. Where the violence is repeatedly and persistently directed against the child, however, even that defense may no longer serve. Inhibition may be his only solution. How ominous a development that may be is indicated by an investigation into the backgrounds of people who have actually committed murder. Wherever the information is available, it is apparent that they fall into this category. The inhibition of fantasy may in some instances therefore not only be regarded as a defense against persistent violent abuse in an unloving environment, it may also suggest a predisposition to commit murder.

Although that concept is borne out both by my own observations and by the findings of researchers concerning the experience of individuals who have committed murder, many writers continue to regard the commission of murder as ultimate proof of the base nature of man and ascribe it to a "killer instinct." In his book *Human Aggression,* Anthony Storr upholds this position with the statement: "The somber fact is that we are the cruellest and most ruthless species that has ever walked the earth; and that, although we may recoil in horror when we read in newspapers or history books of the atrocities committed by man upon man, we know in our hearts that each of us harbors within himself those same savage impulses which lead to murder, torture and war."[1]

Similarly, in *The Natural History of Aggression,* "The current psychiatric evidence seems almost unequivocal; aggression is not merely a response to frustration, it is a deep-seated, universal drive."[2]

When scientists have compared man to other species of the animal kingdom, his standing in the moral hierarchy has plummeted almost to the bottom. It has been pointed out that man cannot match the peaceable natures of the others, who, in most instances, kill in order to survive and, even then, as in the case of wolves, select as their victims only those animals already in a deteriorating state of health; further, man belongs to one of the few species that kills its own kind.

Although on the surface this may seem incontrovertible, if we examine the preconditions that in many instances appear to be necessary before people are capable of killing, we find that, paradoxical as it may seem, they usually do not kill their own kind. Far from being a natural expression of aggressive drives, murder usually has a prehistory that reaches back into childhood and springs from a specific set of circumstances. My examination of the psychological component of governmental efforts in the waging of wars, particularly of wars of aggres-

sion, as well as research into both the early experiences of
individual murderers and the roots of violence in my own
patients, suggests that usually, before people are capable of
killing, a process of alienation must first take place. In that
sense it may be said that, despite appearances, there is reason
to believe that man does not actually kill his own kind.

In his paper "The Attitude of Murderers Toward Death,"
Paul Schilder explains the act of the typical young slayer and
essentially describes feelings of alienation. He states: "It is
rather that life and death do not seem to play an important
part in the manifest content of psychic life. Persons of this
kind seemingly kill as easily as children in their play, and
they are not more concerned about their own death than children are. It almost seems that these 'normal' murderers who
are not otherwise so badly adapted to their reality, show particular infantile trends in their reaction to life and death. One
may say they kill because they do not appreciate the deprivation they inflict on others."[3] In presenting the case of Alvin,
Manfred Guttmacher also describes feelings of alienation
when he reports that Alvin "sees the world as depriving and
divides it clearly into the 'haves' and 'have-nots' . . . He had
no compunction taking from the 'haves' since he is a 'have-
not.' He does not feel that he is wrong because society made
him so. He has been deprived so now it is up to society to look
after him and if they do not give it, he will take it. Stealing
is therefore natural to him. Murder is incidental."[4]

Although there may also be other emotional states that
result in murder, in many instances the repression of feeling
and the inhibition of fantasy are so profound that the murderous act is dissociated. In the study conducted by G. M. Duncan
and others, they reported in one case, "When we saw him, he
was unable to account for his killing her [his sweetheart]."[5] In
another case, discussed by W. Lindsey Neustatter, the man
who committed three separate murders of strangers in three
different locales had complete amnesia concerning how he had
actually gotten to those places. He claimed to kill on impulse
and didn't know why he selected those particular individuals.[6]
In still another instance, a murderer who claimed to be able
to put anything unpleasant completely out of his mind alleged

a loss of memory before his trial and denied making a confession when he had been interrogated.[7] With William George Hierens, the subject of Lucy Freeman's *Before I Kill More,* all murders and assaults were dissociated acts. After two murders, he referred to "waking up," once on the floor and the other time on a chair. Each time he looked around the apartment, noted what had been done with no memory of having done it, and merely deduced that he had done it.[8] In their study "Born to Raise Hell," Jack Altman and Marvin Ziporyn tell how Richard Speck heard about the murder of eight nurses over the radio in a bar and said to the man next to him, "I hope they catch the son-of-a-bitch." Only when they mentioned his name did he realize he was the murderer, and he subsequently tried to kill himself. Later he stated, "I would sure like to know what made me kill those girls. Why would I do a thing like that?"[9]

Although my purpose here is not to analyze the social environment and the system of government that spawns murderers, a cursory examination of the methods governments frequently employ in preparing the psyche for war readily establishes the widespread recognition of the essential role of alienation in killing. From World War I and the characterization of the German soldier as a "savage Hun," who therefore did not qualify as a human, to the Vietnamese "gook," whose "subhuman" status presumably allowed him to be killed with inpunity, alienation has been a primary governmental tool. Perhaps because of the dimensions of the contemplated carnage, nowhere has the process of alienation been carried out on the scale that prepared the German people to participate in the holocaust. Because Hitler lacked the advantages provided by the differences in color, hair, and facial structure that facilitated the alienation of white Americans in relation to Vietnamese or to blacks in the United States, he invented the myth of the Aryan race, a supposedly blue-eyed, blond-haired "master" strain superior to all other peoples. The effectiveness of the approach can be measured by the prevailing colorblindness among his followers in relation to himself and other "masters" of "the master race." He also had a much more difficult task in relation to cultural inferiority. Because the black peo-

ple had been uprooted from their own culture and not permitted to participate in the white man's, there was little difficulty
in inventing the myth of their incapacity to do so. The disparity between the culture of Americans and Vietnamese was
also used to establish Vietnamese inferiority. The Jews, however, had been allowed to share as equals in the cultural life
of Germany and therefore could not be attacked for their level
of intelligence. Culture itself then became the stigma. Said
Marshal Göring, "When I hear the word 'culture,' I reach for
my gun." With both Germans and Americans, victims were
reduced to a menial status and, with official sanction, became
open targets for ridicule and attack. Although every propa-
ganda means was marshaled to persuade both groups of the
subhuman character of their fellow man, it was additionally
necessary to create a sense of difference by segregating the
victims and driving them into ghettos. Even this did not suffice, however. To the credit of the human race, the ultimate
weapon in the alienation of both Germans and white Americans could only be violence and the threat of violence. Whether
it was "the nigger-lovers" in the South who were thus re-
strained, during the period of slavery and later, from educating
black people or from expressing any measure of solidarity with
them, or the Jewish sympathizers in Germany, violation of the
laws that were designed to alienate exposed the "malefactor"
at best to ostracism and at worst to torture and death. Americans who refused to participate in the slaughter of Vietnamese were faced with either imprisonment or exile. Compassion
and justice could no longer be experienced as ego-syntonic;
they placed life in jeopardy.

That this is not the whole story of the conversion of human
beings to murderers or the accomplices of murderers goes without saying. The freedom fighters who struggled against the
Nazi system and our own men in exile who refused to slaughter
"gooks," no less than those who welcomed government sanction to act out their murderous impulses, testify to the presence of other factors. Although the illumination shed by large-
scale governmental efforts during this century in preparation
for mass killing established the importance of feelings of alienation as a precondition for committing murder, in order to

understand why some people needed only a nod to kill and others were ready to sacrifice their lives rather than commit murder, we have to turn to the familial environment. Despite an increasing awareness of the role of violence and the threat of violence as they relate to the structure of our society and its war machines, we are less knowledgeable concerning the part they play in the psychic life of the individual. Although the adult patient frequently appears to be mainly preoccupied with the need to feel loved, the complexities of the psychic superstructure with which he confronts us are very often designed to defend him against his fear of killing and of being killed. As my investigation of the early experiences of people who have actually committed murder suggests, a very special constellation of factors, not the least being alienation, was required before any individual was capable of murder. (Omitted from this discussion were drug-induced crimes.)

Study after study of actual murderers has provided information relating to their early experiences. "Almost without exception," Guttmacher reports, "one finds in their early backgrounds not only economic want, but cruelties and miseries of every kind."[10] In their study of six condemned murderers in Minnesota, which had no capital punishment and where the parents of the subjects were available for interviews, the investigators found that common features were "remorseless brutality at the hands of one parent in the face of compliant acquiescence of the other." In one case the level of brutality was illustrated by the act of a father who held his son nude by the heels and belted him, then dropped him to the floor on his head. Some of those interviewed had been flung bodily across the room.[11]

Stuart Palmer's "Study of Murder" also establishes that "the murderers appeared to have been terribly frustrated during their early lives, suffering extreme birth traumas, serious diseases in infancy and childhood, accidents, physical beatings, severe training practices at the hands of the mother, psychological frustrations, and traumatic incidents outside of the home." He found a significant, positive, functional relationship between the amount of frustration experienced by individuals during infancy, childhood, and adolescence on the one hand,

and whether or not they later commit murder on the other. "In a particularly frustrating situation, their repressed aggression exploded out and they killed the individual whom they conceptualized as their primary frustration."[12]

Interviews with individual murderers establish beyond any doubt the extraordinary dimensions of the brutality to which they were subjected as children. In his book *The Boston Strangler,* Gerald Frank quotes the subject as saying, "I saw my father knock my mother's teeth out and then break every one of her fingers. I must have been seven . . . Pa was a plumber. He smashed me once across the back with a pipe. I just didn't move fast enough. He sold me and my two sisters once for $9 to some farmer in Maine. No one knew what happened to us for six months. We used to have to stand in front of him, my brother Frank and me, every night and be beaten with his belt . . . He used to take my brother Dickie . . . picked him right up and smashed him against the wall . . . My sisters always had black eyes."[13]

Neustatter's study revealed that in one case, where a sixteen-year-old boy killed a woman of seventy-two by repeatedly stabbing her, "the mother admitted she sometimes beat the boy and his father also 'kept on at him.'" The father, an ex-army officer, "insisted he should sit on his pot, if necessary for hours, and he was dry by nine months and trained to put every toy away from the same age." The boy never showed temper; if angered, he would "just go white, clench his hands and say nothing." The boy himself admitted he had a temper, but said that he had always controlled it, and that "he could put anything unpleasant out of his mind."[14]

In his study with the same title, Guttmacher described the parents of a twenty-one-year-old man who had held up a milk delivery wagon and killed the resistant driver. His father had been a well-known athlete and didn't want a child, although he thought he could tolerate a girl. When he found the child was a boy, he became inhumanly cruel. He beat him as an infant, burned his fingers when he pilfered at three, and refused to ride in the same car with him when he was old enough to be taken to his grandmother. Before school age the boy got away while being beaten and thereafter was tied up first. His

mother threatened suicide when he was nine if he didn't re-
form, and she cut her wrists a few years later in protest against
his behavior.

In another case, a thirty-year-old man who killed his sweetheart with an ax had been "the target of the most uncontrolled
brutality on the part of the father." In still another case in the
same study a twenty-seven-year-old man who strangled his
sweetheart and was unable to account for it stated, "Mom
hated me since the day I was conceived . . . She has punished
me ever since . . . I can remember all the unmerciful beatings
she gave me. She is happy now that she has completely destroyed my life." He said she was vicious; she would choke him
and beat him so hard with a barrel stave that he became
bruised and bleeding. She used to say to him, "What did I ever
do that God thinks I deserved to have you wished on me!" She
constantly belittled his father and destroyed any standing he
might have had in the boy's eyes. Her own father had run out
when she was five, and throughout her childhood others accused her of being illegitimate. No mention of the father was
allowed. She was devoid of any sense of guilt. During her
interview she stated that she was glad her son was in prison
and she hoped he would never be released.[15]

Lucy Freeman and Dr. Wilfred C. Hulse's study, *Children
Who Kill*,[16] as well as Freeman's book on William George
Hierens, established the brutal childhood experiences of all
their subjects. Bill Hierens started stealing when he was ten;
at thirteen he was arrested for committing ten burglaries and
sent to a semicorrectional school. At fourteen he was again
arrested for committing nine burglaries. He was finally captured at the age of seventeen, when three murders and two
assaults were ascribed to him. The feelings of alienation that
were quoted earlier had clearly defined dynamics. Bill's father,
"a giant of a man," worked part-time for the Lincoln police
force and, after his business failure during the Depression and
a period of irregular employment, secured work with the Car-
negie Steel Corporation and held a position comparable to that
of police sergeant. He always had a rifle, which Bill saw him
use on cats and rats. Although both parents were native Americans, their families had come from Luxembourg and they

spoke German to each other. Bill studied German in order to "know what they were talking about." Following his final arrest at the age of seventeen, a police search of Bill's room revealed loosely scattered pictures of Hitler, Göring, Goebbels, Schacht and other Nazis, two rifles, and his father's billy club.

The severity of Bill's upbringing is suggested by the history of his toilet training, which his mother succeeded in having him complete by the time he was one. By eight months, he no longer wet himself at night. She did the disciplining as well as his father and used a hairbrush for that purpose. Her history suggests that she suffered from conversion hysteria and during various periods developed what she described as "tetany," a tension in her fingers and toes. At one time, she was paralyzed up to her chest; at another, her face became paralyzed and she had difficulty in breathing. She also suffered a nervous breakdown when Bill was about seven. After an incident when, at the age of nine, Bill was trapped in the trunk of a car filled with live bait and could not be found for several hours, she had recurring dreams in which she drove around looking for him and repeatedly found him dead in that very spot, all decomposed. Bill's father reported that she favored her younger son.

Bill's terror of his father is suggested by his memory of an incident that occurred when he was nine. On a blazing summer day, when he was playing in a park at which his father was employed, he seized a metal trapeze bar, not realizing how hot it would be, let go quickly, and fell and broke his arm. He then sat alone for about a half-hour trying to push the broken bones together. "Like breaking a vase," he commented. "You want to repair it so you won't get blamed for breaking it." A woman finally found him and brought him to his father.[17]

The inhibition of feeling, with its implied component, the inhibition of fantasy, emerges in study after study of the personalities of the people who have committed murder and links them to the children I have treated. In his monograph "Undercontrolled and Overcontrolled Personality Types in Extreme Antisocial Aggression," Edwin I. Megargee found: "In case after case the extremely assaultive offender proves to be a rather passive person with no previous history of aggression

. . . In these cases the homicide was not just one more aggressive offense in a person who had always displayed inadequate controls, but rather a completely uncharacteristic act in a person who had always displayed extraordinarily high levels of control." He states further: "The extremely assaultive person is often a fairly mild-mannered, long-suffering individual who buries his resentment under rigid and brittle controls."[18] Freeman noted in her observation of Bill Hierens his "impassive eyes, controlled gentle voice, outward compliance to authority, and a feeling of terrible repressed power and violence." W. Lindsay Neustatter likewise states: "Murder is the worst crime in the calendar, yet contrary to public belief the tragedy is that it is committed by mild people of previously impeccable character . . . the meek and mild may prove more dangerous than those who can express their inner aggressiveness." He describes a murderer as "quiet, polite, unusually apologetic about his crimes, an extraordinarily neat and orderly man." He had killed four women by strangulation. In another case, the man who was responsible for two murders was "a tall, well set-up, fair-haired young man in his twenties, prepossessing in his appearance, intelligent, quietly spoken, and even when charged with a second murder, showing little emotion."[19]

Although I had recognized that immersion in fantasy and its acting out, as well as its exclusion, appeared to reflect an extraordinary heightening of terror, until my treatment of several children who could neither fantasize nor play it was not clear whether both extremes arose out of similar dynamics. As soon as I explored the relationship between these phenomena and the specific parental environments that gave rise to them, however, I became aware that the decisive factors appeared to be the degree and the quality of the violence as well as of the love that the child had experienced. None of my child patients who were dominated by fantasy, or who had persistently acted it out, had experienced themselves as victims of violence in a parental atmosphere devoid of love. In most instances their fear of infanticide had been enhanced either by witnessing violence or by occasionally being its target in an environment where the hope of being loved had not been completely extinguished. Whereas children with such familial backgrounds appeared to be overwhelmed by a fear of being killed and a need to justify their parents' destructive feelings, the children who were recipients of persistent violence in a nonloving environment frequently appeared to be concerned not with the fear of being killed and the wish to kill in return, but with the fear of the impulse to kill and of losing control. They therefore could not risk the release of their feelings or wishes through fantasy or play.

Although I had encountered various degrees of resistance to fantasizing in the children referred to me, the most striking inhibition occurred in the case of Joan, who refused both to fantasize and to play; at four and a half this was an extraordinary phenomenon. During her initial sessions she remained seated on the couch next to her mother and in a whining voice continually complained of boredom. Whenever I succeeded in luring her into any game or activity, she terminated it the moment it became involving. Like the insomniac who wages an exhausting battle against sleep rather than be engulfed by the unconscious and risk confronting forbidden feelings or wishes, she dared not submerge herself in a medium that might betray what was unendurable. Since play led to fantasy and thence to the unconscious, she defended herself by inhibiting all activity. The particular activity in question was revealed as soon as she had become secure enough in the treatment situation to take risks. She then handed me one puppet and took another and devoted session after session to violent combat. The intensity of the murderous feelings — or impulses — that had required such extraordinary repression was then revealed not only by her difficulty in confining her violence to the puppet, but also by the expression of raw hatred that her play inevitably exposed.

The dynamics that led to her fear of play and fantasy and of the impulses they might liberate were only too readily established. Her parents, both tall, handsome people in their late twenties, had decided to seek help because they were finding her whining passivity increasingly intolerable and because they had been alarmed by her nursery school teacher's estimate of her immaturity and the poor prognosis for her entering kindergarten. They both engaged in a kind of ban-

tering camaraderie that scarcely concealed either their underlying aggression or a seeming lack of any genuine involvement
with their child.

Initially, I responded to their communication with a vague
feeling of confusion that soon turned to astonishment as I
grasped its real meaning. They described Joan's recalcitrance
at performing "simple" acts like climbing a full-scale ladder
or clambering down rocks on her mother's favorite walk
through the park. When Joan's mother saw me without her
husband, she confided that she was constantly preoccupied
with a wish to kill Joan. She is the mother referred to in the
Introduction who reported Joan's clear perception of her
mother's feelings after an incident at swimming when Joan
had stated, "Mommy really loves me; she didn't try to drown
me; it was an accident."

It wasn't long before I also witnessed the partial acting out
of the mother's obsession. When Joan expressed a wish to look
down at the street from my roof terrace during her first session,
before I could indicate a low platform on which she could stand
comfortably, her mother seized her and swung her over the
parapet wall, holding her so there was nothing between Joan
and the street but space. Joan gasped and grew pale. It was
quite clear that in bringing Joan into treatment, her mother
was seeking protection against her own impulses for both Joan
and herself.

With six-and-a-half-year-old Alan, whose mother brought
him to see me because he spent all his time at home "just
lying around," I found similar manifestations of similar dynamics. Although Alan's father appeared to be passive and
detached, his mother confided that she could not control her
violent response to Alan and engaged in lacerating verbal, as
well as physical, abuse of him. In an initial drawing that Alan
allowed himself, he portrayed all three of them with elongated
bodies, massive arms, and spiked hands, which he called "hit-
ters," and substantial feet, which he named "kickers." After
several months of marked inactivity, he revealed his awareness of the impulses that his mother's violence was inducing
by stating during one of his sessions: "My mother is trying to
make me a murderer." His primary concern in "lying around"

and inhibiting all fantasy and play was apparently to immobilize himself in order to avoid killing her.

Two factors whose importance as preconditions for the actual commission of murder is manifest, both in governmental preparations for mass killing and in individual instances, emerged with great clarity in the case of Louis, an eleven-year-old who was presumably referred because he was not functioning at his maximum capacity. After several sessions with both him and his parents, it became clear that his father's understatement of his need for help reflected a wish, not only to diminish its seriousness, but to deny its nature. The alienation expressed in the depreciation of the prospective victim and of the possible consequences of the contemplated crime assumed a chilling character as Louis confided in cold, dispassionate terms his conviction that his mother did not deserve to live.

Louis's parents were separated and did not share their sessions. The father was a lawyer, a huge, burly figure of a man with a shock of thick, curly hair; the mother, who was also tall, but blond and much slimmer, was a painter. Although they were antithetical personalities, violence was a central issue for both of them — the father, very controlled, withdrawn, and calculating; the mother, hysterical, emotionally shallow, and frequently acting out. The father described both Louis and his sister, who was two years younger, as unplanned but accepted children who had seriously disrupted their parents' lives. He characterized the mother's relationship with Louis as "monstrous." She undoubtedly favored her daughter, Mary, a gifted musician who was frequently the focus of praise and admiration. Louis dealt with his jealousy by denying and dissociating it and by proclaiming his concern that his mother was "ruining" Mary.

My impression that the father had concealed more than he had revealed was confirmed when the mother stated during her first session that Louis frequently engaged in a very alarming kind of behavior. He had secretly bought some chemicals about a year before and had set off several explosions, one of which had ripped out part of a wall. He had also put a match to Mary's hair and fortunately had only succeeded in singeing it. The mother found it impossible to get along with Louis and admitted to losing control at his provocations and beating him.

When I first saw Louis, I remembered his father's comment that he had been born "a wizened old man." He was tall for his age, slim and fair-complexioned, with straight blond hair and blue eyes. Aside from his physical immaturity, he lacked any of the qualities generally associated with the concept of "child." I never heard him laugh or saw him smile, and I can't recall a single communication that might be called spontaneous. His overriding exclusion of feeling produced a sensation both of death and of coldly calculated murder.

Louis's central preoccupation was his mother. Although he referred to several incidents in which she had thrown things and hit him or beat him with whatever object was at hand, he had no explanation for the tension he always experienced in her presence. He was convinced she was dangerous and that she was capable of killing him and his sister as a way of getting back at his father. Most people were "normal" like his father, but people like his mother would have to be got rid of to improve the world. She was bad and deserved to die. He had no doubt that if he got mad he could kill her; he could bash her head in. When I asked him about the possible consequences to himself, he assured me that since he was a minor, not much would happen. At worst he might have to live in a detention home until he was twenty-one, but, he asserted, it would be well worth it to rid the world of her. He had a reason, and that would make it all right. He had extended this "reasoning" to the world population and had also worked out a system of "purifying" society. The solution was to gather all the bad people in one place and do away with them. If that happened to each generation, we would begin to have the right kind of people. The odor of Nazi ideology was so marked that it came as no surprise to learn that he was an admirer of Hitler, who also had "killed for a reason."

Although fourteen-year-old Seth did not have Louis's intellectual capacity, his personality was strikingly similar. He was referred by the aunt who had rescued him several years before from a physically abusive mother and taken him to live with her. She now found his delinquent behavior uncontrollable and feared for his future as well as her own. He had never known his father, and his most vivid memory of his mother was being repeatedly beaten over the head by her with the heel of her shoe. Not only was he tall and lean like Louis, but he also conveyed the impression that every spark of feeling had been extinguished except for a rage that had been distilled over the years and had transformed his face into an expressionless mask. Although Louis had reduced his mother and other "bad" people like her to a status that made them expendable, he had retained the concept of another category of "normal" people, like his father, who should be allowed to live. With Seth, however, the feeling of alienation was complete. He appeared neither to want nor to expect approval or acceptance and to feel little inhibition toward the commission of antisocial acts. I had the impression that he experienced himself as not of the same kind, as a different species, and could therefore possibly kill with impunity.

The dynamics that emerged so clearly in the cases of Louis and Seth were further corroborated by Donald, who was referred to me at seven and a half because he had attempted to kill himself. Although his parents had found him in the nick of time, they came to see me mainly out of a desire for assurance that it was not a sign of something seriously wrong. The mother, a slight, dark-haired, and extraordinarily withdrawn woman, masked her aggression beneath a strikingly self-effacing façade. Although the father seemed extremely controlled, the tension revealed in the line of his jaw and the stiffness of his carriage left no doubt about the price of that control. They had both been visibly shaken by their son's attempt, and although they tried to diminish the seriousness of its implications, once I suggested that it unquestionably indicated a need for help, they began to search for precipitating causes, and both agreed that the father's violence must have been a contributing factor.

It appeared that for longer than either of them could remember, Donald had been the nightly target of his father's violent attacks. The accumulated frustrations of the father's day spent at a demeaning task in a tangle of disjointed relationships inevitably found release at the dinner table and in the person of his older son, who, additionally, reminded his father of a hated older brother. The daily ritual that had apparently convinced Donald that his father hated and wanted to kill him had erupted with such intensity on that eventful night as to eradicate all hope of change and of eventually being loved. Suicide seemed to be the only solution.

When I first saw Donald, I was struck by his apelike walk and an air of cynical self-negation that was communicated mainly by a strangely defensive smile. As I had noted in similar instances where children had been the victims of violence, Donald avoided fantasy, but he grudgingly consented to a board game whose rules he manipulated in such a way as to guarantee his defeat. I had never encountered such an investment in failure and initially dealt with it by repeatedly verbalizing my good fortune at having at last found a player who was intent on losing. Gradually, however, I let it be known that from my observations I could tell that if Donald ever decided he wanted to win he would probably have no trouble. It wasn't long before he responded and began to play in earnest. Once again I became aware that we were engaged in no ordinary game. Murder was definitely in the air, and I proceeded to define it within the context of our play as a life-and-death struggle in which there was no question that he was out to "slaughter," "kill," and "demolish" me, words that I employed as often as possible in my effort to elicit verbal expression of the aggression that he had turned against himself and that had invaded the musculature of his body and produced his apelike movements. He relished using those terms, but it soon became evident that he found verbalization too constricting. The first intimation that we had entered a new phase where acting out was his preferred mode of communication was signaled by his knocking my token off the board every time he passed it. Although I had no way of knowing where this would lead, I took it as an ominous sign and soon insisted that he confine his expression to words. As his aggressive feelings were liberated, that became increasingly difficult and the framework of the board game too frustrating. He stopped playing altogether and took up the business of murder in earnest. He informed me quite calmly that he wanted to kill me and now devoted his sessions to this single-minded purpose.

It then became my task to enforce verbalization and to prevent acting out. Since the last thing he wanted was to miss
his sessions, my problem was a manageable one. I became very
exacting in my demands on him and warned that any violation
of the rules would result in terminating the session. I knew
that he would initially find such restraint intolerable and
when I made the error of allowing him to tear apart several
Kleenex, he quickly interpreted that as a sign of weakness
and proceeded to shoot rubber-tipped darts to within inches of
my head. After one warning that he ignored, I had no recourse
but to pick him up bodily and put him out. At another time,
when he persisted in not closing the door to my office on his
way out, I warned that I would have to cancel his next session
if he did not comply. He could not resist that challenge and
drew the promised punishment. Those two incidents were sufficient to impose controls and to eliminate acting out. From
then on, he devoted session after session to verbalizing his
wish to kill me.

Like Louis in relation to his mother, Donald then proceeded
to reiterate and to argue, with all the logic he could muster
and a contempt that appeared to echo the concept of "gook"
and "Hun," that I didn't deserve to live. At the same time, like
Louis, he also established his own immunity from serious punishment because of his special condition as a child. At most,
he informed me, he would get fifteen years for his crime, which,
considering what he would have achieved in getting rid of me,
was well worth the risk.

Whether or not any of these children would eventually have
committed murder is of course purely speculative. The very
fact of their having been brought into treatment suggests a
greater degree of caring on some level than was found in the
parents of actual murderers. Nevertheless, the violent abuse
to which they were habitually exposed and the nonloving character of their environments are strikingly similar to the early
experiences of people who have actually committed murder.

The extraordinary inhibition of feeling and fantasy that I
noted in all of them also resembles the unusual degree of
control that apparently characterizes most murderers. Similarly, the feelings of alienation that seem to result from per-

sistent violent abuse in a nonloving environment, and that appear to be universally accepted as essential instruments in governmental preparation of the psyche for killing in aggressive wars, were also found not only in many of the people who had actually committed murder, but also in three of the five children discussed. In two instances, the children verbalized their conviction that their prospective victims "did not deserve to live." The third experienced himself as outside the pale of human society. The degree of repression that resulted in the inhibition of fantasy in all of them appeared to arise, not from the wish, but from the impulse to kill and from the fear of losing control. The inhibition of fantasy, which serves as a defense against persistent violent abuse in a nonloving environment, may therefore suggest a predisposition to commit murder.

Chapter 7

The Inhibition of Fantasy:
A Case of Infantile Autism

WHEN WE CONFRONT the symptomatology of infantile autism, we are assailed by an even more bewildering picture than that which prevails in other forms of schizophrenia. Although domination by fantasy generally characterizes schizophrenia, infantile autism is marked by what seems to be a complete inhibition of fantasy and feeling and by compulsions and rituals that are often incomprehensible until we examine their probable function. As I have discovered in other instances where children resorted to rigid controls and did not allow themselves to fantasize, the object of their defenses frequently appeared to be the management, not merely of violent feelings, but also of violent impulses. Although other dynamics may also exist, these children had been exposed to violence or overwhelmingly violent feelings and frequently had been their target. In the case of Joey, whom I shall discuss here, his stereotyped behavior led me to conclude that the symbolic violence that constantly engaged him represented a compromise between an overriding impulse to kill and an equally powerful need for restraint.

Despite the achievement of modern techniques, which have established for some time that schizophrenia is reversible and curable, there is still considerable confusion regarding both cure and cause and, beyond that, regarding diagnosis, particularly as it relates to children. In my visit to a school for retarded children, I was struck by the number whom I suspected were schizophrenic rather than retarded. I have also had referred to me a child with the diagnosis of retardation who revealed in the course of treatment a need "not to know" that dominated almost all areas of functioning and masked what I felt was at least a normal intelligence. Although infantile autism is more readily recognizable, it shares with other forms of schizophrenia the still-prevailing bewilderment concerning cause and cure.

The reasons for the confusion about schizophrenia derive not only from the mystifying character of the symptoms, but also from an understandable reluctance to acknowledge that these symptoms, dreadful as they may appear, are defenses and that what they defend against may be terror and the fear of killing and of being killed. The symptom picture itself appears neither to follow any particular pattern nor to have any connection with logic or reason. Within its range we find withdrawal from reality and the world of relationships, regression sometimes to an infantile state, an inner turmoil characterized by a range of expression that veers from complete blankness to constant eruption, an overwhelming rage whose management requires the greater part of the patient's energy, and an extraordinary sensitivity.

The continuing reluctance to acknowledge the presence of environmental factors in the genesis of schizophrenia may be traceable to the feelings of guilt and shame that continue to surround the whole area of the parent-child relationship. The denial of any connection between the child's emotional illness and his response to parental handling, which dominated early psychoanalytic thought, is nowhere more evident than in the study of schizophrenia. The well-meaning "defenders" of parents, by their negation of the parents' role, have merely succeeded in many instances in causing in the parents further repression of feeling and exacerbation of conflict. It is understandable that in order to escape from the intolerable burden of such feelings, many parents find relief in the thought that their children suffer from a congenital, incurable illness in which they have played no part. Were they to allow themselves to think of the possibility of cure, they would inevitably have to confront the probability of cause.

The most poignant expression I have encountered of the pain suffered by the parents of schizophrenic children was the unspoken hope communicated by one mother that I would declare her son schizophrenic, a condition she assumed had neither

cause nor cure. When I indicated after several diagnostic sessions that I thought his condition might be arrested and reversed by psychoanalytic treatment involving a repatterning
of her way of handling him, she left and did not return for
several years. She clearly preferred to think her child was
doomed rather than acknowledge having played any part in
his illness. As in her case, only if parents can be helped to
accept the relationship between the possibly traumatic nature
of their own childhood experience and its influence on their
capacity to fulfill their role as parents can they be led to
understand their children's responses and to accommodate
their needs.

Since many investigators have held the conviction that
schizophrenia is incurable, a great deal of the controversy on
the subject has centered on the question of the dynamics. F. J.
Kallmann's studies of schizophrenic twins have led him to
believe that a person is not born schizophrenic or manic-depressive but has a genetic capacity for such a reaction to
precipitating stimuli; that he has, in other words, a predisposition for the condition, which Kallmann feels, however, can
be both prevented and cured.[1] Bender describes it as a "maturational lag at the embryonic level"[2] and administered
shock treatment to such children. Margaret S. Mahler's concept of "symbiotic psychosis" stresses the constitutional vulnerability and predisposition for the development of psychosis.[3] Psychodynamic factors inherent in the parent-child
relationship and the influence of the "schizophrenogenic
mother" have occupied the attention of an ever-increasing
number, among whom are to be found Leo Kanner,[4] to whom
we are indebted for his delineation of early infantile autism,
Beata Rank,[5] and Louise Despert.[6]

Bridging the gap between those who stress the biological
basis and those who look mainly to its psychogenic origins is
the work of P. Bergmann and E. Escalona, whose studies of
the unusual sensitivities of very young children who later
became psychotic led them back to Freud's concept of "the
perceptive apparatus of our mind," which "consists of two layers: an external protective barrier against stimuli whose task
it is to diminish the strength of the excitations coming in, and

a surface behind it that receives stimuli." To Freud's belief that "ego grows in the place, as it were, of the original protective barrier, and it alone protects,"[7] they add the concept that "the constitutional protective barrier continues to function throughout the individual's life, while the ego adds to the protection." They propose that because of the thinness of this protective barrier, or because of the failure of maternal protection, the infant has to resort to the premature formation of an ego, which, when it breaks down, possibly as a consequence of a trauma, makes way for psychotic manifestations.[8]

This concept has been further developed by Dr. Hyman Spotnitz, whose understanding of the problems inherent in the schizophrenic process led him to formulate an effective method of treatment. His method focuses on the problem of insulation and the development of satisfactory patterns for the discharge of aggression.[9] He compared the human mechanism to an electrical system in which nonconducting materials are necessary in order to confine the flow of electricity to the wires. Where these materials are not present in sufficient quantities and the wires become overloaded, there is likely to be a breakdown. The schizophrenic patient is one who has failed to develop the necessary protective coating or insulation that results when the child receives the proper care, protection, and understanding. When this is lacking, the child is not only exposed to overstimulation, which causes him to withdraw in order to establish the necessary insulation, but he is also prevented from developing satisfactory patterns of discharge. Quantities of aggression build up inside that he dares not release out of fear of destroying the people he loves and depends on for survival. He prefers to turn the aggression against himself.[10]

Indications for treatment therefore follow very clearly from this concept. The therapist must first of all provide the care, protection, and understanding that the child has not known, thus enabling him to develop the necessary insulation so that he can emerge from his state of withdrawal. He is also trained to release his aggression in a new and more satisfactory way, first through fantasy and later through direct verbalization.

I did not have the benefit of Spotnitz's understanding of schizophrenia and his resulting theory of the technique of treatment when, after a year of searching for help, Joey's parents brought him to see me at the age of five and a half with a diagnosis of infantile autism. As I listened to the moving account of their unflagging efforts on his behalf, I was reminded of Bender's description of the parents of schizophrenic children. "Interested parents of schizophrenic children," she stated, "stopped short of nothing, even Bellevue, to get attention for their children." If selflessness and concern could have brought about a cure, Joey would certainly have been restored to health.

The lives of his parents were given over totally to the care of Joey and his younger brother, David, whose abnormality, both physical and psychological, required their constant attention. Since they had to spell each other in the care of David, I never saw them together. Joey's father was a fair, sandy-haired man in his early forties, tall and heavyset. He had been married before and divorced; Joey was his first child. He worked at an automobile plant and valued what was an otherwise uninteresting job because the flexibility of the time schedule enabled him to accommodate the demands of his domestic life. The toll taken by his own early deprivations was reflected by his usually unsmiling face and by the severity of his repression of feeling; his reticent communication was usually restricted to factual information and practical details. His wife, attractive and dark-haired and slightly younger than he, was a freer and warmer parent and more in touch with her feelings and Joey's. Although her upbringing appeared to have been less severe, she also communicated a feeling of dammed-up tension. As I continued to know them, I never stopped marveling at the scale of their selfless devotion to their children. It would have been difficult to find more devoted and more cooperative parents.

They described Joey as a happy, normal child up to the age of two and a half, when his baby brother was born, although in retrospect they recalled some behavior at the age of two that had struck them as compulsive and some irrational fears at about the same time. It had been apparent very early that the younger child was not normal, but a year passed before his affliction was clearly identified. Both parents had been completely absorbed by the problem, the mother searching out one doctor after another in a fever of anxiety, and then, once the irrevocable nature of the illness was defined, sinking into a depression that barely allowed her to care for the family.

Gradually she and her husband had become aware that during this period Joey had undergone a marked change. Although he had already been talking clearly and distinctly and had been a joyous and outgoing child, they noted that at three and a half he had become silent, except for the expression of his needs, and generally avoided people. At four, his speech had deteriorated further, and he had become extremely withdrawn. By the time they began to seek help, his behavior fitted the classic description of early infantile autism. His speech had become a disjointed, repetitious jargon, echolalic in character; when he was asked a question, instead of answering, he merely repeated it. He lived in an autistic world where people and toys were ignored, spending most of his time silently "banging" with a stick and making inarticulate sounds. Ritualized behavior and compulsive eating and masturbation had become the norm. He followed a very complicated pattern of walking, taking three steps forward, two back, and turning himself around.

When his parents made their first appointment to see me, they were in despair about even getting him to my office. Although they had expressed doubt and concern about his ritualized pattern of walking, following his first session he began to lead the way, running ahead until he reached my door. I could ascribe such a dramatic change after such a brief exposure only to the extraordinary contrast that must have existed between the violent tension of his parental environment and the calm, undemanding atmosphere of the therapeutic situation.

Joey was a very handsome little boy whose habitually blank expression sometimes gave way to one of sadness; sometimes he smiled. From the very beginning he appeared not to notice me, but occupied himself with a strange kind of activity that I can only describe as a caricature of violence. He made silent lunging movements, arresting them just before completion, and "banged" noiselessly to the accompaniment of garbled sounds, with here and there a word that was distinguishable.

He struck me as a child who was profoundly and in almost every detail of his behavior "on strike." When it was time for him to leave, for instance, presumably instead of kissing me he kissed the walls and the furniture. After observing his preoccupation with silently "banging," before his second session I placed a toy xylophone where he could not fail to see it. He seized the hammers and "banged" every object in the room except the instrument. He swept to the floor all toys, such as checkers, soldiers, design cubes, and anything else he saw on the open shelves. Although he pretended to ignore the toy, I observed that frequently, even while he was seemingly absorbed in "banging," he was carefully manipulating it with his toe. When he was angry, he beat himself on the head or made motions of hitting his hand against his teeth as though to bite it. He never cried with tears, but only made the sounds that accompany crying.

Not only did he abandon his ritualized walking after the first session, he also readmitted a limited use of speech. When I announced at the end of that session that it was time to go home, he reiterated, "Wanna stay here." By the tenth session, his mother reported that when she got him ready to come to see me, he stated, "You're going to Dorothy." By the fourteenth session, when I had introduced a rubber knife, which he found a very useful instrument for shaking, the announcement of the termination of the session was met with: "Wanna stay here. Wanna play with the knife." After nine months of seeing me three times a week, he readmitted the use of the pronoun "I" into his vocabulary. At that time, in answer to my usual way of ending the session, he declared with vigor, "I don't want to hear 'It's time to go home again!' Don't say 'It's time to go home!'"

Initially I concentrated on winning Joey's attention and establishing communication. Since he obviously pretended to ignore me from the first, I seated myself at the table and busied myself fashioning simple primary forms out of clay that I thought might interest him. His first response was to come over after a length of time, break up the shapes, and thrust into his mouth a piece of the clay, which he proceeded to chew.

I was appalled by the sight of his eating the clay and quickly made available a dish of chocolate bits; in later sessions I presented him with several varieties, which necessitated the verbal expression of his preference.

My handling of this incident demonstrates some of the pitfalls that I encountered. Although he never ate clay again and did verbalize his wishes, it is possible that his angry feelings toward me became less available. As the first session indicated, my greatest area of success was in providing the necessary insulation for him to emerge partially from his withdrawal. By the third session, he sought the physical contact that is a frequent characteristic of autistic children and came and sat on my lap for fifteen minutes while I was occupied with the clay forms, soundlessly "banging" with his stick from that vantage point. Sitting on my lap then became a regular part of every session for many months, his initial activity even after he had allowed himself to become involved in play. It was also his preferred position whenever an occupation, such as water play, permitted it.

The first objects that he accepted as toys were a strainer, which I placed on the faucet, and a hand shower, which I draped over the basin in the bathroom. Two other activities also met with success. I lit a candle and repeatedly doused it using a water pistol, or blew it out. This immediately engaged his interest; he either doused it himself or blew it out or he directed me, "Blow it out, okay" or "Light the candle, okay." In order to catch his attention, I also introduced an air rifle, which fired six Ping-Pong balls with an explosive noise. He was delighted with it, running to retrieve the balls and replacing them himself. Following that session, immediately on his arrival he would rush into the playroom eagerly exclaiming, "Light the candle! Shoot the balls!"

With this method, the rituals disappeared, and eating and masturbation became almost normal. He noticed his parents and played with his father and even with his brother when he thought he was unobserved. He demanded attention in the presence of visitors instead of retiring to his room. He made known his wants and responded cooperatively to simple requests. He bathed and dressed himself and slept in his own bed. He no longer clung to the house, but played outside a great deal and went adventuring into the neighborhood. Eventually he was able to attend a day camp and a school for children with special problems.

It is difficult to evaluate how much more this method might have accomplished had his familial environment remained stable. At one point, however, his mother required surgery, necessitating a week's hospitalization. No amount of explanation could eradicate the memory of her earlier absence and its aftermath, her returning with his baby brother. After her departure this time, he came to his session filled with despair, crying without tears and reiterating, "And now a baby, a baby!" That incident caused a degree of withdrawal once more and was followed by a period during which his brother's condition deteriorated markedly, eventually requiring that he be institutionalized and finally leading to his death.

The impact of these events on Joey's parents was tragic. As David became increasingly unmanageable, they faced the inevitable separation with great courage and once more accommodated their lives to the new routine of periodic visits to the hospital, making those outings as much as possible a family picnic involving Joey. The sadness of the separation and finally of the death took its toll. When, added to that, Joey's father had an accident at work, although it was minor, the stability of the family seemed to go. The father went into treatment for a time, but then the mother broke down. It is perhaps a measure of their devotion to Joey as much as of their basic vitality that they both recovered sufficiently to continue functioning as parents.

In gauging the effect of these developments on Joey, we have to take into account that, at his stage of development, he could only have interpreted them magically, as having been caused by him. He most likely felt he had not only precipitated his mother's hospitalization and her wish for another child, but that he was responsible for David's being sent away, and he feared he might also therefore be gotten rid of. We can only guess at his response to the mounting tensions of his parents as one tragic incident followed another. Nevertheless, although he did not again recapture the enthusiasm expressed by his greeting of "Light the candle! Shoot the balls!" he maintained and extended his other gains.

Although I was unfamiliar with Spotnitz's concept of the nature and treatment of schizophrenia when I saw Joey, in retrospect it illuminates the reasons for both my success and my failure. Although I succeeded in developing a sufficient degree of insulation to permit him to emerge from his withdrawal, my failure to release his rage sufficiently restricted its scope. Because the sessions were very meaningful, the announcement of their termination became a natural means of evoking a direct and verbal expression of his aggressive feelings. His verbal responses during the first nine-month period occurred at those moments when he experienced the highest degree of frustration in relation to me: my announcement that the session was over. That sequence of events therefore suggests that had he been provided repeatedly with situations that elicited his rage, it might have been possible to repattern his rage response to a much larger degree.

Although my method of treating him did not effect a cure, it did arrest and partially reverse the schizophrenic process. At one point my demonstration of a more effective method of dealing with his rage succeeded in reversing its direction, but only by vicarious means and only momentarily. During one session, when he arrived in an obviously disturbed state in which he beat himself and banged his arm against his teeth, crying without tears, I seized a piece of clay and proceeded to pound it violently until it was completely flattened. He immediately became quiet, and when I was finished, he broke the clay into bits and handed them to me for a repeat performance. Prompted each time by his breaking up the clay and presenting it to me, I repeated it several times, a record for cooperative activity up to that time. Although the experience of cooperation was symbolized after that by his carefully making and allowing to remain for the first time a finger imprint in a ball of clay that I had rolled, instead of destroying it as he had done previously, it did not lead him subsequently to direct his rage outward. To have brought this about, it would have been necessary to have expanded those moments of frustration that first moved him to speech and to have provided him with additional provocations.

Joey's response to treatment not only established that, in his case, infantile autism was reversible and, with the correct method, probably curable, but suggested that his autism, with the variety of its symptomatology, was a complex defense necessitated by the threatening character of his environment and his fear of being killed and of killing. Whether or not all children would have responded as Joey did, and to what degree therefore hereditary or constitutional factors played a part, are questions we are still in no position to answer. The importance of environmental factors, however, is eminently clear. The readmission of speech at the end of the first session and the startling disappearance immediately after that of his ritualized pattern of walking inform us not only of the extraordinary effectiveness of a therapeutic atmosphere, but also of the intensity of the threat that necessitated his defenses.

The nature of that threat and his response were dramatically represented by his rituals. His requirement that he always have an object to shake — or to bang without sound — and the silent and arrested lunging movements that punctuated that activity suggest an overwhelming preoccupation with aggression that, at all costs, had to be reduced to safe and unrecognizable symbols. In retrospect, it is also possible to hypothesize that his substitution, at a later stage of his treatment, of a flimsy L-shaped piece of paper for his more solid wooden stick represented a lessening of the internal and external degree of threat he experienced.

The symptomatology of infantile autism, with its retreat from reality and the world of relationships, its compulsive patterns of behavior and its rituals, its garbled and incomprehensible use of speech that kept under repression his perceptions of his parents' feelings and his response to them, became his refuge. The inhibition of fantasy and feeling, which is a function of compulsions and rituals and frequently a reliable barometer of the degree of actual violence or of violent feelings to which a child has been exposed, protected him from his own violent response to his parents' violence or intensely violent feelings. The interruption of the insulating process following the traumatic impact on his parents of the discovery of his infant brother's abnormality caused him to withdraw in order to protect himself against internal and external stimuli. That he was continually involved in symbolic acts of violence might also indicate that he was preoccupied with controlling both violent feelings and violent impulses as well. The atmosphere of his psychoanalytic treatment, which made him feel cared for, protected, and understood, helped him to develop sufficient insulation to emerge from his withdrawal to a considerable degree. To the extent that he was provided with opportunities to release his aggressive feelings, he was able to direct them outward instead of turning them against himself.

PART II

The Later Years

Chapter 8

A Worthless Child and
a Noble Parent

ALTHOUGH I HAD ALWAYS been impressed by a child's ability to create the defensive fantasy required in order to establish a minimal sense of safety, and with the aid of a psychoanalyst to allow it to evolve in play until its resolution, it was not until my analysis of Norma, who was referred at the age of thirty-seven because of a severe neurotic depression, that I was able to understand the powerful role of a defensive fantasy that was not resolved in early childhood. The seeming absence of fantasy during latency had created the impression that it did not perform a continuing function. Norma's analysis revealed, however, that although, with maturation, her fear of being killed by her mother had been repressed along with the fantasy that it had required in early childhood, it remained the secret dynamic behind the unconscious fantasy that now dominated her life. Her insistence that there was something wrong with her came up with startling regularity in the course of her treatment and reflected the undefined hope that her worthlessness had caused her mother's hatred. Her mother's death some years before had in no way diminished the intensity of either Norma's despairing search for some explanation for the absence of her mother's love or of her own ceaseless struggle to win it. Only after the repeated exposure of her fantasy of eventually qualifying by perfecting her character and by doing good works was she able to experience her early terror of infanticide that the fantasy had concealed.

After listening, session after session, to Norma extolling her mother's virtues, I commented on the perfection with which she endowed her. "The nobler I make her, the more understandable it is that she couldn't love me," was her reply. It came off the top of her head, and several years passed before it actually became part of her experience and her understanding.

Norma's investment in feeling worthless was among the most dramatic I have encountered. As many other patients have also taught me since, the most convincing proof of her worthlessness was her murderous response to her mother's murderous feelings. Her need to believe that her mother felt only love for her required that she bury her perception of her mother's hostile feelings. Since that maneuver wiped out any foundation for her own hostility, she was left with the conviction that she was simply a worthless person who hated without reason. In order to maintain the illusion that her worthlessness had caused her mother's hatred, she designed a life-style based on self-defeat and failure. As her story unfolded, the efforts she had made to promote that conviction confounded belief. No significant area of her life had been permitted to contradict it by providing a sense of achievement that might have enhanced her self-esteem.

That the stake involved in maintaining her fantasy was life or death was revealed at those moments when the fantasy was threatened. I soon learned to avoid any expression of either approval or disapproval in my treatment of her. Her response to approval was clear enough — anyone's show of appreciation or affection for her would expose her mother's hatred. But disapproval? She coined a phrase I thought very apt when she referred to her extraordinarily heightened sensitivity to criticism as "a mantle of virtue" that she never permitted herself to discard. Any suggestion that she was less than perfect would have led to the exposure of her greatest imperfection: that she hated her mother and wanted to kill her. If that knowledge were allowed into awareness, it would inevitably have revealed that such feelings were merely a response to her mother's. Her system of self-deception would have been exposed and her defense against her fear of infanticide shattered. She therefore sent out a distress signal at the merest breath of disapprobation and avoided all clues that might have disclosed her own feelings or her mother's.

Some years before, when her husband had asked for a di-

vorce and left her with a daughter who was now eleven, the
resulting feelings of worthlessness were so overwhelming as
to leave no room for the hope of ever establishing her worth.
The suicidal thoughts that followed precipitated her entry into
analysis for the first time. Now once again the violent attacks
of her friend Ada had revived such thoughts. Under the barrage of Ada's criticism her defense against her perception of
her mother's concealed wish to kill her had begun to crumble.
At a point when she had relinquished almost all hope of being
loved and was unconsciously contemplating suicide, she reentered treatment.

Looking back at my first impressions of Norma, I remember
being struck by her self-effacing, ingratiating façade and by
what appeared to be an extraordinary confusion about her
identity. She was a tall, dark-haired, somewhat heavy woman
who appeared to have little awareness of either her intelligence or her charm, but seemed inundated with feelings of
worthlessness. Although I found myself immediately responding to her unusual sensitivity, it wasn't until some time later
that I was able to assess with any accuracy the degree of her
terror and of her distrust. I suspected that she was preoccupied
with suicidal thoughts, and when I suggested it after several
months, she acknowledged it with relief; she had always
known in a dissociated way about her wish for death. On an
unconscious level, she was alarmed by it and had reentered
analysis in a blind drive for survival.

When Norma was first referred to me she was unaware of
the nature of her problem, despite some five years of analysis.
Both the manner and the content of her communications, however, revealed a severe neurotic depression. Through the den-
sity of a thick fog, which appeared to be carefully controlled
in order to perpetuate a sense of confusion, she told me about
her marriage and her divorce and her present friendship with
Ada, which troubled her because of its homosexual overtones.
It was not long, however, before she also introduced the hopeless riddle of her relationships with both her mother and her
older brother Danny.

Shortly after her treatment began, I became aware of her
interest in writing and proposed that, to supplement her ses-

sions, she might find it useful to write every day and make a copy for me. She seized on the suggestion and immediately embarked on an exploration of her relationships with her family from her earliest years. At first she associated the sense of urgency with which she pursued this project with her feelings of extraordinary confusion about herself and her conviction that some buried memory could clear it all up. Later she was amazed to hear herself state that, although she couldn't say what crime she had committed, she wanted to exonerate herself. The resulting record of her analytic experience is a valuable document that she has permitted me to use freely.

Her initial sessions were mainly devoted to the daily barrage of criticism that Ada leveled at her. The blacker the charges, the more they gained Norma's attention; she was constantly involved in weighing their validity. When I finally stated, "You've put yourself on trial; if you find yourself guilty, you're in danger of doing away with yourself," she began to realize that she was engaged in a struggle for her life.

It took some months before she found Ada's prototype in her mother. Although she was aware by now that she hated her mother, she hoped I would disprove it. She brought in a dream in which she saw her parents' flattened image in a concave mirror at Coney Island. Her comment was: "It's a distortion." She wanted them rehabilitated and their "true image" restored after the damaging effects of her previous analysis. Her mother had died a few years before and her father still earlier. Her brother, four years her senior, had terrorized her as a child and still had a crippling influence on her. There were two older sisters — one on the West Coast who Norma thought had little effect on her life and another whose hostility had been nearly as damaging to her as her brother's. There had also been a baby brother, who had died of meningitis during infancy. Rounding out the picture of her family was her haunting awareness of her mother's miscarriages and stillbirths, thoughts of which continually hovered on the fringe of consciousness, as though they contained some secret she dared not probe.

As her sessions progressed, a picture emerged of a shabby, withdrawn child who had no memory of having been held or kissed or caressed by her mother. Her mother's disparaging comments about Norma were part of the daily routine. Although she had some early recollection of her father's warmth, all spontaneous show of affection on his part had stopped when she was six as a result of her mother's ridicule.

The self-deception that had wiped out Norma's perception of her mother's feelings was truly staggering. She was an unhappy child, but her central concern was her mother's unhappiness. The oppressive silence that usually prevailed when she and her mother were together invariably called up thoughts of her mother's tragic life. Her mother's suffering, her nobility, and her martyrdom for her children were her constant preoccupation and served as an ever-present reminder of her own worthlessness.

What confused her most was her mother's seeming ignorance of her brother Danny's violence. She related one abusive incident after another, but found it difficult to concede that her mother must have known of her terror, insisting her mother had warm feelings even though she didn't show them. Despite the evidence of real neglect she presented, she had never consciously allowed herself to think that her mother might have hated her.

Norma's reverent attitude toward her mother, which her brother and sister shared, was complicated by her magical interpretation of an early event. During one session her halting recital of her baby brother's death when she was four left her amazed that, after thirty-three years, it still appeared to be the tragedy of her life. When, acting on a hunch, I suggested that she thought she had killed him, she responded with surprised relief. She had always unconsciously considered herself a murderer.

That preoccupation, however, surfaced only in her dreams. In one, she gave birth to a baby that she then presented to her mother. In another, she was wheeling an empty baby carriage across a street when she met two of her aunts. One was married to a man who "was guilty of all kinds of chicanery" in relation to Norma's father; the other was married to her father's scurrilous brother, who had repeatedly cheated him. Her comment in the dream was "Who are you to accuse me?"

In another dream her mother is blind but leads Norma, who grasps the back of her dress and taps with a cane, as though she, too, is blind. Norma commented, "I must not see what I see in deference to her handicap. She must be strong because I feel so small and weak." During the same session she spoke of her fear, as a child, of going up to the roof alone to join the other children who lived in her building and played there.

Although Norma had always regarded herself as a murderess, she now turned the charge against her mother. Her suspicion that her mother had never wanted children was confirmed when her brother had announced that a friend had just had her fourth child and her mother had exclaimed incredulously, "She wanted them?" In the dream Norma accused her mother of having aborted her children and of having wanted to abort and kill her. It also soon became apparent that Norma's silence during childhood regarding her brother's violent attacks stemmed from her conviction that he was the agent of her mother's wishes. Her own comment, "I must not see what I see," expressed the self-deception she had practiced all her life.

When I exposed her secret and told Norma what she knew at some level — that her mother had wanted to abort and to kill her, that she had been aware of this from her earliest years, and that she had likewise wanted to kill her mother — my disclosure was met initially by despairing acceptance. She wrote:

Tonight I'm assailed by all the old familiar feelings — the emptiness, the longing, the desolation. Life without love is surely the hardest thing to bear. Miss Bloch's interpretation leaves me feeling as stunned as though all of it were completely unknown to me . . . Suddenly things are beginning to clear. What I've always found unbearable is that I should have such horrible feelings about my blameless mother. Now that her destructive wishes are reinstated, I feel immensely relieved.

By the next day she felt overwhelmed by that insight and asked, "Is it possible that a mother wants to destroy her own child?" It wasn't long, however, before she rejected it outright.

She accused me of trickery and deception and the violation of all human feeling. Although she then appeared to accept it and welcomed the freedom to "know" what she knew, it was some time before she was able to experience and to understand the murderous wishes that lay beneath her preoccupation with her mother's virtue and the silence that usually prevailed between them.

In the course of the next few months, Norma's analysis revealed the system of self-deception that had originated with her mother's feelings but extended to all her relationships. Although one part of her took careful note of the evil and the hostility that she encountered, another automatically repressed all awareness of it. Since this process left her own responses unexplained, she was frequently overwhelmed by her own hostility and her resulting feelings of worthlessness. It waited for an incident relating to her husband to bring into focus both the operation of this process and its dynamics. One day, following her separation, Ada had tried to suggest in a gingerly fashion that there were sordid aspects to her husband's character that Norma's manner had led Ada to believe were completely hidden from her. They were both surprised when Norma proceeded to enlarge on her outline.

An entry in her journal records the incident and the insight that followed. She wrote:

> To know — and not to know — a process by which I erase my perception of evil in others. All that "I knew" had not prepared me for Ada's revelation, and it took some months before what I "knew" and what I knew began to come together. I had been defending myself against something I wouldn't define, just as some years ago I had known that in order to survive I had to stay away from my mother, without acknowledging I felt she wanted to kill me.

That last sentence startled and shocked Norma and finally led to the exposure of her system. She wrote:

> Suddenly something seems to have opened up that I don't want to go near. This "process" which has become so much a part of me is the result of a daily confrontation with knowledge I didn't dare let myself know. It hadn't occurred to me until this moment that

a precedent had already been established for the feelings that
existed between my husband and me. The measureless rage and
the wordless guilt belonged to my mother.

Her system of self-deception was designed not only to en-
hance her image of others but to diminish her own. When she
finally allowed herself to perceive Ada's destructive character,
she became aware that she had no idea of her own identity.
When I stressed the difficulty of finding it at her age, she felt
relieved. She later described an experience related to her ensuing search for it:

> I woke up with a start and a feeling I had been dreaming about
> my brother Danny. Ada suddenly popped into my head and the
> clear awareness that she hated me. I had no feeling of anguish or
> grief, just a crystal-clear realization that it was true, that on one
> level, I had tried to conceal it, and on another, to work ceaselessly
> to overcome it. Suddenly, I saw it and felt no anxiety. Apparently,
> first it's necessary to find someone who feels as ambivalent and
> destructive towards me as Danny or my mother; then I search my
> soul to discover what there is in me to provoke such feelings. I
> concentrate on my faults to explain away the hatred and also to
> maintain hope. The fantasy, I think, has been that, if I can be a
> better person, I will no longer provoke such feelings, and I will be
> loved. It seems so simple. Now I see that once I remove myself as
> the cause of other people's hatred, I can begin to live. Finding my
> own identity then becomes a very different experience. At some
> points in the past months I recognized the absurdity of my fantasy.
> It was a child's dream — you'll see, I'll be good, I'll be very good,
> and then you'll love me.

In order to preserve her self-image of worthlessness, she had
also developed a technique that she called the sifting process,
a method of screening out from any experience, no matter how
positive, some particular detail with which she could attack
herself. As she explained it, "A moment's exuberance could
seem shockingly inappropriate and provide the ammunition
for endless self-flagellation."

In addition, she permitted no significant area of her life to
provide a sense of achievement that might increase her self-

esteem. When she began to examine her efforts to establish her worthlessness, she enumerated instance after instance that clearly indicated her unusual abilities and at the same time her enraged rejection of other people's recognition of them. Her need to maintain a diminished self-image was still so great that even now this unprecedented admission of worth was followed by a strong reaction. She wrote: "I've had a strange sensation in writing this; I feel I'm not telling the truth. A counterpoint of mockery on a nonverbal level accompanies everything I write. I know that everything is absolutely true, but I don't believe it."

Although I was already thoroughly familiar with the phenomenon of resistance in psychoanalytic treatment, I don't think anyone taught me more than Norma about either the dimensions of the investment in remaining dependent or its meaning. At a stage where a great deal of the debris that had cluttered up her life had already been cleared away, freeing her to move forward, Norma suddenly evinced absolutely no intention of budging, beating a retreat at the slightest recognition of her creativity. One day she brought her latest painting in to show me. This was not the first time I had seen her work, which I found very impressive, and I took this opportunity to express my genuine feeling. My praise apparently inspired her when she arrived home to confront what struck her as an extraordinary concept: she had talent. She spent hours delving into the history of her system of self-deception that had been designed to conceal it. To her amazement, this was then followed by complete numbness and inactivity; she felt paralyzed. During her next session she got the first inkling of the real meaning of her avoidance of achievement.

Although many patients have ascribed to their fear of failure their reluctance to attain, or even to define, a goal, Norma's experience reinforced an already strong impression that in many instances the more corrosive and inhibiting factor may be the fear of success. It has been recognized that success may precipitate acting out in a suicidal patient, but it has not been so apparent that passivity, the stifling of creativity, the inhibition of effort, or the blunting of aspiration may simply express an unconscious determination to avoid exposing the system of self-deception and risking being killed. The terror that took over with the first tentative steps toward accomplishment exposed the nature of the conflict. Norma's analysis revealed that buried in her unconscious was the conviction that achieving success meant risking death. Not only would her mother's hatred of her be exposed if she established her worthiness to be loved, but also the fantasy that it was her worthlessness that had provoked it. The hope of eventually winning her mother's love, her primary defense against her fear of being killed by her, would have collapsed.

Not only would achievement expose the reality of her mother's hatred by enhancing Norma's self-esteem, however; it would also threaten her concept of how to win love. Since being herself had elicited only hatred, she had unconsciously concluded that to win love she had to wipe herself out. Another patient once stated, "If I'm me, nothing will work," and yet another, "I became someone else so I would be liked." Many had avoided relationships rather than meet such requirements. With Norma this concept emerged with particular clarity in her relationships with men. She had reported becoming aware of a strange kind of lethargy throughout her married life, a loss of all feeling of volition that affected both intellectual pursuits and even the memory of any creative interest. At a later point, when her overwhelming discouragement about ever finding a man had momentarily decided her to end the search, she was astonished by what followed and wrote: "A cloud seems to have lifted, a weight which has kept me paralyzed. I now see that for me finding a man means relinquishing all interest and condemning myself to mindlessness, the price of being loved. No wonder I regarded it as hopeless. If I had relinquished any more, I would have been dead. With Sol I gave up everything that meant anything to me. I repeated with him what I had learned from my family was the requirement for winning love. It hadn't occurred to me that it still permeated my life. As soon as I decided to stop looking, I was all energy; I could do what I wanted, go where I pleased. There's still something, though, that doesn't want to believe any of this, that wants to think it's phony. And that's the part that wants to keep me paralyzed. Perhaps if I expunge enough of myself . . ."

For Norma, as for many patients, the problem of identity was complicated by still another factor. She was convinced that a precondition for winning love was not only "expunging" herself but remaining dependent. The memory of being cared for in the early years was her only experience of being loved. She therefore ascribed its loss to growing up and being independent and yearned for a return to that early state. By maintaining the illusion of helplessness, she had tried magically to revive her only experience of her mother's love — her physical care during infancy and childhood. She wrote: "What has always infuriated me when I've been praised is the fear of what would follow — the declaration of my independence; I would no longer be considered a candidate for loving care. I've never believed in my wish for dependence. Now, suddenly, it explains a major part of my life; dependence has been the price of love. Another thought occurs — dependence and lack of identity are intertwined."

This revelation led her to conclude: "Until now, all my efforts were expended with only one end in view — to win love, and, in particular, my mother's, a truly hopeless project. For over three decades I've concentrated on meeting what I felt must be the requirements, and now at thirty-nine I'm faced with the bitter knowledge that I've never known it."

The examination of the relationships within her family inspired by this last insight led her directly into the realm of homosexual feelings. Although she recognized that these feelings expressed her search for love, she was mainly preoccupied with what she considered their abnormality and spoke with great difficulty. After listening to her unyielding insistence that she was responsible for her mother's hostile feelings, I finally made an interpretation that dramatically revealed her enormous stake in maintaining her system of self-vilification. I stated, "The only thing wrong with you is your determination to believe that everything is wrong." The violence of her reaction paralleled her response to my statement concerning her mother's wish to kill her. Again she accused me of manipulation and trickery; this time I was trying to conceal from her

that she was really a homosexual. Her eventual acceptance of
my statement was followed by black despair. If nothing was
wrong with her, all hope was lost. She wrote:

> I can't believe what's happened, but some part of me has already
> understood, and the rest waits in a state of wonder. I'm not sure if
> I can recall Bloch's exact words, although I remember telling her
> she ought to make a tape-recording of them instead of repeating
> them what seemed like a dozen times. I know I felt stunned. Fi-
> nally, she made me repeat, "My feelings are completely normal;
> my problem is I think everything that has to do with me is wrong."
> They plunged me into a sea of desolation. Once more I was sure
> she was trying to mislead me and I interpreted this completely
> new diagnosis as an attempt to deflect my attention from what I
> concluded must be a really hopeless homosexual problem. Thirty-
> six hours and a severe migraine later, and I'm beginning to enter-
> tain the possibility that she really meant what she said. Whatever
> is, is right. It seems too wonderful.

By the following day she was again ready to take it all back.
"Today I look upon it as a fantasy. When Miss Bloch tells me
that my feelings are normal, and I have such a paranoid reaction, I wonder what she means by 'normal.' For a slug that
has lived under a rock, an absence of coloring is 'normal'; fish
that live at the bottom of the sea are also 'normally' blind. I
wonder if she means that I've responded in a 'normal' way to
the conditions of my life and have emerged with the predictable distortions."

Her gradual absorption of the concept that she was all right
led her to accept not only her feelings of rage but also other
people's, especially Ada's, and for the first time she allowed
herself uninhibited expression of her hatred of Ada. She was
then amazed to receive an affectionate note from Ada; after
the shock wore off, she answered in the same spirit, but then
noted a surprising development.

> I keep having all kinds of dreams about women. Every woman
> I've ever known, it seems, is coming back to impress me with her
> good will. On Monday night, my mother and my sister brought me
> flowers. They're all very happy affairs, except when I wake up, I
> walk around in a dull rage. Can it be that my rage is my response

to being loved? For the first time in weeks I abandoned all interest in my diet. I felt I had lost. That seems curious — what had I lost? It seems I need to feel hated. It may be if I feel loved, then I've lost my case — that's what I've lost. I have no justification for my hatred. Another thought occurs — if anybody finds me lovable, then my mother stands convicted; she hated me just because she hated me.

That concept led to an understanding of a major part of her struggle. Her journal states:

It seems unbearable to me that I just wasn't loved and that nothing I can do will ever change it. That the major protagonist in all of this has been dead now for some years seems to make little difference. There must be something wrong with me; I can still change and then all will be well — I'll be loved. The thought that I'm all right, which at first seemed so filled with promise, transforms all hope into empty desolation. At moments I find myself poised as though on the brink of discovery; perhaps there really is something wrong and Miss Bloch is concealing it from me. The hope that springs up at such times is my only measure of what's really wrong. During my analysis I'm aware of having pursued a fixed idea, that there was some secret, some mystery, which, once revealed, would transform my entire life. What I searched for was the weakness in myself that made me unloved — it suddenly occurs to me that the secret has been found at last and I'm refusing to acknowledge it, the secret that there was nothing wrong with me, only that I was unloved. I've really found the key to my life.

That was a milestone in Norma's analysis and led her to review the history of her struggle. She wrote:

What a difficult time it's been and how much has been accomplished. To have identified at last the longing that never had a name or a dimension, but enveloped my spirit in boundless desolation from the beginning of time. I never knew what I lacked nor what I wanted, but wandered blindly over completely unmarked terrain simply in search. I stumbled often and often had the feeling of returning to something already familiar, to places I thought I had left, but I recognized no guide-posts, and all that I came to know was confusion and a despair for which I had no label. That this was a hunger for which my experience had given me no definition hadn't occurred to me. I felt the emptiness, the sense of a void, but I didn't know why it was there, or perhaps even that it was. I called it "despair," "desolation," "hopelessness," but without understanding what hope had been eclipsed to give rise to such a feeling. This is the confusion that has beset me all my life. Finally, to understand it, to know, when the feeling is upon me, what it means, however black the despair, is to have restored to me some small measure of human dignity, to have found the beginnings of my identity. That I never knew my mother's love, but spent my life in a blind search, unaware that it was missing or even that I searched — suddenly this brings into focus so much of my experience. I always feared homosexual feelings; they meant to me that I was unnatural, that I had an affliction, a disease with which I had been born. I think I believed this even when I knew such feelings are shared by all of us. Even while I defined them to myself as a search for identity, a longing for acceptance by members of my own sex, and even while I acknowledged that I feared women and had experienced rejection at their hands, that still didn't mean to me that I had never known my mother's love, or that my homosexual feelings expressed my wish to find it.

The "fantasy," however, was not so easily abandoned. Some time later she became aware that she identified with her father and again returned to the conviction of her abnormality. When I again exposed her determination to believe there was something wrong with her, she became aware once more of the intensity of her need to cling to the hope that in reality there was something wrong, that she could change, and in so doing still qualify for her mother's love. The despair into which she sank finally laid bare her monumental preoccupation with establishing her worthlessness in order to explain her mother's wish to kill her and to keep alive the hope that if she could make herself more worthy, she would be loved.

Her new, dramatic insight into this investment soon led her to reassess and to terminate her relationship with Ada. She recorded the event as follows:

> I have at last relinquished my desperate attachment to the image of my mother as the source of all love, of salvation. I recall Friday's session when I stated that I was through with Ada and her jealousy which allowed no room for my growth, and Miss Bloch had asked

insistently, "How can you give her up, when you have nobody else?" I replied with conviction, "I can — I have you." I didn't recognize it then, but that was a milestone, my declaration of independence of a preoccupation which had kept me tethered to all the destructive experiences of my past and made it the inevitable condition of the present. It seems nothing short of a miracle — I have come through, out of the dark tunnel. I can't describe the feeling of being here, at this moment, in full possession of my faculties, my life for the first time stretching ahead of me, no longer absorbed in the backward glance, "the lengthening chain," the past. I literally feel I've been born, not an infant birth, but into being. I ascribe this final definition of myself to my parting from Ada. When I put her out of my life, I was born — at last! With one stroke, I got rid of Danny, of my mother and of that dreadful image of myself as a creature without shape or form, a female Caliban doomed to live out her life in darkness and mire. And there I was, like the lady of the legends, or Papagena, who needed only love to disclose her true identity. For the first time in my life, I think I know who I am.

Until this point, Norma's analysis had dealt mainly with her need to feel loved and her response to feeling hated. After she had succeeded in experiencing her rage and had established the beginnings of her real identity, she began to feel and to define the terror that lay beneath her unyielding preoccupation with winning love. Although there had been some earlier intimations of it in relation to her creativity and to her sexual activity, her terror did not emerge full-blown until she became interested in finding a man. Norma's unconscious perception of an important requirement not only for qualifying for her mother's love, but, as her early magical thinking had led her to conclude, for staying alive, had been the exclusion of men from her life.

Her earliest recollection of the origin of this conviction was at around the age of four and a half and concerned her father. Norma had written about him: "It's likely my father was never more than a shadow which had certain outlines that I filled in out of a need for something solid." Two early memories of him that also involved her mother, however, suggested that the reduction of the early flesh-and-blood image of her father to a

mere shadow was the result of a complex process that her
mother had set in motion.

She described the first one as follows:

> I was playing on the floor — my brother and sisters had already
> left for school — not far from the sounds of my mother busily
> getting the day's cooking under way, and dimly aware of my father
> standing with his back to me, putting on his trousers, when sud-
> denly he sprang around, and there, dangling in front in a kind of
> pink glow, was his thing! I nearly burst with joy as I squealed
> delightedly, "Shame! Shame!" Grownups could be so careless! He
> quickly tucked the offending member out of sight, blushing with
> embarrassment and pleasure. Suddenly, my mother burst in upon
> us, her round belly quivering with a rage that seemed to travel to
> the very tip of the wooden cooking spoon that she seemed to bran-
> dish in her right hand, her face a study in contemptuous fury that
> powerfully swept before it all trace of pleasure and left nothing but
> a wave of angry red. "What's the matter with you?" she hissed.
> "Don't you have any other place to dress?"
>
> "Yah! Yah! Yah!" he replied, mocking her. But I understood. My
> father had been bad, and there was something strange about his
> badness. And my mother was a witch.

By itself that image of her mother might have been sufficient
to imbue any relationship with her father with a sense of
danger, but a year and a half later another incident effectively
reduced her father to the shadow she remembered. The joyous
ritual of the day was lining up with her sisters and brother
and waiting expectantly for his kiss on his return from work.
On this fateful occasion, just as Norma's turn came, she heard
her mother's voice from behind: "What's all the kissing? What
are you, a kissing bug? You have to kiss them every night?"
That ended all spontaneous show of affection by her father
and placed any meaningful relationship with him out of
bounds.

The image of the "witch" brandishing the cooking spoon
continued to haunt Norma throughout her life and enforced
her mother's prohibition against her relationship with her
father and with all men. At one point, after a particularly

intense sexual experience, Norma had the distinct impression that the walls had suddenly become paper-thin and this incarnation of her mother was slowly mounting the stairs to her apartment. In a desperate effort at survival she dashed across the room and turned on the light. Following that night, she felt she had no choice but to terminate her relationship and it was many months before she dared to have another one.

At the point in her analysis when she again felt ready for a heterosexual relationship, she had a dream that represented an extraordinary condensation of the dynamics of her terror. It actually consisted only of a frightening sound, high-pitched and thin, a blackened smokestack and a kind of kiosk that contained the door to the roof that she recalled from her childhood. Her ensuing associations summoned forth one terrifying memory after another, ending with her experience at the dentist the previous year. "That seems to come closest," she wrote. "The feeling of hysteria, that I won't manage. It suddenly occurs to me that the prospect of forming relationships with a man has always filled me with terror."

The kiosk brought back her earliest fantasy, from around four and a half, of a similar structure that she had presumed was inside her and was continually guarded by a jovial little man, one of the seven dwarfs. Norma had always been too ashamed of what she felt was its abnormality to reveal it to anyone, and only now, when she was clear enough about her real identity, was she able to approach it. Its significance becomes apparent with the realization that the first time her abusive brother took her up to the roof of the building to which they had just moved, she suspected that he might kill her there. The roof became the symbol of death and was represented in her fantasy by the door. To insure her safety, she selected as guardian to the door the "jovial dwarf," whose endearing statue she saw every day in her home. Although that early fantasy vanished along with her need for it, she continued to be haunted throughout her life by the nagging sense of its grotesqueness, which was enhanced by her complete amnesia concerning either its origin or its function. Only now did it become clear that this bizarre perception of what was inside her had defended her against her terror and had guaranteed her safety at all times.

Her fantasy also had another unconscious determinant. Although "the roof" was an important symbol in Norma's dreams and fantasies, she was unaware of its symbolic meaning and expressed surprise when I reminded her that "falling off the roof" is a common expression for menstruation and represents abortion. The repressed feelings and memories that this particular dream about "the roof" liberated proved to be the key to her fear and to the central issues of her life.

In recalling the fantasy of the incorporated door and the "little man" who guarded it, she suddenly revived an early image of herself standing in the dark, crowded new apartment to which the family had moved after the death of her brother. She is all alone in the unfamiliar house and gazes out in terror at what seems like acres of furniture. Since she was convinced that she had murdered her brother, she apparently had interpreted all subsequent experiences in the light of her "crime." At the moment of abandonment, when, she now assumed, her mother had left her to go shopping, her expectation that her mother would retaliate by killing her appeared to have reached the point of realization. In the extremity of her fear, she then created the protective fantasy.

It wasn't long after this insight that Norma experienced that terror on a conscious level in relation to her creativity. At one point during her session, while she was reporting her triumphant resumption of painting after one of her periodic setbacks, I caught a note of fear in her voice and commented, "You seem scared." To quote from her own account of that session: "I was surprised by Bloch's response," she wrote. "Had she not called my attention to it, I mightn't have noted a feeling that was so familiar — I was frightened because I felt she didn't want me to paint. Pursuing it further, in answer to her 'Why nots,' I arrived at 'You don't want me to do anything,' and then, 'You don't want me to live' — 'You want me dead.'"

After a lifetime of searching for her mother's love Norma finally experienced her terror of being killed by her. The feelings that she projected onto me expressed her unconscious perception of her mother's wishes. Although she had appeared to accept the validity of my early interpretation of her dreams and other communications, until now she had been unable to experience them. Only after she had confronted the reality of her mother's hatred and the hopelessness of her struggle to win her love could she develop a sufficient sense of her real identity to allow her to know the terror that she had defended against since her earliest years. Experiencing it liberated her from the necessity of maintaining the ingratiating, self-effacing façade that had been her lifelong defense.

The suffering experienced by Norma has frequently been referred to as "masochism" and its motivation, the achievement of pleasure.[1] Theodor Reik summed up "the essence and aim" of masochism as "victory through defeat," stating, "The masochistic character has expanded its suffering to cover the whole of life. He faithfully believes that misery, humiliation, disgrace will be made up for by what comes afterwards."[2] The "afterwards" reaches out indefinitely to include the time after death, the prize being "future appreciation" and "the praise of posterity."

His concept of "victory through defeat" comes very close to describing the investment in worthlessness, but his theory of the nature of that "victory" bypasses an important issue that Freud referred to in 1927 when he stated, "There is no doubt that there is something in these people that sets itself against their recovery as though it were a danger."[3] That the stake in the investment in worthlessness could only be life or death has been brought home to me by my treatment of Norma and of many other patients. I soon learned that any suggestion that Norma was worthwhile or any experience that might imply it could throw her into a panic by indicating that she was not to blame for her mother's hatred of her. Since she was still convinced that her life depended on her mother's love, such a suggestion would have exposed the uselessness of her struggle to win it and have thus placed her life in jeopardy.

It is not possible to measure with any degree of accuracy the herculean efforts that had commenced in her early childhood and continued throughout her life to promote the illusion that she was unworthy. She had idealized the image of her mother and devalued her self-image in a process that was intended to lay the groundwork for eventually being loved. What might appear on the surface to be a perverse and irrational pattern of behavior on analysis stemmed very logically from her earliest perceptions. Since her life appeared to depend on her mother's love, her safety demanded that she maintain a potentially loving image of her. She therefore tailored her self-image to justify her perception of her mother's negative feelings by establishing her own worthlessness, resting her hope of being loved on the possibility of changing and becoming worthy.

That the investment in worthlessness is essentially a way of maintaining hope, as Reik implied, was corroborated not only by Norma, but by many patients. The "hope" goes far beyond praise or appreciation, however. Whether a child conceived of himself as "a giraffe" or as "a dog that doesn't deserve to be a child," or whether at age thirty or forty or fifty he flagellated himself, insisting that he was "a bastard," "a cheap character," that he was bad, worthless, or inadequate, and developed a self-defeating life-style to prove it, it became evident that he was engaged in the same struggle that Norma's story so dramatically illustrated: to maintain the hope that since his worthlessness had caused his parents to hate him, whenever he changed and became worthy he would be loved.

How little that fantasy is ever allowed to be tested was also established by Norma. Since she unconsciously knew the truth, she had devised a system of self-deception that required the agility of a tightrope walker. If she proved beyond a doubt that she was worthy, she would have exposed that she was not to blame for the way her mother felt about her. On the other hand, if she unequivocally established that she was unworthy of her mother's love, she would have lost the last shred of hope. Either unqualified success, which exposed her intrinsic worth, or abysmal failure, which destroyed all possibility of becoming worthy, threatened her system of self-deception. At any point in her life that either was demonstrated beyond the shadow of a doubt she was in danger of committing suicide. She could therefore not allow the conflict to be resolved; she had to trick herself into living.

The dual function of Norma's façade — to defend her against the fear of being killed and to win love — suggests the complexity of the process of liberation. In one of her last entries she wrote: "This is the whole story — that I was a slave, and now at last I'm free." The courage that she derived from her new understanding freed her from the need to defeat herself and permitted her creativity to come to the fore. That she had not yet given up the struggle, that underlying all her new productivity was the unconscious fantasy that her efforts would be rewarded by her mother's love, became apparent with each new effort. Survival was still experienced in the terms that had been set in early childhood. Only after her fantasy had been exposed again and again was she able to accept that not only had her worthlessness not caused her mother's hatred and her wish to kill her, but the proof of her worth would not win her love. Gradually she was able to abandon her fantasy and the self-deception that had made it impossible for her to discover either her mother's identity or her own. She was then ready to look elsewhere for love and to approach her search for it with maturity.

Chapter 9

The Need for a Distorted
Parental Image

THAT A DISTORTED PARENTAL image may be essential to the psyche's defensive system has emerged with great clarity from both my work with children and my psychoanalytic treatment of adults. The more familiar defensive distortion is the idealization of the parents, which is a universal function of children's fantasies and a dominant factor in neurotic symptomatology, along with the devaluation of the self. Norma herself presented the dynamics of that investment in almost classic terms. When I marveled at the nobility she had ascribed to her mother, she stated, "The nobler I make her, the more understandable it is that she couldn't love me." She devoted her sessions, as she did her life, to establishing her own worthlessness. That these distorted images were a defense against the fear of infanticide and essential elements in the fantasy of eventually winning her parents' love through change was established again and again in the course of her analysis.

It has not been so evident, however, that when there has been a shift from the idealization to the depreciation of the parents, the patient might paradoxically still be dominated by the same defensive fantasy. I have found that when the liberation of the patient's accumulated rage and the establishment of the beginnings of his real identity have led to the exposure of the parents' hostile feelings and the crumbling of the idealized parental image, what has frequently followed has been an equal but opposite distortion. As I have listened to the impassioned and unyielding denunciation of the parents in some instances, I could not help relating its intensity to the previous attacks upon the self, and I suspected that the earlier devaluation of the self and the current devaluation of the parents might serve a similar function. Whereas the patient's efforts to establish his own worthlessness had been part of the fantasy that promised that when he changed his parents would love him, the monstrous transformation of his parents' image appeared to carry with it the demand that they change. Implicit in the attacks was not merely a sense in many instances of the very real wrongs and injustices the patient had suffered, but the belief that if only the parents had wanted to — or even more, if only they still wanted to — they could change and give the patient the love that he had required in the past. Carefully buried was the perception of the parents' limitations and their possible incapacity to fulfill a need that had been set in the patient's early years, when life or death had actually appeared to be the issue. That life still depended on the parents' love was the unspoken conviction that hid behind the attacks. It has been my experience that very often only when a patient has been able to relinquish his devalued self-image for a more realistic one and has succeeded in improving the conditions of his life has he been able to surrender his fantasy of securing his parents' love and, with it, his need to attack them. The reluctance to accept his parents' reality until that point has been reached suggests that a distorted parental image may be an essential factor in the psyche's defensive system.

Integral to that defense appears to be a singular lack of any meaningful curiosity about the dynamics of the parents' personalities. In only rare instances have patients I have known sought out the information that would clarify their parents' feelings and behavior or allowed whatever they knew about them to influence their emotional response on anything more than a superficial level. In a letter written several years after her treatment began, one patient, who knew almost nothing of her parents' backgrounds and evinced even less interest, put the problem very succinctly: "I don't want to grow up and realize that my parents are just goddamn people — because I want to hate them and hate myself and be mean and terrible and hated." And the ending of that statement reveals the secret wish: "because I want to be loved."

To fathom that seeming paradox, it might be helpful to know

that for the first two years of treatment this patient had presented a saintly image of her mother and had assumed that
she herself was responsible for her father's violent rages. Her
own feelings had been rigidly repressed, and when they came
tumbling out, they were understandably intense. That the
hope of eventually being loved was still tied to maintaining
hate suggests that acceptance of her parents' limitations would
inevitably have meant, not only relinquishing that hope for
the present and the future, but acknowledging that she could
not reach into the past and transform the hatred of those early
years into love. When her improved self-image and her more
gratifying life-style allowed her to abandon her investment in
winning her parents' love, her previous underlying conviction
— that she couldn't survive without it — became dramatically
clear. Her unconscious perception of her parents' personalities
was then allowed to surface, and her expectations and demands to conform to their reality.

Only rarely have I been in a position in which my knowledge
and understanding of the parents of my adult patients have
enabled me to appreciate the scale of the distortion that appeared essential to the patient's defensive system. Because
Norma's journal provided so much information about her
mother's life, her mother's personality and the reasons for
her very real mistreatment of Norma, the measure of her
inability to fulfill a parent's role emerged with some clarity.
As I attempted to see her in perspective during the initial
phases of Norma's treatment, I became aware that Norma's
need to maintain an idealized and potentially loving image of
her had precluded any possibility of establishing her reality
or of understanding the dynamics of her concealed wish for
infanticide. Norma's investment in feelings of worthlessness
in order to explain and justify her mother's hatred had not
only denied Norma's real identity, but had also required the
blotting out of her mother's.

Although Norma was preoccupied with the early conditions
of her mother's life, she rarely allowed herself to establish in
any real way a connection between those conditions and her
mother's personality. To have acknowledged the existence of
cause and effect between her mother's familial environment

and her capacity to love would inevitably have revealed the hopelessness of Norma's struggle. Her refusal to recognize her mother's real identity indicated that she experienced as a danger any challenge either to her own self-image or to her image of her mother. Not until the end of her analysis, when she had freed herself of her worthless self-image and of her conviction that her life depended on her mother's love, could she begin to experience in depth the reality of her mother's feelings or attempt to search for their origins in the details of her mother's life.

In her first efforts to establish her mother's reality, Norma wrote: "I can't think of her without pain; I can't separate her pain from mine. When I try to approach her image, I have to find my way through a dense fog over a vast gray plain that has become so sensitized that every step is an abrasion and the entire area an aching sore. As far back as I can recall I was preoccupied with my mother's unhappiness, blindly and without comprehension. I was an unhappy child, but I was constantly absorbed by the details of her unhappiness."

The "details" started with a scene when her mother was five and was directed to give the only food in the house, a single roll, to her younger sister because she was "only a baby." Norma was to wait several decades before she inadvertently discovered that her mother's concentration on this incident was her secret justification for an extraordinarily tragic occurrence that followed soon after. To present it in Norma's words:

> On a wave of optimism resulting from my analysis, I had planned an assault on the familiar unbreachable wall of silence and told my mother that I'd always considered myself responsible for my baby brother's death. In return I was rewarded with the shocking information that when she was five she had dropped her infant sister, who injured her head and died soon after. The neighbors had accused my mother of killing the baby. "How could they accuse me?" she ended passionately. "I was only a child."

This disclosure of her mother's early tragedy initially merely aroused Norma's indignation that once again her mother's misery had topped hers. It was some years before Norma allowed it to bring into focus some of the dynamics both of her mother's hostility and of the fabric of her mother's personality and the direction of her life.

Norma's mother was the oldest of five, the youngest of whom was fifteen years her junior. The family's poverty forced her to work at an early age and doomed to bitter failure her repeated efforts at an education. Because of her own mother's illness, the care of her younger siblings became her responsibility until her marriage. Norma noted early in her analysis:

> I remember thinking she confused us with them. I didn't realize until this moment she didn't treat us any differently. We were actually all her children. Her brothers and sister communicated a kind of feeling about her that was very similar to what my sisters and brother and I also experienced. It was compounded of awe and respect and contained the same sense of distance one would observe in approaching a religious symbol. I think that for all of us, uncles and aunt alike, it was impossible to get past my mother's virtue; she was the original martyr.

The "martyrdom" of Norma's mother was not far removed dynamically from Norma's "mantle of virtue" and merely reflected in its larger dimensions the enhanced sense of guilt deriving from her actual relationship to the death of her younger sibling. Remembering how profoundly Norma's own relationship to her mother had been affected by, in her case, the unfounded conviction that she had caused her brother's death, we can only speculate about the feelings resulting from the reality of her mother's tragic situation. Not only was Norma's mother dominated by boundless feelings of guilt, but it was reasonable to suppose that her own mother's feelings toward her might also have registered a change following the baby's death. Although Norma's mother's acceptance of a role that amounted to virtual slavery may have been dictated by necessity, it may also have been an attempt at expiation that prevailed throughout her life.

Although we have to rely on speculation to some degree in relation to Norma's mother, an examination of the impact on Norma of her conviction that she was a murderer might also lead us to a better understanding of the dynamics of her mother's feelings. From time to time during her analysis, Norma recalled incidents that appeared to dramatize a feeling for which she had no name. Her earliest recollection of the presence of something strange that appeared to set her apart from other children occurred somewhere between the ages of five and seven. To quote from her journal:

> The children were all playing in front of the house on a late spring or summer afternoon — spring, because Lena Goldstein came along wearing a checked suit. We all loved Lena. She was young and we thought she was very pretty and she smiled very readily, so that whenever we saw her rounding the corner on her return from work we'd stop our play and run towards her. She'd meet us with out-stretched arms, embracing as many of us as could fit, the others crowding in on the children who were lucky. The particular memory which has stuck is one in which I run for a short distance with the other children, then stop shyly and watch with joy as they receive her embrace.

Perhaps we might consider this a very normal response in a child who had never known her mother's embrace, but the quality of Norma's feeling about this memory as well as its further definition in a much later one suggests that we are dealing with something very different. During a later stage in her analysis, she wrote:

> I have always had a feeling of separation from others, a sense of difference, perhaps of not being completely — or at all — identified with their goals and aspirations. I keep thinking of Ada, of her valiant struggle for a relationship with a man that would give her what she wanted, of her wish and need for love. I remember a conversation with her and the sensation of a chasm which her discussion of her experiences or desires immediately defined. As Ada spoke, I recall a curious sense of concentrated effort, a selfless determination to transcend some feeling in order to be where she needed me to be. I didn't keep completely buried my wish also to be preoccupied with similar problems, but I perceived it as though from a great distance. Perhaps it was as though I should say, "This is what I also would want if I were a person like Ada."

The feelings of alienation for which Norma had found no name during the major part of her life may have been a re-

sponse both to her own experience and to the feelings that she
absorbed from her mother. I have frequently found such feelings in children who have been the victims of repeated violence. Early in her analysis, Norma had described the overwhelming shame and humiliation resulting from her brother's
abusive attacks, which she was incapable of warding off. Even
though she recognized the disparity in their sizes and
strengths, she still experienced her continual defeats in her
struggle with him as a measure of her cowardice and worthlessness. Her conviction that she was a murderer may very
likely not only have set her apart from the rest of society, but
may also have served as an unconscious rationalization of both
her brother's physical and her mother's verbal abuse.

Although Norma had frequently found comfort in the
thought that her mother had treated her no worse than she
treated herself, she had never permitted herself either to assess or to question the true nature of her mother's self-neglect.
The details of her mother's familiar house attire presented a
picture of a seriously depressed woman who took no pleasure
in her body and who had never been taught to take care of
herself. From Norma's account of what she knew of her
mother's life, and of her uncles' and aunt's, it is possible to
hypothesize that in addition to all the other determinants that
may have made Norma's mother such a poor mother, she herself had received very inadequate mothering. That she had
been entrusted at the age of five with the care of an infant
might indicate a serious lack of either concern or judgment on
the part of her mother.

Although we can only surmise that Norma's mother experienced feelings of alienation, Norma has supplied us with
enough information to establish a fairly reliable framework.
Her mother was known to have had only one friend prior to
her marriage. During all of Norma's lifetime, there had been
none. Her mother had never exchanged visits with any of her
neighbors and, except for her sister, restricted exchanges of
visits among relatives to two or three a year. Her resulting
isolation was further reinforced by her almost complete lack
of participation in her children's lives. Norma had no memory

of her mother ever visiting her school except at graduations. It was her father who donned his best clothes to deal with the rare problems that arose in that connection, just as it was her father to whom Norma appealed for the purchase of her first doll. When we consider that Norma had only one recollection of ever having a conversation with her mother but mainly recalled her silence, whether alone with her or at the dinner table, the extraordinary degree of her mother's withdrawal becomes apparent.

It would be difficult to gauge the enormity of the effect on a five-year-old of being charged with murder, particularly against a background that must have seemed to her to have provided incontrovertible proof. Just as Norma had interpreted all subsequent events in the light of her expectation of punishment, her mother must have also, but to an extraordinarily intensified degree. Once those feelings of alienation were established, there was little in her family's treatment of her that did not serve to exacerbate them. To have been the oldest child and a girl in a family where poverty dictated the terms and where there was a paucity of loving feelings was to have known the meaning of deprivation and oppression.

The resentment and jealousy that the oldest child may normally feel toward the younger siblings may, in the case of Norma's mother, have thus been enhanced to an unusual degree. Not only did the burden of caring for them fall on her, but it was also her misfortune that the family religion granted importance only to males. Accordingly, although she hungered for an education, only her brothers were taught Hebrew and encouraged to go to school. Norma's aunt, the youngest in the family, also appeared to have no cares and must have seemed to Norma's mother to have led a charmed existence. There was no one in the family whose lot did not seem better than hers and therefore enviable. The resulting vindictiveness and the jealousy that became a consuming force in her life were merely natural consequences of this array of circumstances.

That Norma's mother transferred her feelings of jealousy to her children emerges from Norma's communciations. Since her jealousy, like her rage, was never given free expression, however, we are left to establish it mainly by its unmistakable imprint. The scene in which she ended all spontaneous expression of affection between her husband and her children raises the question of the identity of her target. Since she herself never kissed her children and therefore never received their kisses, she may well have envied him their embraces. On another level, she may have competed with them for his affection, as she had competed with her siblings for her father's.

That the jealousy that originally belongs to siblings should be transferred to children is a frequent occurrence in my experience and may be less strange than it appears. At some point I became aware that early sibling relationships may, under certain circumstances, determine the character of the parent-child relationship. In many instances, which I shall discuss later, where the parents had a strong, frequently pre-Oedipal fixation on the parent of the opposite sex, they not only projected the image of that parent onto their mates, but in order to reinforce that projection they experienced their children as siblings. We can therefore speculate that Norma's mother may have fallen into this category and have found in her youngest child the focus of the jealousy that was originally directed at her youngest sibling.

It was in the nature of Norma's problem that she could not allow herself to perceive her mother's jealousy. Even after she had confronted her mother's hostile feelings and had accepted their reality, she did not permit any broad inquiry into their origins. It was only by chance that very late in her analysis an uncle disclosed to her that her father had adored her as a young child. For the first time Norma permitted herself to weigh the possibility of her mother's jealousy. Her mother's mockery of her father's show of affection had by necessity remained unexplained, as had all her mother's other expressions of hostility. To have recognized that jealousy played a role in her mother's — or her brother's — hatred would have exposed Norma's system of self-deception. The admission that her father not only loved but favored her would have established that she was lovable and thus intensified her sense of danger by exposing her mother's true feelings. It would have challenged her concept that her worthlessness had provoked her mother's concealed wish to kill her and robbed her of any hope of eventually winning her love. She therefore had to repress it.

Norma's mother's jealousy was directed not only at any expression of affection between her children and her husband but at almost every area of their lives. It almost succeeded in preventing the marriage of her oldest daughter and conveyed to Norma that friendships or any other relationships were undesirable. It also played a paradoxical role in relation to their achievement. On the one hand, it was quite clear to Norma that it was her mother who insisted that they obtain a college education. On the other, Norma had no recollection of her mother ever evincing any interest in her progress at school. Any reference to Norma's aspirations was met with sarcasm and disparagement. It was only in relation to her mother's stifling of any interest of her brother's, however, that Norma was able to unleash her most intense expression of outrage and indignation. She wrote:

My mother always played a silent game and revealed herself only at rare intervals. I knew only too well how a simple phrase, a pointed question, a smile that was always acid at its roots and bitter in its comment, could reduce hopes and dreams to ashes, make wishes stillborn and convert all feeling to chaotic rage. I retain one indelible image of my mother, one eyebrow raised, her mouth screwed into the mockery of a smile. Volumes could be written on what she managed to convey with such economic means; it might be simpler to communicate its effect — whatever before had bloomed now withered and turned to dust.

The dimensions of her mother's rage can be measured by what appeared from Norma's description to be conversion symptoms. She described her mother's mystifying seizures during her childhood that left Norma frozen with fear and reduced the family to agonized helplessness. One afternoon, when they were about to terminate a happy family picnic in the park, her mother was suddenly unable to stir. Norma remembered the terror of that moment, but not its resolution. It was followed by a prolonged period when her mother could also not get out of bed. She recalled her mother's anguished cries at what she had interpreted as her father's heartless insistence that she try to walk, but she also remembered that, soon after, the illness had disappeared as mysteriously as it had come. Norma also recalled the severe pains that had partially immobilized her mother's arms. From what we understand of conversion symptoms, it is possible to assume that by this means Norma's mother was defending herself and others against the violence of her rage.

Except for Norma's mother and her Uncle Max, Norma's mother's family were violently acting out and intimidating people. Although Norma remembered seeing her grandfather only twice, the tales of his violent character and his brutal beatings of his rebellious sons suggest the origins of his children's violence. A scene from her childhood in which she watched her aunt mercilessly beat her five-year-old son for getting himself badly sunburned had left an indelible impression. She felt that her Uncle Max had probably withdrawn and concealed his violence in order to curry favor with his father as a protection against his hostile and much more imposing brothers.

Norma's mother's concealed wish for infanticide may therefore be traced to her traumatic childhood, which was marked by feelings of alienation arising from the death of her baby sister and the accusation that she was a murderer, by severe deprivation resulting in enormous quantities of rage, and by exposure to scenes of violence. That she did not respond to her experience of violence by acting out this violence may be ascribed to the effect on her of her baby sister's death. The magical conviction of children in general that their rage is the cause of whatever death occurs in the family was heightened in her case by her actual role and may have necessitated an extraordinary degree of repression.

Norma's unconscious need to perpetuate a potentially loving image of her mother had precluded any possibility of establishing her mother's reality or of understanding the dynamics of her wish for infanticide. When Norma finally allowed herself in the course of her analysis to admit and to experience her mother's hatred of her and her own rage, she was still a long way from acknowledging who her mother really was. Her previous insistence on her mother's nobility was merely transformed into an equally absorbing concentration on her hatefulness. Although Norma's self-image gradually yielded in response to the accumulating evidence of her real identity, her idealized image of her mother, with its concentration on saintliness and martyrdom, exploded with her rage and came together again as a monstrous character. Not until Norma's new sense of self had been consolidated around a new and more gratifying life-style was she ready to relinquish her struggle against her perceptions and to confront and accept the reality of her mother's life and of her resulting bitterness and hostility. Her newly established ego strength then enabled her to give up her fantasy of winning her mother's love and the need for a distorted parental image.

Chapter 10

The Unconscious Fantasy of an Abandoned Child

ALTHOUGH IT HAS NOT BEEN UNUSUAL to find that a patient's life was directed by an unconscious fantasy, it was the case of Jonny that demonstrated for me the relationship between the intensity of the threat of infanticide and the scale of the unconscious fantasy required in order to accommodate it. The effect of the violence to which he had been exposed had already been made evident, but that the completely mystifying course of his life was being dictated by an unconscious fantasy, and what that fantasy actually was, did not become apparent in his treatment until he had gained a sufficient sense of his own identity to reveal it.

Unlike most patients, whose inhibitions may seriously limit or even prevent them from achieving success in any area, he embarked on one career after another, only to abandon each one as he approached the point of professional competence. In retrospect, I realize that part of the confusion I experienced in attempting to understand this phenomenon stemmed from the extraordinary range of his talents. His ability to perform with distinction in whatever art he selected created a smokescreen that effectively concealed his unconscious motivation.

Jonny was an illegitimate child who was referred to me by his adoptive mother in early adolescence. Although there were several interruptions of considerable duration in his treatment, caused by his mother's illness and the family's leaving the city, for over fifteen years I was in a position to learn at first hand about his psychological development and not only to assess the impact of his early experience but finally to help him uncover the unconscious fantasy that had directed his self-defeating behavior. In addition to his verbal communications, the weekly installments of the journal he kept during the last five years of his analysis permitted me to understand his emotional conflicts.

During her first interview, Jonny's adoptive mother told me the following story. All that was known about Jonny was that his father was Irish, or part Irish, and that his mother was Italian and was sixteen when Jonny was born. He spent his first two years in an infant home and was then assigned by the agency, to which he had been delivered at birth, to a foster home, where he remained until he was almost seven. At that time the agency declared the foster parents "unfit" and took Jonny away. Following the separation, Jonny's behavior became a problem of such dimensions that in the next year and a half he was sent to ten different foster homes; in one he was allowed to remain for only one night, in another, a few weeks. He spent the intervals between homes at an agency, mystified, as I learned later, both by what appeared to him to be a routine of being sent away and then being brought back and by the role of the social worker.

When his adoptive parents first saw him, they were enchanted by his charming manner and his handsome face. He was as fair and diminutive as his adoptive mother was tall and dark-complexioned. Both adoptive parents responded immediately to Jonny's poignant request to go home with them. According to his mother, the agency was glad to get rid of him, and the adoption was speedily arranged. There was no counseling from the agency concerning Jonny's care nor any suggestion of the need for therapeutic help. Although friends were so impressed by his uncontrolled behavior that they immediately made such a recommendation, the parents were convinced that all he needed was love. They soon became aware, however, of his unusual responsiveness to music. When a friend who was a violinist offered to teach him the instrument, they therefore readily agreed. What followed amazed everyone. His talent was so extraordinary that a musical career appeared inevitable. He was later admitted to a school that specialized in music, which he was attending at the time of his referral.

The problem that his mother presented was Jonny's inability

to work, either at his academic subjects or his music, which he loved. She also reported that his behavior at home was immature and frequently resulted in what seemed like an excessive amount of destruction. It was not until I had seen Jonny for several weeks that I was able to grasp how much his problems had been understated.

The mother, who was in her late forties when I met her, had been married twice. She had had several miscarriages and had despaired about ever being able to bear a child. Therefore, soon after her second marriage, she had decided to adopt one. She was a librarian and, after her second husband's death, had a hard time making ends meet. The illness that was to strike some years later, and to necessitate her living with her sister in Connecticut, had not yet become evident. Although I never met Jonny's adoptive father, I eventually learned that he was a difficult man who had had little understanding of either his own feelings or Jonny's and who had perpetually urged him to forget the past and to "force" himself if he didn't feel like working. Although Jonny's mother was much more sympathetic, the intensity of her own repression of feeling dictated an equal intolerance of Jonny's. She described Jonny as uncooperative and hostile and warned that he would probably complain a great deal about her. She also spoke admiringly of Jonny's ability to make friends and his capacity to love. I saw her periodically during the first year and a half of Jonny's treatment, and throughout that time her intense anger at Jonny's extremely provocative behavior never outweighed her dedication to helping him.

When I first met Jonny I understood his parents' initial response to him. With his curly blond hair, blue eyes, delicate features, and disarmingly gentle smile, he appeared wraithlike and angelic. His sexual immaturity reinforced the impression created by his size that he was not an adolescent but a child. Without hesitation and with the utmost grace and charm, he launched into an account of his difficulties at school, confining his communications to the current moment. When, after several sessions, I suggested that sometimes past experiences helped illuminate present problems, he appeared to hesitate a moment, and then said, "You know, I'm adopted."

He then proceeded to tell me the following story. He knew that he was an illegitimate child and that his mother was sixteen when he was born, but when he was six and a half, he had been stolen from his parents. He remembered the day very clearly. Some people came and dragged him out of the house while his parents looked on, helplessly weeping. In his desperation he clung so tenaciously to every piece of furniture between his room and the door that time and again they had to pry him loose to get him out. Then they put him in an agency where there was a social worker who was very nice but who continually tried to get rid of him. She kept taking Jonny to new homes that inevitably sent him back. Jonny had thought she might be his mother but didn't want him. Then, after a while, Jonny was adopted.

When he finished, I asked if he would like to hear the story as his mother had told it, and with his assent, I related it. He greeted it with vituperative rage, insisted that he was stolen from his real parents, and refused to acknowledge any inconsistency in his own account. He also castigated a society that not only actually permitted children to be stolen from their parents but condoned such acts. I did not argue any point with him and emphatically agreed on one — I had the impression that these parents had actually loved him and he had loved them. This was confirmed some years later in an entry in his journal when he wrote:

> I like the name Jonathan. The Reillys must have called me that. I like the name and I'm beginning to like the person. I wanted so much to be able to ask someone what I was like as a baby. When I went down to the agency and they told me there was a boy named Jonathan who was there for two years, I knew I was alive. I'm crying, but I'm not crying about being alive. I'm crying about the person who called me "Jonathan." Her voice made me feel loved. It's funny. I knew just how wacked out she was, but I didn't care.

In subsequent sessions, I learned that his first reaction to his separation was to find some way of getting back to the Reillys'. He recalled running away several times in the hope of finding them. The misbehavior that resulted in his repeatedly being returned to the agency was also calculated on one

level to achieve that objective, although on another he was
mystified by the rejections, a confusion that suggests that his
behavior with the Reillys may have already exceeded the
bounds of what was considered acceptable by others. The im-
possibility of achieving his goal, however, became increasingly
clear to him.

Even while he was still absorbed in maneuvering to get back
to the Reillys', he was also preoccupied with the other traumatic aspect of his experience: his discovery that his real
mother had abandoned him. In all the years that I knew Jonny,
although he speculated from time to time about his real father,
all his yearning and rage were centered on his mother. We can
only guess, from his interpretation of the social worker's role,
the dimensions of the confusion resulting from the abrupt
disclosure of his origins simultaneously with his violent separation from the people he had assumed were his parents. His
immediate need to establish some form of relatedness to someone in order to secure a minimal sense of safety was revealed
by his assumption that perhaps the social worker was his
mother and didn't want him. In the further hope of finding his
mother, he then turned to examining the face of every woman
he encountered. This search also proved unrewarding and with
time seemed to have been relinquished. As I discovered years
later, however, it merely went underground where, as an unconscious fantasy, it became the governing force in Jonny's
life.

The scale and the intensity of that unconscious fantasy were
also reflected in other defenses that Jonny required in order
to deal with a fear of infanticide of extraordinary dimensions.
Not only did rejection in his case spell abandonment, but, as
Jonny saw it, the violence with which that was accomplished
represented not merely one person's wish to kill but a whole
society's. Since it is not unusual for children, or even adults,
who leave for whatever reason, to feel that they have been left,
it would not be unreasonable to hypothesize that Jonny interpreted his separation from both his real parents and his foster
parents as abandonment. Similarly, we can conjecture that the
violence that accompanied the later separation may have been

projected onto the earlier one and that Jonny experienced the original abandonment as an act of violence.

Only such suppositions make understandable the scale of Jonny's defenses. The self-defeat with which children frequently attempt to justify their parents' feelings assumed a violent character, and the self-punishment involved not only psychological and emotional deprivation but actual physical self-abuse. In order to accommodate a scale of rejection that was magnified immeasurably by violence, and to shore up what little hope he could of eventually being loved, he had to depreciate his own self-image to an extraordinary degree and to perform acts that would establish his worthlessness. His self-hate was so intense that he took to hitting himself at night, a practice he resumed periodically even in adulthood. As a child he managed always to provoke punishment on his birthday and so be denied the planned celebration.

Suicidal fantasies and suicidal acts dominated his life. He constantly courted danger. Whether it was to establish his powers of omnipotence in the face of his terror or to expose himself to bodily injury and possible death, crossing the street became a challenge to his skill and ingenuity. Like a bull-fighter and his intricate capework, he flirted with passing cars to see how close he could come to being hit and yet escape. When, some years later, I had finally impressed him with his unconscious drive to suicide, he reviewed his behavior and counted fourteen different incidents when he had tried to destroy himself in only the recent past. One summer, when his parents took him to visit an aunt in Texas, he repeatedly exposed his right eye to the direct rays of the sun in an effort to blind himself and succeeded in impairing his vision.

Immediately after his final move to New York, he disclosed to me that he had managed to secure a revolver. When I informed him I couldn't treat him as long as he owned one, he pleaded with me for several sessions, insisting that he had to have it but would never use it. Only when he had finally agreed to get rid of it did his investment in its possession become clear. At one point he wrote in his journal: "I don't feel like killing anyone else but myself . . . I'm miserable. I'm glad

I got rid of the gun . . . I felt I was keeping it for my own execution." At another point: "I think one reason I kept and in fact got the gun was nothing to do with killing anyone — but it was meant for me . . . All of a sudden I feel at a loss . . . As long as I had the gun, there was a way out. That does not exist any more . . . Things will have to be solved another way."

Murder was almost as compelling a drive as suicide, but in the main his homicidal wishes were confined to fantasy and dreams. His only memory of actually making such an attempt was when he was around ten. A boy had cheated and then hit him. In a fit of blinding rage, Jonny had gotten his arm around the boy's neck and started squeezing until a policeman came and took him to the police station. As he was choking the boy, he kept thinking, Die, you rat! But he didn't really want to kill him and didn't know why he was doing it.

In order to cope with his terror, he also needed to believe that he had supernatural powers. Both in his waking and his sleeping life he became preoccupied with the fantasy of flying. He imagined himself soaring over cities, observing people far below, and occasionally descending to perform deeds of mercy. Such fantasies not only had sexual connotations, but derived from his feelings of helplessness and the wish to transcend his condition and control the overwhelming forces that had destroyed his security. At a later point in his analysis, he acknowledged, "The main problem I had was not wanting to live in reality." And still later: "Reality reared its beautiful frightening head and said, 'You can live. Like Peter Pan, fly. All you must do is believe.' Well, fly I shall, but it will either be on the ground or in a plane."

The ability to experience and to handle feelings became a major casualty of the traumatic events of Jonny's early years. Whatever his behavior patterns prior to his separation from his foster parents, his response to the violent and incomprehensible manner with which that had been accomplished, accompanied by his abrupt discovery that his original parents had abandoned him, produced in him unmanageable feelings of outrage and humiliation. In addition, the sudden feeling of belonging nowhere made it imperative for him to find a place. Whether it was his recognition that his behavior resulted in the unwillingness of any subsequent foster home to keep him or the persistent rejection by prospective adoptive parents, as he put it in his journal, "I became someone else so I would be liked." Elsewhere he wrote: "I would sell or give away my own feelings for anyone who would take care of and like me."

It would be difficult to estimate the damage to Jonny's psyche from the need to repress and to camouflage his feelings. By the time he was originally referred to me, they were no longer available to him. He had cried every night until he was adopted because he couldn't ask for his "real" parents, but then he had stopped. From that time on he regarded crying as a sign of weakness and not crying a symbol of power. Several weeks after beginning treatment he stated, "Terrible things can happen, but my face never changes. If somebody told me my mother and father died, my face would be the same." At the funeral of a friend who was very dear to him, he felt despair that he couldn't shed a tear. Some years after he had entered treatment, however, he saw a boy thrown from his motorcycle in a collision with a car. He lay bleeding and crying pitifully. Jonny wrote: "I felt the pain of that boy for an instant. The crying still remains in my mind. It cut through me like a beam of light that could enter my body without interference." He felt sick afterward, but rejoiced that he had been able to react.

The feeling that gave him the most trouble, however, was his rage. He had repressed it so successfully that it became completely dissociated and expressed itself in seemingly unmotivated acts. Soon after the session in which he had disclosed his version of his origin, he arrived with a note that he asked me not to look at until after he had left. It read as follows: "I feel lonely depressed and not knowing what to do. I feel like a baby crying for self-pity as if I should not have done it. I just feel miserably and at one point felt like committing suicide. I need help very badly. I can't seem to control myself. I keep crying at times."

When I questioned him about its contents the following session, he told me that while visiting a friend over the weekend he had stolen some money. He then revealed that he stole every day of his life, and that it had started a long time before, when he used what he stole to buy the friendship of other children. Now he didn't know why he did it. When he came in during a following session with a golden figurine that he had just taken and related with righteous indignation the infuriating incident in the shop that had preceded the theft, I commented that he seemed to feel he had a right to steal. He summed up his understanding of a phenomenon, which on one level left him feeling profoundly ashamed and worthless, with the statement: "People have stolen from me; I have a right to steal from them." When I asked him to name what they had stolen, he said without hesitation, "My mother and father." When I pursued it further and asked whether everyone was responsible for it, I drew the reply: "Yes, everyone is, all society is."

As he related one incident of theft after another during the following months, it became apparent that there was a definite pattern to his stealing, and that each time it was precipitated by an incident that filled him with rage and that he experienced as humiliating. Whenever it occurred, for whatever reason, his only recourse was to steal. In his words, it was like "a shot in the arm." He himself compared it to an alcoholic's drive to drink. The aftermath, as his note had indicated, was also, inevitably, depression and suicidal wishes.

Although I succeeded in helping him track down the motivating cause in incident after incident, one particular event finally enabled him to achieve effective insight and to break the pattern of his response. His mother had given a party to which she invited a friend and the friend's daughter, who was Jonny's age. In the course of the evening, Jonny was called upon to play. Each time the girl belittled his performance, asserting that her brother was a better violinist. During his recital of this experience, Jonny maintained a very friendly manner and reiterated how nice the girl was. When he came to the end of the story, however, he related that he had later gone into the bedroom where the coats and pocketbooks had been left and stolen ten dollars from one of them. The theft appeared to be completely unmotivated. Further questioning, however, revealed that the purse from which he had taken the money belonged to the girl's mother.

The effect of this revelation on Jonny was astounding. Since he had been so unaware of his response to the girl's insulting comments, his sudden impulse to steal had been completely mystifying. Now, finally, he realized that his feelings of rage and humiliation were so intolerable to him that he had repressed and dissociated them. It had not occurred to him that he stole for a reason, not, as he had thought, merely because he was just "a cheap character." For the first time he began to understand his behavior and to develop the beginnings of feelings of self-esteem.

More puzzling than his stealing was his investment in self-defeat. Although I was very familiar with that phenomenon, I had not encountered before either the scale or the particular form it took in Jonny's case. The problem that initially brought him into treatment persisted through most of the years that I knew Jonny. At first it appeared to resemble the usual need to establish worthlessness as a means of justifying the parents' hostile feelings and so maintain the hope of eventually securing their love, with its concomitant dependency needs and its avoidance of success.

In retrospect, I now realize it was the extraordinary range of Jonny's talents that repeatedly obscured its meaning even in high school. My first intimation of something strange occurred during the first period of Jonny's analysis when he was clearly on his way to becoming a professional violinist and suddenly decided to switch to the clarinet. I suspected that he was avoiding success for the usual reason — the justification of his mother's rejection of him — but I listened to his rhapsodies about the clarinet and had to admit they seemed convincing. In addition, it soon became apparent that he was equally successful in his choice of a new instrument.

I then lost track of him for a time, but had the impression that he was pursuing his career. When he reappeared after a five-year hiatus, however, I discovered that he had abandoned all thought of music, that he had been married and divorced, and that he had been earning his living as a mechanic. Soon after his reentry into analysis, however, he began to take music lessons again, this time in singing, and once more to train seriously. He stated that since he had been a little boy

his one ambition was to be a singer and at last he was going
to gratify it. He spoke with some bitterness of his adoptive
parents' early disapproval of a singing career and their successful efforts at preventing it. He described once more with
convincing eloquence the feeling of fulfillment he derived from
singing, and once more he underwent intensive training and
showed an equal aptitude for this new field of expression. He
appeared to have some intimation of an unconscious design,
however, when he noted in his journal: "And the stage lights
are up once again, and a new act is about to begin."

Perhaps because Jonny had already resolved some of his
problems and was much more in touch with his feelings, and
for the first time was in continuous psychoanalytic treatment over a long period, his pursuit of singing not only finally
revealed the underlying dynamics that had led him to abort
his previous careers, but exposed the unconscious fantasy that
had directed him. Jonny was also approaching thirty, and the
sense that time was running out also began to goad him. For
a while Jonny was once more carried along by the intoxication
of developing his new talent. In less than a year, however, he
noted in his journal: "My teacher again said, 'You are going
to be a singer.' Anyone else with this news would be ecstatic.
I, no. It seems as though, with all the fighting I have been
doing, to avoid doing well has not worked. Such despair. Feel
like running, hiding, killing myself."

A little over a month later, he noted: "My lesson was great.
I feel it getting closer and closer. The dream of really singing
is so near, it is as though not too long ago I had wondered
what it was that I was going after, but now I have the tiger by
the tail, and I shall not let loose." Surprisingly, however, in
the same entry he added: "I wanted to register for an acting
class today, but I did not."

It soon became clear that history was repeating itself. The
entries in Jonny's journal during the next months read: "Today my teacher said that I should start singing songs. This
scared the daylights out of me. Because it meant that I was
getting closer and closer to being able to sing." A month
later: "This past week has been very difficult. It has evoked
all my fears of succeeding . . . I sometimes want to believe

that this is all a plot to destroy myself." And still later:

> This past Friday I had a very good lesson and also taped it. Saturday morning I listened to it. From that time until this evening I have been in and out of a depression. What the cause, I am not sure. (1) It could be that I liked my voice. (2) That I didn't and I was disappointed that it still sounded like me and since I hate myself that was all I needed. (3) That it really did displease me . . . I cannot get over that you and my teacher like that sound. I sound just like me and I hate it. I wanted another voice.

The following week produced:

> I want to give up singing. Why? I do not know . . . When I think of my singing I get very melancholy. Can it be just that I heard my voice? . . . I have no right to like anything about myself. Because I am not worthy. Why? Because my mother did not find me worthy enough to keep me.

Never before had Jonny pursued a career with such determination or with such awareness of his unconscious drive to defeat himself. His fight to win this time became so intense that the unconscious opposition required a new form and Jonny began to speak of "my little axe lady." He wrote: "When I practice today, I must do well even though I don't want to. I must now exert more pressure against the 'Axe.' 'She' knows that I'm gaining strength . . . There is one way to beat her and that is — write about my feelings, talk them out with you. She *depends* on my not expressing feelings and thus is able to continue the confusion. By bringing thoughts and feelings to the surface, I steal the show from her."

"She" was not easily defeated, however. "I finished my lesson. It was one of the best in a long time . . . I forced 'her' out. She tried to ruin it, but I did not allow it." On the following day:

> I started thinking. Here I am so talented. I could act just as well as anybody. That is when "she" reared her ugly head and tried to depress me. But again I fought back and won. I am a singer. Remember, Jonny? "She," the fiend, would love a whirl at disaster and destruction, like "put a little torment in your life." "She" thrives on self-destruction . . . Friday I had a great lesson. So on

Monday I managed to do everything wrong. "SHE" was doing a
great job. I felt her presence so clearly. She was in the same room.
So today I must not allow it to happen . . . I find it difficult to begin.
I can start to say the past lesson was the best I ever had. We made
a tape. Had some fantastic sounds. The first time I played it back
I was very worried. I did not like it much. I was surprised it
sounded so well. I must learn to really like and to accept myself
(my sound). I must again be very careful today when I practice. I
must not undo. Like not hate . . . I have just finished practicing. I
didn't do too bad. I tried to foul things up a few times, but pulled
myself out of it. But I did ask myself, "Why am I practicing, why
am I working to become a singer?" That's enough to discourage
anyone who's practicing anything . . . If I don't practice I feel like
killing, destroying myself, wasting my life. If I do practice, I get
depressed when I improve and get all hung up over it . . . Some of
the old ways of "SHE" working on me have been abandoned by
"HER." New and more powerful guises are being used . . . "SHE"
is putting up a death struggle to kill me. It is hard to believe that
I can hate myself so much and still know that I am not a bad
person. It all reverts to lack of love. The child saying that maybe
the reason for me not being loved is because I do not deserve it,
that "I" am no good . . . My ears do not want to accept the sound.
They rebel against the past. They do not want "him," the unloved,
unworthy, hated person to emerge. I begin to feel the pains of this
boy who couldn't find love, who if he were anybody else, a girl,
rich, he would indeed be loved; if he were dark, if he had dark hair
and dark eyes . . . Yesterday and this morning I hit myself
unmercifully.

The "axe lady" scored. The acting class to which Jonny had
referred from time to time finally materialized. Although I
clearly recognized once again the presence of the unconscious
need to defeat himself, I was frankly puzzled by certain features of its expression. Usually in my experience, self-defeat
has taken the form of not permitting achievement in any area
or of restricting its scope. To allow one's talent to be developed
to a point of professional competence and then abruptly to
abandon that career for a new one was unprecedented. Jonny
himself offered the usual explanation in another connection,
when, noting his compulsion to lose in tennis, he asked, "Could

it be that I lose because when you lose you are taken care of, just like a child?" Since most children who have been deprived equate being cared for with being loved, independence — or success — frequently means abandoning all hope. Jonny developed the theme still further. "If I were to lose — legitimately," he wrote, "I would know it was because I tried everything, but my opponent was better." "To try everything" and to lose, on a deeper level, meant giving up hope. In most such instances, the issue that is being decided unconsciously is one of life or death.

It was still not apparent, however, why Jonny threw himself into perfecting one career after another only to abandon it at the point of realization. As his conflict about singing began to grow more intense, I again called to his attention the pattern that I had observed, and just before his actual switch to acting it finally hit home. It would be difficult to communicate the sense of shock with which I heard Jonny finally reveal his secret fantasy during one session: "Whenever I think of making my debut, I picture the audience. Everybody is applauding and suddenly my mother stands up and comes forward to acknowledge me."

At last it all became clear. Jonny had not been able at any point and still could not allow the debut to take place because he knew the fantasy would never be realized. In his early years, as the possibility of returning to his foster parents gradually disappeared, he had defended himself against the terror that had followed his violent separation from them with the fantasy that if only he could make himself visible to his real mother and prove that he was worthy he would be claimed. When his adoptive parents offered him violin lessons, he unconsciously seized on them as an opportunity to achieve "visibility" and proceeded to work toward that goal. At another point he surprised me by coming in with the shortest crew cut I had ever seen. Again, although it was an unusual hair style at that time, with his handsome features and well-shaped head, it was becoming. Only later did he reveal that his unconscious design was to make himself more recognizable to his real mother who had seen him only as a baby, when, of course, he had had little hair.

Following the revelation of his fantasy, he now wrote:

> Here I am in music and want and am driven, attracted to acting.
> For the first time in a situation, I don't feel I'm copping out on
> myself. I am being drawn towards it and I *am* going to follow it. I
> will try not to do it destructively . . . My acting teacher feels great
> things are in store for me. I do not interpret this as fame, glory or
> such, but as aiming at myself, and because of that — boy, am I
> happy hearing that. I feel myself truly in that direction, and not
> only am I anxious for ends, but am delighted with the journey
> itself, as though the journey is the happiness.

His new emphasis on "the journey" rather than on "the ends"
suggests the dimensions of the complicated task that still lay
before him. Although his statement is a conscious acknowl-
edgment of the exposure of his unconscious fantasy and of his
abandonment of his investment in directing all his energy
toward the goal of winning his mother's love, it implies that
he had not yet found any other motivation for achieving
success.

To what extent Jonny's problems were caused by his
mother's abandonment of him at birth, and how much the
agency contributed through its handling of him, is a matter
for speculation. The original assignment to a foster home that
after four and a half years was judged unsuitable raises questions about the method of selecting foster parents. The omission of any apparent instruction to those parents concerning
the revelation of their status to Jonny was a major factor in
his later confusion. In addition, the suddenness and the violence with which the agency carried out the separation produced a trauma from which Jonny never recovered.

The extent of Jonny's self-destructiveness and self-defeat
was a measure of the intensity of his struggle to remain alive
under the conditions thus created. The agency's belated judgment of the foster parents catapulted him in a state of terror
into a world with neither parents nor relatives. Except for the
defenses that the care of his foster parents had helped him
develop, the very foundations for survival appeared to have
been undermined. He therefore had to employ all the ingenuity
his psyche could muster in order to stay alive. Not only did he

find it necessary to assume responsibility for his abandonment — a need shared by all abandoned children in order to promote the illusion that if they changed, their mothers would want them — but in addition he had to transform his personality in order to win new parents.

We also cannot underestimate the effect on Jonny of the violence of his separation from his foster parents. It is possible that he later experienced the violence as coming not only from them but also from his real mother. Maintaining feelings of worthlessness in order both to justify them and to hold out the hope of eventually being loved was therefore not sufficient. In addition, he had to resort to self-destructive behavior involving self-abuse and suicidal acts.

On a conscious level he endowed himself with supernatural powers, and on an unconscious one he defended himself with a fantasy that made it possible to remain alive. Since he felt that his life depended on his mother's finding and acknowledging him, he repeatedly engaged in extraordinary efforts to distinguish himself by proving his worth and by being "seen." Because, unconsciously, he knew his fantasy would never be realized, however, he had to abort every career before the fantasy could be tested. When he felt he was actually coming close to that point, the danger to his life of exposing the fantasy required the additional creation of an inner voice, his "axe lady." Her function of discouraging his efforts at success appeared on the surface to be destructive. Since he felt that his life depended on maintaining his fantasy of being acknowledged by his mother, however, the "axe lady" was another desperate attempt on the part of his psyche to enable him to survive.

We can only speculate about the effectiveness of psychoanalytic treatment in early childhood in resolving the fantasy that later caused so much havoc in Jonny's life. Once the fantasy had become unconscious, a major task of psychoanalytic treatment was to enable Jonny to develop sufficient ego strength to face the reality of his mother's abandonment of him and of her absolute rejection. Only then was he finally able to allow the fantasy to surface so that he could begin to relinquish it.

Chapter 11

A Girl's Obsession with
Marrying Her Father

IN HIS PIONEER STUDY of neurotic illness, Freud concluded that the central causative factor was the Oedipus complex, the universal desire of the son to marry his mother and to kill his father. Although his discovery of the universality of such wishes and feelings was an incalculable contribution to our understanding of psychic functioning, his assignment to them of a nuclear role in the genesis of emotional problems created a formidable obstacle to further exploration for many years. In my own experience with patients, I have found that where the Oedipus complex becomes pathological, it is the result of an imbalance in the familial relationships and is frequently a measure of the parents' hostility. Where children feel loved, they appear to take the Oedipal situation in their stride.

Although I had always suspected that a pathological Oedipus complex might represent a defense against the terror of infanticide, it was not until my treatment of Janet that this concept was dramatically confirmed. When I finally understood her obsessive fantasy of defeating her rival for her father's affection and of then actually marrying him, it was clear that I was being confronted with a response to violence as well as an Oedipus complex. For several years no amount of logic could persuade Janet that fathers in our society do not marry their daughters. Only after analytic treatment had succeeded in diminishing her fear that her father would kill her could she relinquish her fantasy of controlling his violence through seduction.

Janet was a preadolescent who was referred to me because of what appeared to her parents to be increasingly irrational behavior, and her most immediate rival was not her mother but her sister Anne, two years younger. I had already noted in instances where parents reject each other, or where the parent of the same sex is absent for long or frequent periods, that the child's fantasies concerning the availability of the parent of the opposite sex develop without the usual restraints imposed by reality. As I learned later, Janet had no doubt that her parents hated each other and that her mother had absolutely no sexual interest in her father. She and her sister therefore had an open field. She eventually presented her perception of their relationship in these terms: "Women are so much the grasping vine creeping over the cold male who thinks women are cotton candy horrors." How they related to her she summed up in her description of "the nightly ritual," referring to herself as "a beanbag with glazed button eyes, sitting at the dinner table eating dust and drinking mud and getting darted by the two war lords at either end of the table."

Initially, the mystifying factor in Janet's obsessive fantasy of marrying her father was that she did not love him but hated him; not only did she hate him, she lived in daily terror of his abusive attacks, which were mainly verbal where she was concerned, but were physically violent against her brother, who was three years older. Janet remained in treatment until her early twenties, when she and her husband moved to the West Coast, and in all that time her fear apparently froze any expression of tenderness or affection for her father. I therefore concluded at an early stage in her analysis that her determination to marry him was a defense against her terror. This was clarified much later when she recalled taking a shower with him at a time when his erect penis was at just her eye level. Following that memory she became aware that seduction played a major role in her father's way of relating to her and provided her only sense of mastery over him.

Unlike Norma, who had never experienced violence from either parent but unconsciously regarded her brother as the agent of her mother's concealed wishes, Janet's exposure to her father's violence was soon established as a regular part of daily life. Janet also lacked the ameliorating influences of Norma's environment — her father's genuine loving feelings and her mother's complete absorption in the physical care of

the family, which Norma experienced as love. Janet's mother
was ill during part of her childhood, but even when she was
well she left the care of the family to household help. When
Janet was able to confront her feelings about her some years
later, she stated, "She has black insides and no love." Her
father's violence and his seductive charm therefore operated
in an atmosphere that offered little protection. A neurotic
depression with its disguised identity rooted in feelings of
worthlessness, which met Norma's needs, could not accommodate Janet's. Her unalleviated terror had carried her to the
brink of psychosis, and by the time of her referral she was
beginning to find refuge in a psychotic depression.

Because of Janet's age, I had the advantage of periodic contact with her parents, which enabled me to learn at first hand
about them and their relationship both to each other and to
Janet. In addition, circumstances provided me with the opportunity of understanding Janet's experiences through her written communications. About three years after her treatment
began, her family's move to another city made even weekly
visits impractical. After a year of sporadic sessions, she was
able to arrange to see me on a biweekly basis. Since that
scarcely met her needs, she attempted a partial solution by
writing voluminous letters. This correspondence permitted her
a freedom of expression that she had not yet been able to
achieve on the couch and allowed me a glimpse into her emotional life that might otherwise have taken many more years
to acquire. Like Norma's and Jonny's journals, her writing
provides us with a vivid record of her fantasy and her efforts
at survival.

Remembering the Janet of later years, I find it difficult to
summon up that earlier image of a very slight girl with honey-
colored hair, large sad eyes, and set, unsmiling face, frightened
and secretive. Her distracted, unhappy expression and her
ugly school clothes scarcely prepared me for the unusual
beauty that she revealed one day when she came dressed for
a party. Early in her treatment I also noted a curious quality
in her manner of communicating, which took several years to
define. It appeared to be a distillation of concentrated intensity
and yet of distance, of a kind of tonelessness that related not

only to sound but to color, perhaps of a lifelessness that was carefully maintained.

Her mother was a tall, fairly attractive blond woman in her early thirties with a queenly air that proved to be a formidable defense. Her unrelenting affability, her persistent demonstrations of concern and good will, permitted the emergence of not even a shadow of either the rage or the terror that one could only suspect lurked behind that armor. Although, as Janet's treatment liberated her fury, it became very clear that her mother could expect little immediate joy from her daughter's cure beyond the satisfaction of seeing her well, she never wavered in her support of the analysis.

Although she never stated it directly, my monthly sessions with her soon established that she felt she had given birth to an abnormal child, that there was, and always had been, something mystifyingly wrong with Janet. At times, she suggested, Janet's communications did not seem rational. The only hint that Janet's problems might be related in any way to her response to her parents' feelings surfaced only in her reference to Janet's rivalry with her sister. Her husband had originally favored Janet, she stated, but had later transferred his affection. Although a battery of psychological tests revealed a wide gap between Janet's superior intelligence and her functioning, her mother felt that Janet's problems had never interfered with her progress at school nor affected her social relationships.

My first session with Janet's father has always remained vividly with me and contained all the elements with which I became so familiar. He was a lawyer, a tall, heavyset, bearded man in his late thirties, extraordinarily charming, and radiating warmth, candor, and good will. It was therefore with something of a shock that I heard him comment on his way out that he was "a bad character" who sometimes lost his temper. That was the first hint of the explosive violence that both Janet and her mother later reported. During that first session he also volunteered the information that Janet had been left too much with baby sitters during infancy, the only suggestion that Janet's problems were not congenital and, like his wife's, involved the other parent.

I saw him only a few times in the course of Janet's treatment, and beyond the fact that he had one older brother, I learned almost nothing about his background either from him or Janet. I was kept equally in the dark about Janet's mother despite her more frequent visits. Perhaps my own lack of success in penetrating the mystery of her origins explains to some degree Janet's almost complete ignorance of her history. Except to say that she was the youngest of a large midwestern family whom Janet never met, Janet's mother disclosed nothing about herself. Not only were Janet's parents unknown to her, however, but in all the time I knew Janet, she evinced not the slightest curiosity about the factors that could have created their destructive personalities.

Although I have very often been struck by a seeming lack of interest on the part of many patients concerning the kind of life experience that could have produced their parents' way of relating to them, the crucial reason for it was nowhere more clearly demonstrated than in Janet's case. I don't think I have encountered a patient who knew less about her parents' early lives or was less inclined to know more. Her investment in camouflaging both their identities and her own apparently demanded that they remain undefined.

As in most instances, self-deception operated in Janet's case as a way of maintaining the fantasy that it was her worthlessness that had caused them to hate and to want to destroy her, and that as soon as she changed they would love her. Her devalued self-image and her assumption of responsibility for her parents' feelings as well as her idealized parental image served to obscure her parents' limited capacity for love. Her hope of eventually being loved rested on the denial of their reality and of the validity of her perceptions.

At first I was bewildered by a quality in her communications that could not be explained until I realized that it was simply a consistent omission of any reference to herself. It was like being presented with a puzzle that was incapable of solution because the salient pieces were missing. I gradually became aware, however, that her secret conviction that she was the mysterious cause of all that went on in her environment was not only a constant preoccupation and an unverbalized fear, but also a major defense. It was the hidden source of all the questions she brought to her sessions.

There was one girl, for instance, who sat beside her on Monday but on Tuesday selected a seat several rows away. Why? The daily struggle with her sister, which appeared to date from the beginning of time, was reported in a similarly flat, matter-of-fact way. It started with each new day and subsided only during sleep, and then sometimes only partially. They set traps for each other, plotted and betrayed, and constantly sought some new excuse for conflict, which was mainly verbal or confined to spiteful little acts. Janet would not have said it was she who initiated the conflict, only that she was often blamed for it. Neither would she have admitted that she was jealous of Anne or knew that Anne was their father's favorite. Her ideal of feminine beauty, however, invariably took Anne's black hair, dark eyes, and fair skin as its frame of reference. As for their father, it would never at that point have occurred to Janet to admit that she wanted his or anyone else's affection, or that she felt she didn't have it. The marked absence on a conscious level of any defined objective in the all-absorbing competition with Anne was another facet in a way of life that was rooted in a need not to know.

During the first two years of her treatment, her presentation of the nightly turbulence at the dinner table also had the character of a weather report that registered the heat, the humidity, the barometric pressure, and the wind velocity without any reference either to their impact on her or to the dynamics of these seemingly natural phenomena. Just as she never inquired about the source of her father's constant rages, she also accepted her mother's persistent silence at his abusive attacks, which both robbed Janet and her brother and sister of any sense of safety and, further, appeared to lend an air of respectability and appropriateness to his violence.

Although she kept her inner functioning a secret during the initial period of her analysis and only gradually relinquished her constriction and constraint and withdrawal, at first tentatively and then with mounting intensity she finally gave vent to the repressed rage that had kept her paralyzed. It then became clear that no matter how severely she castigated her parents, the direction of her attack inevitably reversed itself and found a more acceptable target — herself. No matter how much she lashed out at them, she invariably ended by insisting it was her worthlessness that made them hate her and offered as incontrovertible proof her intolerable murderous response to their murderous feelings.

"I am a mistake," she wrote, ". . . a great growing octopus that's unwanted and hateful and hating . . . ugly, and ready to explode on people who want to tie me up and stick me in a closet and kill it . . . shut it out of love . . . Love is a stupid illusion. Who loves? No one. Not me, I don't. And no one loves me. Why should they? Just look at what I am!!!"

As I had already noted in other instances in which actual violence had created an overwhelming fear of being killed, self-deception was not confined to psychological reality but was extended to the physical world. Through Janet's correspondence I learned for the first time that the elusive quality that kept nagging at me from the very beginning stemmed from her concentration on maintaining the fantasy that she was invisible. It was with a feeling of recognition that I read: "I feel so uncomfortable with myself whenever I think anyone else knows I'm alive." In further clarification of the device she employed in order to create a feeling of safety, she wrote: "It's really strange that the possibility exists of you seeing the actual people I know, because half the time I have the feeling I'm talking about imaginary people. I think of you as completely separate from my everyday life, and if you should chance to enter it by seeing someone I know, that's strange and scary, because that means I'm a person. I can't get away with pretending I'm invisible, because apparently I'm not." She explained: "I used to think, and sometimes still do, that I'm not real. And only when I thought I and others were not really communicating and being real that they could like me and I could stand them."

In order to establish her reality, sometimes she had to invent exercises for herself: "The other day I couldn't believe I was real, so I had to write down all the things I do that no one else does. Sometimes I wonder who is the person living in this room here, who arranged everything this way, who chose what to do with it. *Someone* did. Must be me. But I have trouble feeling this."

The problem of concealing her own forbidden feelings and of defending herself against her parents' was met by the development of what she called a glaze, stating, "In my family, glaze was essential in order to keep myself together in one piece. It's like a big campaign to have everyone like me and the way to do that is to efface all my qualities good and bad so they won't make people not like me . . . If I'm me, nothing will work — the glaze makes me tolerable to myself — inside it I think I am perfect and pure and I don't think about my humanness."

Such descriptions already heralded the cracking of the "glaze." There were statements at this time such as: "I want to be me all the time with no compromise for anyone." Or, "The whole problem is that it's gotten to the point where I don't even realize the thickness of the wall I've surrounded myself with — although I feel the pain of the vacuum inside . . . I want to believe anything bad I hear about myself and am always busy making up things in addition." At moments, panic ensued and fears of insanity came to the fore. "If I didn't preserve that last ounce of consciousness and control I would really disintegrate," she then wrote. "I just want a big soft answer to everything wrong with me, like a mother!"

The "pain of the vacuum inside" created by the "glaze" drove her at a certain point to toy with drugs. She was attracted to people who smoked marijuana, used mescaline, and took her to parties where heroin was also in evidence. She didn't succumb, however. "I don't even realize what the danger of marijuana is for me — except that I might really screw up problems now by finding a false way out. *That's* the only thing that keeps me from giving in to my curiosity . . ." At a particularly bad time, she stated, "I really feel awful and have started the crimes against myself again which are making me more miserable than I can imagine . . . If I had given in to pot, which I am *not* going to do, I would have been smoking for the past three days." And again, "I've been vaguely thinking about mescaline, but I just realized for the first time *really* that I don't want drug visions because that would wreck the strength and excitement of the ones I already have . . ."

In the service of the fantasy that dictated that she conceal her brilliance and thus justify her parents' feelings, she spent her first two years at college neglecting her work and just getting by. Although she permitted her talents to come through during the next two, she still maneuvered to create academic chaos by allowing papers and examinations to pile up. She wrote at this time: "The more I realize how completely deranged I could let myself be, the less I am able to let myself approach it . . . These rather extreme terms (sane, etc.) are not exaggerations of how I feel. So I'm insane and a little foolish to get myself into such a totally unnecessary mess when I could be brilliant and happy." And a month later: "If it weren't for analysis, I'd have been dead long ago — not really, but I would have definitely been insane if I feel I come so close to it even now sometimes. I can look over the edge and not fall in, though."

Suicidal thoughts and wishes were also a frequent preoccupation. She wrote:

> Do you realize what it means to be alive and yet be dead for someone else? What a *curse that is!* My life feels like it's been one long series of smashes on the head. No wonder I want to be dead, or neuter. I'm afraid to think it, but I really do exist — in spite of my father — (and because of him). I'm here and nothing he can do can deny it. He sure tried, or so it seemed. He's not fit to have children. I'm glad I was had, because I don't have to accept this shit, but — It's so easy to be dead. Everyone thinks it takes such guts to commit suicide, which is crap, because all you need is insistent desperation. Which I don't have.

At another time, she wrote: "Tonight I was just thinking that I could never commit suicide — ever — because I love life (trite as the phrase may be)." At a very low point some months later, she added: "No, there must be a better way — like leaving forever . . . the worst thing is I can't stand anybody. Because nothing likes me . . . and if they do, I don't believe it anyway . . ."

Later, when her suicidal impulses again came to the fore, she said, "The whole problem is that I don't want to admit I have any emotions or that I care about anybody because no one cares about me. Parents don't. It's so easy and horrible to sag down and down into a murky mudpile and die and rot and stink." Loneliness, "the anguish of separation from people," the feeling of being deserted or rejected, invariably brought this theme to the fore. "I really want to die," she reiterated. "But I won't do it."

Janet's search for identity appeared to start from scratch, beginning with the very fact of existence, of visibility and reality, of being human and a person. In this connection, her ability to perceive me as a person was a very important factor. At one point, when I revealed my summer plans to her, she responded, "Really, you have graduated in my mind to the full status of a Person! This is a hard thing to allow because it means that: (1) I am also a person. (2) Someone knows me. Before, if I thought anybody knew me well, it would be terrible. But the great thing is finding out that it's not so terrible." A few weeks later, she added, "I really like you quite a lot as a person (now) not just my sounding board. Oh, boy, I feel like a person too!"

An important aspect of my being is clearly presented about a half-year later when she wrote:

> What I would like to do now is go over to a certain attractive boy . . . He's leaving . . . Crap! Now I feel deserted. Can you believe that? I feel deserted when anyone whether I know them or not leaves me alone. Are you still there in that eternal chair? I guess you are. At least I believe you're listening, that you exist from one appointment to the next, as opposed to everyone else in this horrible world who even when they are talking to me have their god damned broad inscrutable (father?) back turned to me . . .

A month later, my status — and hers — were further defined: "Sometimes it helps to think of you as a mother, a real person, and that maybe a real person (I used to think you were a machine or a pillow who didn't even know I was there) could like you. You are really nice and you must like me, judging by things." At another point, she can admit: "You are an unbelievably tremendous help to me" and "I'm gradually beginning to trust you, which, believe me, is miraculous, because

I trust *no one* . . ." And then, tentatively: "I don't really think you'd like it if I wanted you as my mother, because that's a hell of a burden." This was not yet a sustained feeling, however, and in another mood, a month later, she charged me with: "The whole trouble is you, who I don't trust. But then, who have I *ever* trusted?"

She revealed, however: "I'm not *really* so screwed up underneath. All this resistance to you is to make you care enough to turn into my mother and then everything'll be All Right. You should schedule appointments to read my letters. Hope you like them. How could you, actually. All these sickening outpourings. I get sick of hearing other people's . . . But maybe you don't mind because you're doing something for me — " And further: "If I ever recognize that you're human, that'll be a big step, but it's a hell of a lot easier not to."

Her growing awareness of me expressed itself in a concern about the burden of these letters: "I wonder if you mind reading all these letters. I'm afraid of what I want, i.e., I want you to want to read them and that's sticking my neck out pretty far — where the guillotine usually falls (fell)." A half-year later, such compunctions are gone. At the bottom of one brief note, she added: "This is a rude note — I wonder if it's all right to be rude to you." Another letter was addressed to "Miss Dorothy Blah." She also dared to become insistent: "What I wrote . . . about my father and mother is extremely important. Don't forget it! Just this last sentence, a demand on you, makes me feel like *myself* because I am asking you to recognize me as a person and remember something I think is important."

At another time, when she was overburdened by unfulfilled assignments and having to make important decisions regarding being a writer, she projected all her fears onto me: "Either you're a fake or I'm a fool to think you care . . . you are unchangeably another person which means complete alienation and oppression. So stop fooling around and come out for what you are. Parent-type, fake. I hate you for being a shitty fake." Some months later, when for the first time she had allowed herself to express fully her ideas and feelings about writing, she again turned on me, but with a difference, and said: "I have too many of my own ideas (oh, God — am I presuming?) not to get them out in some form — my own vision and feelings about things. What do you think of this? What the hell do you . . . think? You are a mound of silence. God. What do you think of me? Do you like me, do you think I'm worth existing? . . . *Answer* for Christ's sake. Wow. Who the hell am I? The ignored is asking for something."

A very impressive aspect of Janet's struggle for identity — and for love — was the extraordinary energy she brought to it. It is possible that Janet's early memory of her father's love became the igniting force that drove her to find again what she lost when Anne replaced her in his affection. In addition to this early experience, and despite her parents' limited capacity for love, her mother's preference for her brother and her father's for her sister also clearly informed Janet of the nature of her loss.

As one of Janet's letters tells us, however: "Being away from my parents . . . does wonders for my self-image." There is evidence that she made that discovery at a very early age. Although her father was probably correct in ascribing some of her problems to the early absence of her mother and the presence of baby sitters, it was Janet's good fortune that one of them was a very warm, creative woman who loved her and communicated a feeling that Janet later sought to duplicate. Her most dramatic experience of a different self-image occurred, however, as a result of her summers at camp. They were her most joyous memories and provided her with another standard by which she could judge people's responses to her.

As her analysis progressed, she repeatedly placed herself in situations where she might discover what relationships really were and where she fitted in. She wanted to find out about families, how they worked or how they would respond to her, and so for two summers she went to live on a farm.

Her fixation on her father was of such staggering dimensions that it was very fortunate that she brought to its resolution such determination. It affected all her relationships. In order to understand the maze through which she tried to find her way, it is important to grasp fully first of all that she couldn't get it through her head, as she said, that men love women. In addition, she continued under the influence of the early per-

ception that there was no love between her father and mother
and the conviction that if only Anne could be gotten out of the
way her father would be hers.

Her problem with Anne was the first to yield. During the
first years of treatment, she didn't dare seek out girls who
reminded her of her sister in any way; invariably her friendships were repetitions of the cold rejection that she felt she
had experienced at her mother's hands. Her reports of the
social situations in which Anne was present inevitably alluded
to the established fact that nobody noticed Janet at such times,
to Janet's consequent withdrawal in advance, and to the pre-
dicted response from the others present: she was ignored. By
the time she entered college, however, she had thrashed about
with her feelings about Anne and had come to understand her
selection of friends sufficiently to shift to choices whom she
referred to as "softheads," who were no threat to her. They
were clearly modeled after Anne, who, aside from being experienced as more attractive by Janet, was considered by her
to be generally passive and intellectually her inferior.

Boys, however, were her major preoccupation. Her early
relationships with them followed a familiar pattern. She selected boys who were hostile and rejecting, felt paralyzed in
their presence, and routinely blamed herself for whatever went
wrong. There was one exception, a boy who was committed to
another girl at that time. She found herself extraordinarily
free with him. When he broke off with the other girl, however,
Janet's "paralysis" returned.

These relationships inevitably reflected her feelings about
her father. During the early years of her analysis, her sexual
fantasies about him, when broken down, invariably sought to
establish her power over him. Her concept that her father was
also absorbed by the problem of making a choice between her
and Anne was revealed by her response to her parents' temporary separation at a later time. Anne was already engaged
by then, and it appeared the prize was finally Janet's. At that
point it became apparent that she was terrified her fantasy
might be realized. During that entire period, she refused to
see her father and only gradually worked through her obsession. At one point she had a dream in which her father called

for her at school in his car. She entered the car and began to disrobe, then realized that her behavior was inappropriate and put her dress on again.

Her statement "I am afraid of being swallowed up and killed and hated and destroyed by men" is basic to an understanding of her relationships with boys. She became aware of her concept of love in a daydream that she described as follows:

> . . . if I scream the truth of how I feel, he'll hurt me physically as thinking of Dad's pent-up violence every minute. Every time Don hits me in one of these dreams, I try to change the ending to me hitting or walking out on him, but it's never believable that way. If I have the last word, I get very frightened that the other (Don, Dad) will hate me, and that if I let them slug me next time, they'll like me again. I think of love in terms of hitting! I can't recognize that this isn't love!

The boy in the daydream was homosexual, took drugs, and was given to violent forms of behavior.

Her relationships until her last semester at college are best summed up in her own words:

> The boys I know are absolute fags. I guess I like them because I don't want to be a woman, and they aren't very good at making me feel like one . . . But I don't even want to be a person, to exist, so how can I admit I have a body? Especially a female one — if I want to be a boy I can escape myself even more, so I don't have to exist. So I pick boys that are like girls . . . Even though I would never get involved with Marge, but every so often the great desire to have an affair with a girl recurs and I get *scared!* If I ever did I'd hate myself no end. Now suppose you were just a kind of person who thought homo — or at least, bisexuality was okay to try, and you said I should go ahead "if I felt like it" — and I went ahead and got all screwed up. I mean, in other words, I don't know what to do myself, and I listen to you, but who says you're good to listen to?

Such summations already represented the beginnings of her acceptance of femininity, as do speculations like the following:

> I also wonder sometimes how you don't feel terribly burdened with listening to people who want like hell to lean on you and get

answers (like me) and have you run their lives. I'm feeling sort of castrated when I don't feel I'm running my own, like on and off, now. That's probably a very revealing and dangerously unrestrained thing to say, but it just got said. Sometimes I wonder what it would be like to have a penis, and I think it would be great . . . I think I would like being a boy as much as a girl . . . I admire boys too much, and I'm afraid I want to be one. I hardly ever admire girls the way I do boys, because I don't want to be one and don't see good things in being one. Boys have a lot more freedom sex-wise, mainly. They can also grow beards, which is a nice choice to have. Girls have advantages too, though, like wearing colored clothes, having long hair, wearing perfume and letting boys take risks. I don't know if Artie is exactly risking the way he should in this thing with me . . .

From there, it was just a step to: "I've sort of realized that boys are people. I used to think that only girls were . . ." And then: "I found that the minute I admitted to myself I was a woman . . . I wasn't afraid of people. It's a lot of fun — There are all kinds of possibilities, like having children. And I like men, then, too. People look at me. Maybe they look at everyone, but I notice people seeing me — and some of them *always* look." And finally: "Johnny said I was a good woman and that I seemed to enjoy being one. You can't imagine how happy I was to hear that!"

It is important to note that Janet's struggle for her identity as a woman was accompanied by a struggle for identity on all levels and that at its core was the battle to overcome the self-image that she had absorbed from her parents and that helped justify their hatred. A change in the family's fortunes brought them back to the city after their five-year absence and put an end to Janet's correspondence at the same time that it enabled her to resume regular sessions. As I had already learned from her biweekly visits, she was not yet capable of the same freedom of expression in her verbal communication. That took some time. In my presence her projection of the feelings she experienced in relation to her mother resulted for a time in a negative transference. She came in raging, session after session, and imputed to me all her mother's negative responses to her. Gradually, however, as her creative forces were simul-

taneously liberated and a sense of her real identity began to
emerge, other feelings came to the fore. For the first time since
I knew her she was able to release her tears as well as her
rage. She became bolder in defining the area of her interest,
and her persistent search for a viable relationship with a man
finally resulted in success. She found the man she wanted and
married him.

It would be tempting to report that they lived happily ever
after. We might expect, however, that marriage might revive
and crystallize all of Janet's early fears of her father. Although
she married a man who had a capacity for meeting her needs
on all levels, he resembled her father sufficiently for her to
project onto him all her early feelings. It is also not surprising
that her distorted responses to her husband were as tenacious
as her earlier conviction that she could actually marry her
father, and for the same reason. The paranoia resulting from
her terror of her father's actual violence frequently led her
during the early years of her marriage to ascribe hostile in-
tentions to her husband's behavior toward her. Similarly, her
sexual experience with him initially was constricted by her
anticipation of violence. The comment about her daydream
contained in one of her letters continued in force: "I think of
love in terms of hitting." She brought the same determination
and courage, however, to the resolution of her marital problems as she had to her earlier struggle against psychosis, and
forced herself to separate her husband from her father.

Following her marriage, however, I became aware of a new
and unexpected and mystifying development. Janet became a
little girl. Not only did she experience herself as diminutive
in a world of grownups, but as the "bad" girl who had mysteriously provoked her parents' hatred. She searched for disapproval and found it in the nuance of every word or expression.
"I'm bad!" she reiterated session after session. I was frankly
puzzled by this turn of events, but suspected that this new
obsessive fantasy was related in some way to her earlier one,
and that her father, if not both her parents, was involved. The
unyielding insistence that characterized this new image had
all the earmarks of the defense against terror, but I realized
it would be a mistake to ignore the wish that might underlie

the fear. I wondered if it could be a proclaimer of innocence and a denial of sexual maturity, and therefore a protection against her father's — or her husband's — violence and her mother's retaliation. Just prior to and following her marriage, Janet had also begun to write seriously, and I had to allow that this new preoccupation might also be intended to protect her from her mother's jealousy and retaliation.

My analytic experience had already informed me that frequently the investment in trying to turn back the clock is linked with a wish to change the past. Although in the course of Janet's analysis her increasing ego strength had allowed her to abandon the constriction of the "glaze" that had protected her against her terror, to liberate the rage that it had also held in check, and to search for and establish the beginnings of her real identity, it had not yet permitted her to confront her profound yearning for her parents' love. Now, when her marriage proclaimed her maturity, she was suddenly thrown back to that early defense — her "badness" was the cause of her parents' hatred and their wish to kill her, and when she changed, they would love her. Only after patient and persistent confrontation of her fears established an increasing sense of her identity, with its consequent feelings of gratification, could she begin to allow herself to know her parents' reality and to relinquish her investment in winning their love through self-negation. The process that permitted her to detach herself from the early self-concept created by her responses to her parents also enabled her to acknowledge her husband's identity and to separate him from the destructive image of her father.

We have seen in the case of Janet that her response to her mother's concealed wish to kill and her father's violence and threats of violence, undiluted by the feeling of being loved, brought her to the brink of psychosis and resulted in an Oedipal fantasy of extraordinary dimensions. Her fixation on marrying her father, which was stimulated by his seductiveness, defended her against her terror of his violence and her fear of being killed by him. In order to survive she also fantasized that she was nonexistent, invisible, and unreal, engaged in a campaign of self-vilification and self-defeat, and developed a "glaze" designed to hide her true identity from herself as well as from others.

Her entry into psychoanalysis at an early age saved her from psychosis and led to her emergence from her illness by helping her to release her murderous rage and to confront her fantasy. She was then able to establish her reality, her existence as a person, a "human," and her identity as a woman, as well as to liberate her creative energy. Although her marriage revived her terror of her father's violence, which she projected onto her husband, her persistent struggle for health gradually enabled her to separate them. By forcing herself to acknowledge her father's current reality, she was able to defuse her terror of him and to relinquish the fantasy of sexual gratification from him that had defended her against it. Her conviction that her life depended on her parents' love and that her "badness" had caused their hatred and their wish to kill her yielded as her persistent challenge of her fears resulted in the establishment of her real identity.

Chapter 12

The Persistence of Childhood
Fantasies in an Adult

IT IS A RARE EXPERIENCE to find an adult patient entering treatment with her early childhood fantasies intact and available. In the case of Sandra, an only child, who was referred in her early twenties, it was possible to trace back to its specific source and to resolve each of the component parts of the still-current fantasies we found were already well established when she was four and a half. As her analysis unfolded, it became clear that she had maintained the fantasies, which were her original defense against her fear of infanticide, because the terror that had given rise to them was still undiminished. Both the character and the early incidence of the violence that she had experienced in relation to her parents as well as the quality of their loving feelings had apparently rendered a defense of either neurotic or psychotic depression inadequate. In order to provide a minimal sense of safety for herself, she had found refuge in schizophrenia.

Danger was the central issue of Sandra's life. It started in the intimacy of her family and radiated outward to encompass the entire world. It invested both what was seen and what was unseen. Reality had not been large enough to contain it, and so she had blended in an unreal world that became an inseparable part of daily experience. Every area of her life had been shaped to accommodate it, and almost every facet of her personality reflected in some degree its all-pervasive character. To make survival possible she had projected the danger onto imaginary creatures and adopted the fantasy that she was invisible. Fantasy for Sandra had become a way of life and defended her against an ever-present terror.

As far as Sandra recalled, it started when she was three and a half and her parents had bought a candy store in Chicago behind which they made their home. Beyond a vague feeling of something that had come before, which only later began to take on some distinctness, everything else that Sandra knew of her first years was told to her. Three factors became the focus of her attention. Two years before she was born, her brother had died of pneumonia at the age of five, and her mother had revealed: "You would not have been born if he had not died." The other concerned her father, who had been a successful merchant but then went bankrupt. That event and her brother's death had occurred at about the same time as the death of his mother and had brought about what her mother described only as a "change" in her father that she couldn't understand. The third concerned Sandra herself, who had been nursed until she was almost one year old and then, her mother had related to her sadly and accusingly, had vomited every time she saw her mother's breasts.

Sandra was a small but beautifully proportioned girl who, except for the traces of illness in her face, was very attractive. Her appearance was that of an adolescent, her manner of dress very plain and shorn of any decorative function. She wore her blond hair drawn tightly off her face in a knot at the back. Her manner of sitting and lying on the couch was marked by great rigidity and by sudden changes of position in which her arms and legs described unusual angles. She might suddenly clasp her hands behind her neck or the small of her back and maintain them there for several minutes, her legs meanwhile intertwined in a curiously acrobatic way and thrust to the right or the left, her toes outstretched, a general tautness investing her entire frame, which then would give and reorganize itself in an equally rigid manner. She also had a way of drawing in her breath as though to sigh, but then retaining instead of expelling it. Only later did I discover that her concentration on body movement stemmed not only from a continual state of tension but from the need always to keep herself on the alert and ready to go at a moment's notice. My questioning drew the reply: "I could be out of here in ten seconds

flat." Although her communications were always expressed
with great precision, she frequently prefaced them or followed
them with the comment that she knew she wasn't clear or that
she was afraid it wouldn't come out right or that she spoke in
a jumbled way.

She had many disturbing and mystifying symptoms. For
instance, she found it difficult to judge distances. When she
stepped off a curb, she never knew just how far to put her foot
down. She was also confused about the distances of cars or
even of our relative positions in the room. An object might be
five feet away or fifty, she was never sure. She had the same
trouble with time. She couldn't remember if an event had
occurred yesterday or last week or three weeks ago, a year ago
or several years. At times objects had a heightened clarity as
though they "vibrated." Sometimes she had the sensation that
people were behind glass walls and very far away, or she felt
she was floating. She went out of contact and sometimes it was
a week or several weeks before she returned. She was clumsy
and often bruised herself against objects; at work she was sure
to knock into a desk or basket. My questioning elicited the
information that she did not, however, bump into people. She
also couldn't remain in one room for more than a half-hour or
at most an hour at a time.

Relationships were an agony to her. Usually they were
structured so that she sat and listened while the other person
did the talking. She found it very difficult to be with groups
of people because of what she described as the necessity for
"watching," which required her complete concentration and
which she found impossible with more than one or at most two
people at a time. She allowed no detail about the other person
to escape her, but where there were several, she lost the thread
of the conversation and became confused because there was so
much to keep track of. She conceived of relationships as ar-
rangements where she was expected to take care of the other
person. There is one other factor that must be included among
her symptoms. As the weeks progressed, I noted that Sandra
seemingly had no wishes. When I commented on it, however,
she promptly replied that she wanted to be "a ball" and proceeded to give an accurate description of a fetus, a little ball

which, without any apparent human intervention, had all its needs taken care of.

Sandra and her mother had moved from Chicago to New York two years before, after her father's sudden death from a brain hemorrhage, and had settled in a dilapidated part of the city. Her mother, at sixty, appeared to be a monument of helplessness and avoided leaving the house except under Sandra's escort. Conversation with her was an uninterrupted monologue, an endless recitation of all the details that made up her ill-starred and miserable life. At the commencement of her treatment, Sandra experienced their relationship as unbearable.

When Sandra first came to see me, she stated that she was afraid she might end up "staring into space." "Nothing had ever happened" in her life, and she was at a loss to understand why she felt so upset. The "nothing" that had happened appeared at first to center only on her father, whom she described affectionately as "a sweet, helpless and passive man." At that point, her memory of him started with the candy store. He spent most of his time sitting immobile in a dim room and could be roused only by vigorous shaking. He was her playmate. Whenever Sandra's mother was busy, she shunted Sandra in to play with her father, and Sandra pulled and tugged, kicked and pinched him, tweaked his nose and ears until he became aware of her, when they proceeded to play the game that he liked: they were Hansel and Gretel, who were pursued by the witch in the dark forest. Until she was seven or eight and her father took a job for two years, this was their daily activity. When he returned, Sandra, who meanwhile had started playing with children, no longer found this game satisfying, but it was not until she was eleven or twelve that she rebelled. From then until she was sixteen she refused even to talk to him, and she recalled that any contact with him during that period sent her into screaming fits. When Sandra was ten, she made her first real friend, who came to visit and, to Sandra's surprise, indicated that there was something very strange about her father. It had not occurred to Sandra, but it was true; he was strange.

Although Sandra had never thought of her father as

"strange," she was aware of certain definitely strange phenomena in her world. When she first entered treatment, she stated that she had had the impression that when her father was withdrawn he was thinking of her brother, and it frightened her. Sometimes she thought that he was with her brother. She admitted to some peculiar concepts about this brother. For instance, she believed that if she had been born because he had died, then if she died he could return. She conjured up feelings of anger and resentment in him because she had taken his place, and a rage to do away with her so that he could come back. She had created the image of a revolving door with him on the outside and her on the inside. As long as she kept it firmly closed she was safe, but should she relax, he would swing her out and himself in.

In fact, it turned out, Sandra had always lived on very familiar terms with the dead. They assumed peculiar forms and were very dangerous. There were the paper-thin black "shades" whom she had always known; they inhabited the cracks and crevices and in her childhood were especially thick in the dark hallway that led out into the street. The world was alive with them. They were allied to the "creatures that dwelled under the ground" and the "black chiffon things" that were always alert and watchful and could swoop down without warning and attack. *They were all especially bent on destroying children.* Sandra had formulated the only possible way to deal with them: to be so quiet that she would pass unnoticed, but even in that quiet, she also had to remain alert and watchful, ready to spring into action. Any quick movements or unusual display caught their attention. She had to be very careful. When she was four and a half, some workmen gave her a bracelet that they had found while digging next door. Although she wanted it, she had felt obliged to take the safer course of throwing it back into the ground lest she stir up the ire of the "creatures" who might come in pursuit of it.

She had also always believed that all dead people, when they got tired of their graves, came back to stay among the living, and she still believed it, even though on another level she appreciated its absurdity. Several times in the course of her treatment she reported in terror having seen one of these "dead" people, whom she described as rigid and withdrawn. Once it was a man on the street, another time, an instructor at a course or the student who sat next to her, a man in her office or, most recently, a supervisor. Although the "creatures" and the "shades" and the "black chiffon things" had disappeared as her terror diminished in the course of treatment, after each encounter with one of these "beings" they returned. On questioning, it also became apparent that they inspired her with the same feelings that she had experienced in her father's presence when he was withdrawn. At such times she had always been prompted to take some desperate action, to tug him, pinch him, pull his ears or his nose, or hit him on the head until he came back to "life." It was clear that she had always thought of him as "dead" when he was withdrawn and as "alive" when he was in contact; her concept of the ease with which the dead could pass to and from the land of the living stemmed from this impression. It also appeared that the "shades" and the "creatures" and the "black chiffon things" were all related to her father, but how was it possible to reconcile these deadly figments, which were all "especially bent on destroying children," with her "sweet, helpless" image of him?

The perplexing contradiction began to assume some clarity one day when Sandra admitted hesitantly and with a great deal of guilt that she had been a very mean, nasty, and ill-tempered child, given to irrational outbursts of rage, and who from the age of eleven or twelve refused to participate any longer in the games with her father, leaving him to his uninterrupted stupor. When I commented on the unusual circumstance of a "sweet, helpless" man and a raging child, she was suddenly amazed at the memory of another image that had not come up in all that time. At first she recalled merely that, except for the times when they played games, when he was not withdrawn he was a very irascible, ill-tempered man, given to violent outbursts and incapable of brooking any disagreement. Her own rage was clearly provoked and a method of defending herself. This memory was reinforced by her exaggerated responses to a man in her office whose sadism she felt knew no bounds and whose contacts with people were

unmarred by any human feeling. She realized that he reminded her of this other image of her father, which she feared
and hated.

It was difficult for her to acknowledge it, but she then remembered that she had always thought him dangerous. Whenever he cut her hair, for instance, she feared that he would
kill her with the scissors — not intentionally, but only because
they were "handy." As a matter of fact, she had always thought
he would kill her, but inadvertently, if the opportunity presented itself. There was also the memory of their outings in
the park, where he favored a grove of huge trees, dim and
isolated. Although she had never connected this feeling with
her father, at such times she always feared that a woodsman
would step out from behind a tree and kill her with an ax.

As she described this persistent conviction that her father
would kill her, but with the curious modification that it would
be inadvertent or in response to an opportunity, I began to
suspect the existence of an actual incident that she had repressed. Previously she had also spoken of her fear of him
even in his withdrawn state because then "he wouldn't know
it was she." An experience that followed soon after corroborated my suspicions of a traumatic incident and threw additional light on her conviction that she would be murdered.
One day she arrived at her session straight from work in a
greater state of terror than anything I had ever seen. It appeared that that day a new supervisor, a large and rigid
woman, had walked into her office, and Sandra had immediately had the conviction that if a child had been in her path
she would have trampled on him. I immediately recalled the
image she had conjured up when she had spoken of her fear of
her father when he was withdrawn, "because then he wouldn't
know it was she," and was amazed by the realization that I
had always gone along with her presentation of him as seated
when he was withdrawn. Obviously he had moved around.
Taking my cue from her description of this woman, I commented that her father had also moved about with the same
stiff, relentless motion. She replied quickly, "I never let him
come near me when he was like that." That was an astounding
statement in view of the way she had always presented him,

and she herself was taken by surprise. She had no idea where it had come from and could recall no incident that answered such a description. It was clear, however, that her response to the supervisor was a repetition of an early experience.

I continued to probe, to repeat the words she had used, and bit by bit over a number of sessions the following picture emerged. She recalled first of all that her mother had told her that when she was very small, perhaps two or two and a half, she screamed hysterically whenever she was left alone with her father. Then she had an image of his face against the light, the eyes bloodshot and staring, the expression wooden. She remembered a strange kind of movement to which she referred a number of times, very stiff and exaggerated, as though he were expending more energy than he needed. In this memory she placed herself on the floor, with him approaching but at some distance. She also added a distorted mouth and throaty, guttural sounds, but wasn't sure if she was making them up. That was as far as her recollection ever took her and even that underwent periodic repression. Her conviction that her father would kill her because "he wouldn't know it was she" obviously stemmed from such an experience in which his violence appeared uncontrolled but not aimed specifically at her.

Gradually, as Sandra became increasingly aware of the connection between the reappearance of the "black chiffon things" and the terror that was revived by people who reminded her of her father, they disappeared. They were replaced, however, by the sensation of her father's actual presence, impalpable, but nevertheless there. Sandra's interpretation of her father's withdrawn states as "death" and his periods of contact as "life" had led her to regard his actual death as a temporary state from which she had no doubt he would return as soon as he got tired of it. She also lived in continual fear of the rage he would experience on discovering that she did not want him back.

Her unyielding conviction about her father's immortality also brought to the fore her impression of his unmitigated malevolence. His "presence" was betrayed by disaster. This first came to my attention when Sandra developed a foot infection and stated ruefully that her father was "up to his old tricks." It then became clear that whenever Sandra was ill, she was convinced he was "around." Each time she announced his presence and we traced her sensation to some specific unhappy event, it became clearer to her that she was experiencing her old terror of him, and gradually this too disappeared. The most dramatic "shedding" of him occurred in relation to her magical interpretation of her own anticipation of disaster. She arrived at her session one day in what had become by that time a rare state of terror. A cousin had given birth, and although both mother and child were fine, the mother had had an extraordinarily difficult period of labor. The disturbing element for Sandra was not the fact of the difficulty but her own foreknowledge of it. She had kept the pregnancy secret from me because she feared that such a revelation would magically reinforce the possibility of disaster. When I explored the real grounds for her fear, it became clear to her that her cousin's abnormal physical condition had led very naturally to Sandra's anticipation of trouble. She was completely taken aback by this simple cause-and-effect explanation that had nothing to do with her father's powers. Following this session, she stated that for the first time she felt her father was really "gone." Until its sudden disappearance, she had been unaware of a pervasive, scarcely definable sensation that had always been with her. Now for the first time she felt strangely and completely relaxed.

Although it scarcely seems conceivable, Sandra's mother was perhaps even more terrifying than her father. Although Sandra was in a constant rage at her mother at the beginning of treatment, rarely spoke to her, and turned a deaf ear to her endless dronings, once she was helped to reduce the tension between them and stop the outpourings, she rarely made any reference to her. As time went on I began to suspect that Sandra's silence about her early experience with her mother was a barometer of her terror.

Sandra's earliest recollection of her mother was of "a smiling shiny cardboard figure with a bread knife in her hand." Later, she added that sweeping out from behind the figure were "winds of almost hurricane force which threatened destruction." Some years after this addition, she recalled the image of herself as a small child seated in terror with her back against the wall while this huge shiny cardboard figure of her mother with the bread knife glided over the surface of the kitchen floor. Sandra then recalled that this was an actual memory of her mother when she had lost control, seized a knife, and in Sandra's presence whirled about the room making chopping motions in the air.

Sandra never doubted that her mother might kill her. Just as she was convinced that her father would do it because "he wouldn't know it was she," she also felt that her mother would never do it in a premeditated way but impulsively. Sandra was particularly watchful when her mother washed her hair. On these occasions she feared that her mother might just push her head under the water and hold it there until she drowned. Whenever her mother came outside to watch her cross the street when she was very small, Sandra had also assumed it was not for her protection but in the hope of seeing her lying dead in the street, sprawled beneath a car. For years Sandra would not eat any food prepared by her mother but confined her diet to canned goods and salads. She thought of her mother as a witch who could turn happiness into disaster. The idea of what would please her mother immediately called up the image of a bombed-out world in which not a single human being survived.

Sandra finally related this in an uncomprehending way, as though she could not believe the reality of her impressions, much less their validity. She did recall an early childhood incident, when she had asked her mother to choose which animal she would like to be; her mother promptly selected a tiger so that, in her words, she "could eat everyone up." She disclosed that attempts to approach her mother with any of her needs were met by a flood of tears that soon silenced her. Complaints or any reference to problems inevitably unleashed a torrent of memories of misery and disaster that was not spent until her mother's entire life had been dredged through. When provoked to anger, her mother became speechless and could emit only weird sounds.

In exploring Sandra's conviction that her parents not only wanted to kill her but actually would, I discovered that in addition to her response to their violent feelings and the actual threat of violence she experienced from each of them, several other factors played a very important role. When she first voiced her belief that she would be killed, I proposed that she was convinced her parents had killed her brother. She was surprised by my suggestion, but even more surprised that she didn't immediately reject it; it "sounded" right, even though she knew he had died in a hospital. She recalled the strange feeling she experienced whenever her mother spoke of her brother. He was always sickly and whiny, and her mother described how, when he started school and for some time afterward, he insisted that she remain right outside the door of the classroom. In relating this to Sandra, her mother spoke with anger and annoyance, as though she still resented it. Sandra was convinced she didn't love him, and she always felt uneasy when her mother referred to him.

Another factor underlying her conviction that she would be killed was related to the violent Chicago neighborhood in which she had grown up and to the number of people whom she knew who actually were killed. In response to my questioning, she mentioned four right off without thinking and led me to believe that she might come up with additional memories if she gave it time. The earliest occurred when she was four; the man next door, whom she visited often, pushed his wife through the window in a drunken fit of rage and killed her. Then there was the man who was found murdered in an alleyway across the street. Around the corner, a man had clubbed his wife to death, and another killed his wife by throwing acid at her. It didn't seem unusual to Sandra for people to kill each other.

A third factor emerged in the course of her treatment when she and her mother moved from a small brownstone in the city to an apartment house and she expressed a fear of big buildings. When she was a child of five, she stated, she had seen a big building that "quivered away." There was a loud noise and they ran and arrived in time to see the debris. Again, two years later, someone suddenly announced that a building was about to collapse, and again they ran and arrived as the dust was settling. Just before they had left Chicago, she had also gone to a favorite restaurant that she hadn't visited in some time only to find that it too had collapsed. It was clear that the "big buildings" Sandra was afraid of were seen from the vantage point of childhood and were considerably smaller and less substantial than the brick apartment building that was inspiring so much fear. Once again, the detailed description of the frightening experiences of early childhood was followed by a radical alteration in Sandra's physical sensations. For the first time, her neck and shoulders felt relaxed and without tension.

Just as Sandra had responded to her father's murderous feelings by projecting them onto a world that became inhabited by "creatures" and "shades" and "black chiffon things," all of which were "especially bent on destroying children," and by "dead" people who walked the earth at will, she developed another fantasy that was the projection of her mother's equally murderous feelings. When she first came to see me, she reported that one of her problems was her inability to remain in the same room for any length of time, a symptom that actually ruled her life since it determined her choice of job as well as all her other activities. On investigation, it appeared that she feared she would be smothered, that the walls would close in. She had mentioned, as noted earlier, that her mother rebuked her from time to time with the story that, from the age of one, she had always vomited at the sight of her mother's breasts. From this, I was able to reconstruct with her the possible "smothering" sensation that she might have experienced as a nursing infant beneath their weight. In addition, she related that when she was ill as a child, she frequently slept with her mother. At such times she was in terror that her mother would roll over and smother her. Following these explorations, she no longer needed to project the "smothering" sensation onto walls. The symptom disappeared, allowing Sandra to return to school and to find employment that required that she remain in the same room for many hours.

Besides projecting onto the world the dangers that she absorbed from her parents, Sandra defended herself by reducing her vulnerability to attack. She accomplished this by fragmenting her self-image and, like Janet, by creating the fantasy that she was shadowy or even invisible. Early in treatment it became evident that she experienced great anxiety at the necessity of describing anyone, a task that required that she present a unified impression of the person. It developed that the image of herself that she preferred was the memory of her shadowy and splintered reflection in an old blackened mirror of her childhood. Later, when I called attention to the carefully restricted nature of her communications, she admitted that not only were there certain areas she would not discuss with me, but also that she made it a practice in all her relationships always to omit a segment of her experience, usually a different one, so that no person in the world obtained a complete picture of her. As long as nobody "had all the pieces," she felt she was less likely to be destroyed.

The need for self-deception, which had transformed her father into "a sweet, helpless, and passive man" and herself into "a nasty, mean, ill-tempered child," kept her involved, as it had Norma, in establishing a simultaneous image of both her worth and her worthlessness. In order to maintain repression of the knowledge of her parents' murderous feelings, Sandra too had to conceal from herself the equally murderous feelings that they provoked in her. To that end she had to maintain a sense of her worth. The intensity of these feelings was of such magnitude, however, that in order to deal with them she had to resort to extreme measures. The sensitivity to criticism that served Norma and the "glaze" that defended Janet did not suffice.

Sandra defended herself additionally against any awareness of her rage by two alarming physical sensations: "going out of contact" and experiencing the world through "glass walls." At the beginning of treatment, she reported she was unaware of what precipitated these states, which might last for five or six weeks at a time. Each time the symptoms recurred, it was possible to trace their origins to particularly enraging experiences, the inevitable outcome of her carefully structured social situations. Since they were designed to reproduce as faithfully as possible her original relationships with her parents, they kept her in a state of perpetual turmoil. It soon became clear that Sandra's greatest fear was that her accumulated rage would become uncontrollable and that she would kill. Her wish to kill and her fear of killing became so intense at such times that they required a repression that resulted in the eradication of all feeling and left her with the sensation of "going out of contact."

There is also no doubt that experiencing the world behind "glass walls" served a similar function: to protect the environment from her murderous impulses. *Webster's* defines a wall as "a structure . . . intended for defense or security." If we speculate about what or whom Sandra was trying to "defend" by her "walls," we know from the precipitating incident each time she experienced "glass walls" sensations that it was clearly not herself but "the world." But why "glass"? Two major properties of ordinary glass are transparency and fragility. Apparently both were necessary for Sandra's purposes. In order for her to function minimally if she were to place the world behind "walls," they would have to be transparent. Their fragility, however, was probably even more important. If she felt driven to commit mayhem and simultaneously wanted to stop herself, placing the objects of her destructive desires behind something as breakable as glass might assuredly do it. When we consider that Sandra created this fantasy whenever she had an impulse to kill, then it appears that her choice of glass could only have been designed to help her maintain control.

That this is not pure speculation emerges from the information Sandra provided during several sessions. It appears that Sandra's efforts to control her impulse to kill started at a very early age. As great as her fear that her father would kill her, it may have been matched by the terror inspired by her perception that, not only did she wish to kill him, but that, despite her size, she could do so with ease. She described her terror whenever she was shunted in to keep her father company and found him in a catatonic stupor. In order to rouse him so that he could dispel her fear and play with her, she had to "kick and shake and pinch" him. At such times, moved by feelings of fear and frustration and helplessness, she was often tempted to seize some heavy object and hit him over the head with it. That she never yielded to that temptation may have some bearing on her later creation of "glass walls" when she was overwhelmed by a similar impulse to kill.

Sandra's choice of "glass" also appears to have other ramifications. On a number of occasions, when I tried to put her in touch with the rage that was keeping her immobilized, she stated that she felt like "smashing glass." The particular "glass" that immediately came to mind was the storefront of her parents' candy store in Chicago, but that was as far as her associations went. We therefore have to speculate that the temptation to vent her considerable rage at her parents as a child assumed the form of wishing to shatter their store window and was then repressed. The ease with which such a deed could have been accomplished reminds us of the similar challenge her father presented and suggests the degree of control she must have exercised in order to restrain herself. It is therefore possible that whenever she later felt a similarly overwhelming impulse, she unconsciously summoned up that earlier image that had demanded so much control and so kept the "world" safe by placing it behind "glass walls."

As her feelings of rage were exposed and understood in relation to their cause, her right to such feelings and her ability to tolerate them began to be established. At the same time, her need to maintain relationships that inspired so much rage diminished so that the amount of rage with which she had to deal also decreased. The first symptom to go was the "glass walls" sensation. This was accompanied by a less and less frequent need to "go out of contact" and by a briefer duration of such periods. Finally, after about two and a half years, Sandra ruefully stated that she was no longer able to accomplish this feat at all. At most, when her rage overwhelmed her, she felt "distant" and "remote."

As in the case of Norma, simultaneous with Sandra's need to maintain her worth in order to conceal the murderous feelings evoked by her parents was the equal necessity of proving her worthlessness in order to justify her perception of her parents' hatred and of their concealed wish to destroy her. In order to create this worthless image, she had originally explained her father's violence by conceiving of herself as a "mean, nasty, ill-tempered child." She also insisted she never did anything right, and in reality she felt that she should always be doing something else, although it wasn't clear just what that should be. Although she expressed her thoughts with precision, she was convinced that she made little sense. Her extraordinarily accurate perceptions of other people were rejected as distortions at the slightest challenge, with the ready admission that this was merely additional evidence that something was wrong with her. She also avoided any opportunity that might establish her true worth. One time, at a friend's suggestion, she wrote an article. When an editor immediately offered to print it, all further writing stopped.

The intensity of her need to maintain a devalued image of herself and the magnitude of the stake that was involved were dramatically revealed on several occasions. At one point, when I was truly astounded by her tale of how she had managed to secure a college degree despite her terror, I commented on her unusual effectiveness. For weeks after that she lived in a state of panic that warned me of the caution I had to exercise in exposing her system of self-deception and in challenging her fantasy of a devalued identity. When she emerged, we both agreed that "effectiveness" was a dirty word, to be avoided at all costs.

As her fears diminished and she was able to permit herself to be effective, however, an incident occurred that threw into perspective all her previous revelations. She worked at a day care center with a group of very difficult children whom her intuitive approach permitted her to handle with great skill. Although any questioning repeatedly persuaded her that she had found the only possible way of dealing with them, she remained convinced of her inadequacy. One child, for instance, defied all her efforts. When I suggested that perhaps he didn't belong in a day care center, she readily agreed that of course she knew that, but she had assumed that since he had been placed in her group, she should have been able to find a way of handling him. When she referred him to the director, who, after consultation, agreed that she was right and recommended hospitalization, she experienced a profound sense of shock. The suggestion that "she was right," in which not only he, but all the other teachers concurred, plunged her into a state of despair. If she was right, then what she had perceived about her parents was true. The unexpressed hope that her perceptions had always been wrong, that her parents hadn't really wanted to kill her, but that her own worthlessness had produced this image and that at some unspecified time, perhaps when she was no longer worthless, the image would change and they would show her the love and the care for which she had waited — all of this could no longer be maintained.

There was still another ramification to her investment in denying her perceptions, however. The concept that she "should have been able to find a way" led directly back to her father and her conviction that it was her ineffectiveness that prevented her from "finding a way" to make him love her. She assumed complete responsibility for his catatonic withdrawals and reasoned that he would not "go away" if he loved her. Since she could not prevent his withdrawing, in order to "join" him, she engaged in the very serious practice of inducing herself to withdraw, but never succeeded in producing more than a bad headache. Had she been effective, she was convinced she would have discovered a way of either joining her father or of keeping him here. To admit effectiveness therefore meant to admit defeat and to surrender all hope of dealing with her father's withdrawal so that he might love her.

Not until another incident occurred some months later, however, did Sandra's insight into the handling of her perceptions finally liberate her repressed knowledge of her father, freeing her from the world of fantasy in which she had dwelt all her life and from the need to distort her own identity. For some years she had maintained a friendship with an extremely disturbed young man whose need to be taken care of was only too familiar. She experienced any prolonged exposure to his presence as oppressive and traced the feelings of guilt that he instilled back to her own early experience with her father. As with her father, her friend's interest in creating a world of fantasy provided the more enjoyable moments of their relationship. As Sandra became healthier, however, she found his company increasingly intolerable and saw him less and less.

One day he introduced her to a male friend with whom he was planning to live. During the session at which she reported this meeting, Sandra presented her impressions of her friend's relationship very vividly, but without giving it a name. When she met him after an interval of two months, she found him very upset about the impending rupture of the relationship, which he openly described as homosexual. To her amazement, Sandra realized that only after her friend had admitted it could she acknowledge her clear perception of the nature of his relationship. Although she had known it from the very first moment, she had not permitted herself to "know what she knew."

Sandra's realization that she devoted a great part of her energy to concealing what she knew enabled her to recognize its origin in her repression of her knowledge that her father was "crazy" and had wanted to kill her, which she could now freely admit. This new awareness was accompanied by a strangely unfamiliar sensation of relaxation. All the tension that had kept her body in a constant state of motion was gone. She also found herself freed of the necessity to "watch" people. "Knowing" what she knew apparently also meant "seeing" what she saw. She became conscious of what she called "background," that is, her true orientation in space. She saw objects instead of stumbling over them. The lack of coordination that had previously accompanied her movements appeared to be gone. Her ability to experience on a deep level the awareness that her father was "crazy" and had wanted to kill her had at last defined the real source of danger and removed it from the world. The fantasy of another unreal dimension no longer appeared necessary. For the first time in her life she felt safe.

Although Sandra's stake in maintaining both her worth and her worthlessness was presented in the same muffled way all her feelings were, it nevertheless became clear very early in her treatment just what that investment was. Her experiences with both parents had left her at the age of twenty-five with only one conscious wish, to be what she called a ball. On an unconscious level, however, she also tried to structure her relationship with her mother in order to create the illusion of being taken care of, the closest she could come to feeling loved.

At the beginning of her analysis, I began to suspect some
hidden meaning in her method of paying me. Although she
herself was paid once a month, she dutifully handed me my
fee at the end of each session. When I explored it, I discovered
that she was repeating with me a strange ritual that she forced
her mother to perform. She gave her mother all her earnings,
but insisted that each morning her mother dole out to her just
enough for lunch and subway fare.

That the motivating force underlying all of Sandra's defenses was the conviction that survival rested on the hope of
someday winning her parents' love was demonstrated, not only
by her investment in establishing both her worth and her
worthlessness, but by the disaster that threatened when this
system of self-deception appeared to fail. As in the case of
Norma, whenever either her worth or her worthlessness was
in danger of being proven beyond any doubt, her wish for
death came to the fore. Just as all her other feelings were
carefully understated and masked by such terms as "gray" or
"edgy" or "bland" or "drifting" or "numb" and never identified
as anger or despair or depression or terror, her suicidal wishes
were equally camouflaged. At various times, when her rage
became overwhelming and threatened to expose her image of
her worth and to reveal her murderous feelings toward her
parents, she expressed a wish to "fade into the couch" or to
"go through walls" or "float" or "disappear." Similarly, late in
her analysis when her first real wish — to do work that interested her — endangered her image of worthlessness and, with
it, the repressed knowledge of her parents' murderous feelings,
she spoke of her desire "to lie at the bottom of a pool." As she
was able to admit into awareness both her own and her parents' feelings, her symptoms disappeared.

At a point in Sandra's treatment when her major symptoms
had subsided or vanished altogether, I began to suspect that
more than terror was involved in the periodic and persistent
reappearance of the "black chiffon things" and in Sandra's
sensing her father's presence. It became apparent that they
represented not only fear but profound longing. I recalled her
initial presentation of her father as "sweet and helpless," but
it wasn't until she began to discuss a relationship she was

having with a man that I understood the nature and the depth of her involvement with her father. She had selected a man who, she stated unequivocally, she could not have tolerated for a moment if she had had any real fear that he would kill her. She recognized, nevertheless, that his suppressed violence and his silence were sufficient reminders of her father to enable her to re-create the illusion of his presence. She also experienced his frequent absences from the city as she had her father's withdrawals — as death — and his anticipated returns as a continual revival of the hope that her father would come back.

It took another, more gratifying relationship, however, to clarify her persistent attachment to a father who filled her with terror. Although she realized sadly that whenever she tried to summon a fond memory of him, within minutes it was transformed into something unpleasant and menacing, the mystery was not cleared up until one day when her father's image suddenly appeared in the midst of her lovemaking and filled her with rage. She then recalled the sexual excitement she had experienced as a child while lying in bed with her father on one of the many afternoons when they took a nap together. Nothing she had experienced since had recaptured the marvelous sense she had had at that moment of wonderful things about to happen, of transcending reality. Her indignation at his intrusion into her current life and his interference with her pleasure finally dissolved her attachment and her need to revive her image of him. She also was then free to seek mature relationships.

As the cases of Norma and Janet demonstrated, there appears to be a direct relationship between the intensity of the destructiveness of the parental environment and the scale of the fantasies required as a defense. Whereas Norma was able to create a system of self-deception that remained within the framework of reality, Sandra, like Janet, found it necessary to develop defenses that appeared to enable her to transcend it. In her case, the intensity of her parents' violent feelings and the occurrence of actual incidents that could have caused death produced a state of terror of such magnitude that apparently only the symptoms of schizophrenia could accommo-

date it. She created an imaginary world onto which she projected the danger that her father represented and endowed
structures with the threat of smothering that she feared from
her mother. In order to escape attack, she adopted the illusion
that she was shadowy or invisible and continually held herself
in a state of readiness either by training her body to remain
on the alert or by keeping in motion to avoid being a target.
She designed not only her activities but all her relationships
to escape what she experienced as the imminent and ever-
present danger. She further defended herself by going out of
contact or developing the sensation that she was surrounded
by glass walls whenever she felt overwhelmed by her rage.
She thus not only enhanced her sense of safety by concealing
from herself the precipitating cause of her anger and so avoiding identifying her parents as the source, but she also protected them from the possible consequences.

That her early childhood terror had remained undiminished
is traceable both to its early intensity and to the concept of
death that she had formed in response to her father's catatonia.
Since she had always thought of him as "dead" when he was
withdrawn, his actual death did not remove him as a source
of terror. Similarly, her mother's agitated state, which, from
Sandra's description, sounded like psychosis, persisted until
some time after Sandra had entered treatment. Sandra therefore continued to require the same defensive fantasies as an
adult that she had needed as a small child. As she was able to
admit into awareness both her own and her parents' feelings
and as her reexperiencing of them permitted her to separate
the past from the present, the fantasies that had defended her
against both her fear of being killed by her parents and of
killing them in return were resolved.

Chapter 13

The Fear, the Fantasy, and the
Hope of Being Loved

As WE CONTEMPLATE the fantasies presented here, we cannot fail to be impressed by the monumental scale of the patients' struggle to win their parents' love as a primary defense against their fear of infanticide. Depending on the intensity of the violence and the love and on the incidence of traumatic events, in varying degrees they were all afraid their parents would kill them or that they would kill their parents, and they pinned their hope of staying alive on eventually being loved. From Ellie's "monster" to Sandra's "black chiffon things," their fantasies served, not only to master terror, but also, by projecting it onto imaginary creatures, to maintain an idealized image of their parents, from whom it was therefore possible to receive love. The "dog that didn't deserve to be a child," the child who "didn't come out of his mother's stomach," and the array of "worthless" people who otherwise would have been loved by their "noble" parents all attempted to explain and justify their perception of their parents' hostile and aggressive feelings by blaming themselves. Their implicit hope, since their worthlessness had provoked those feelings, that whenever they changed and became worthy they would be loved can be found even among the children who attempted suicide and the abused children who later committed murder.

This delusion both sustained them and perpetuated their suffering. My treatment of adult patients frequently revealed that it invested their entire lives and eclipsed time and reality. In its service, infancy remained the anchor of their being, life was made to seem eternal and age meaningless. The passing years were only dimly noted and the reality of death itself scarcely entered their awareness. Even the eventual knowledge that their parents had already died was carefully buried so that survival, which was still experienced as dependent on their love, was not threatened.

The hope of being loved was such an essential part of their defense that, to preserve it, they created a system of self-deception that involved the distortion of their parents' and their own identities, a system they maintained by means of fantasy. Their security demanded that they seek within themselves the causes of the parents' anger or hatred or their wish for infanticide. That necessity, along with their magical thinking, made it inevitable that they tailor their image of themselves to explain and justify those feelings. The process that was represented so dramatically by Ellie at three and a half with, "I don't like to think of myself as a giraffe," was revealed in every instance as the method adopted by the psyche to insure its safety. Janet's perception that both parents hated her and wanted her killed found this justification: "Who loves?" she asked. "Not me, I don't. And no one loves me. Why should they? Just look at what I am!" In order to promote their self-deception, attractive people very often insisted that they were ugly, brave people that they were cowardly, the generous and compassionate that they were ungiving and unkind; people with fine minds frequently considered themselves mediocrities and children, inevitably, that they were "bad."

The last outpost of this system of self-deception, with its depreciation of the self-image in the struggle to win love, must surely be the fantasy of being "not human." That fantasy was employed by several patients as a defense against their perception of their parents' hatred. In all the instances presented here, the rejection was reinforced by varying degrees of violence. Norma traced to the ages between five and seven her first awareness of a "nonhuman" identity, which she retained until well into her analysis. Although she never forgot the few times the fantasy had surfaced in the course of her life and continued to speculate about its meaning, she was unable to understand what she described as a "phenomenon." Her memories of allowing herself to enjoy only vicariously the experiences that gave others pleasure continued to recur until one day, to her amazement, she found herself writing: "This is what I also would want if I were a person like Ada."

A second entry defines it more clearly. After an evening of painting, overwhelmed by feelings of loneliness, she wrote:

> I suddenly became conscious of a presence that has continued to haunt me, forcing its anguish, its agonizing self-negation upon me. I don't think I can capture with any degree of accuracy the quality or the content of that pain. I think of it as a creature, defended in every part of itself by a smile, behind which cowers, in supplication and in terror, bloodless and bodiless, a shadow having only the outlines, the appearance of living substance. It denies all — thought, feeling, creativity — and accepts itself as something other, alien not in the sense of being strange or foreign, of belonging to some distant land or people, but of having no connection anywhere, a non-being. Through the years I have from time to time had intimations of this other-state, of the distance that, in the magnitude of its dimension, had transformed quantity into quality and produced an other-being who could only listen and observe and find vicarious enjoyment in the ordinary pleasures, the day-to-day living-in-the-world of the exalted ordinary ones. To be surrounded by love and warmth, the celebration of a family — how could such a one even conceive there was a connection between herself and these evidences of being human?

When we consider the feelings of alienation of the children who were victimized by their parents, we can see the similarity between their response and Norma's. According to her report, the most important factors in establishing her "nonhuman" identity were the bottomless feeling of humiliation and the unalterable sense of helplessness that resulted from her brother's abusive treatment of her, which she felt had her mother's approval.

Although Norma's fantasy of a "nonhuman" identity was confined to the unconscious until late in her analysis, in the case of Patty a similar fantasy was acted out. As I recall my first impression of her, slapping her feet, robot fashion, as she proceeded down the hallway to the playroom, meanwhile maintaining a stream of chatter in a curiously high-pitched artificial voice, and then, once seated, bringing her nose down

to a sheet of paper as though that were the normal distance
for reading or writing, it seems clear that she was responding
to her parents' treatment of her by acting out the identity that
she felt explained and justified it. Her conviction that she was
"not human" defended her against her fear of being killed by
providing the hope that when she became "human" she would
be loved. Her inability to resolve the fantasy of "the dog that
didn't deserve to be a child" by becoming a "child" suggests
that she perceived the near-hopelessness of her struggle.

It is also possible that Bill Hierens, who was brutalized
as a child and killed three people, was also acting out a "nonhuman" identity. That he experienced himself as "nonhuman"
is established in the following entry in his journal: "Just who
am I? I begin to wonder, after all, I could be human as the
rest are, but to myself, I would laugh at such a thought. Others
seem much more superior. In plain words, I think I am a worm
. . . You goddamned nincompoop. Why the hell do you live is
all I can wonder. You're one of the most unworthy persons I've
understood to be able to live."[1]

Implied by this self-image is the hope that if only he were
human, he would be loved. I therefore surmise that his rejection of that possibility defended him against his perception
that even if he achieved that goal his parents would still not
love him. Just as Jonny failed himself in one career after
another in order to maintain the fantasy that his mother would
find him, Hierens needed to believe, and possibly to prove,
that he was "not human" as a way of justifying his parents'
savage treatment of him and of preserving the hope of eventually being loved.

As Patty demonstrated and as Bill Hierens's experience
suggested, where exposure to violence increased the child's
terror beyond a certain magnitude, a fantasy that merely devalued the self and idealized the parent did not suffice. Under
conditions of heightened terror, when life appeared suddenly
to be imperiled, the fantasy of a different identity was acted
out. When Larry saw his father hit his mother and smash
several objects, he felt so threatened that he immediately "became" the all-powerful character he had seen on television.
Mighty Mouse didn't remain a fantasy but was acted out and

adopted as a new identity when the already considerable sense of danger created by his unloving and violent environment was immeasurably heightened by the scene of violence that convinced him he would be killed. The terror of the four children who insisted they belonged to the opposite sex had also passed the point where a fantasied identity would suffice as a defense. As in Larry's case, when a highly threatening incident attacked the defenses they had created to achieve some sense of safety in what they experienced as an already perilous situation, they acted it out.

With most patients, the self-deception usually affected only psychological reality. In instances of extreme terror, however, the perception of physical reality appeared to undergo change. Ellie's cry, "Help! I'm disappearing!" and her report that objects were also "disappearing" occurred during a period of heightened terror. In Larry's announcement that Mighty Mouse was "sitting on his shoulder" there is also a suggestion of a similar distortion. Both Janet and Sandra responded to scenes of violence by creating and acting out the illusion that they were invisible. Norma defended herself with the fantasy that inside of her she carried the door to the roof, which was guarded at all times by a jovial dwarf. When Jonny's singing was approaching a performance level that would lead to the exposure of his fantasy that his mother would find and acknowledge him, he created inside himself the "axe lady," whose function was to defend him by defeating his efforts and thus preserve the fantasy.

With many patients, the distortion of the perception of physical reality was not merely confined to the body image. Where the intensity of the terror became even sharper, the perception of the physical environment also underwent change. Janet described her sensations in these terms: "When I let everything frighten me, like loneliness and unreality of friendship, I lose myself in a panic that comes out in wildness and screaming and laughing and feeling sick and empty, and everything looks like papier-mâché and I can't trust anything . . ." Although we can only speculate, it is possible that "papier-mâché" figures were less frightening than real ones. After Danny's terror had been considerably reduced, he also stated about that earlier period: "Everybody was putting on a show for me. You weren't Dorothy Bloch. People were posing as my parents."

Sandra's terror may also be measured by the extent to which her perception of the environment became distorted. The "paper-thin black shades," the "creatures that dwelled under the ground," the "black chiffon things that could swoop down without warning and attack," "all of them especially bent on destroying children," were present by the age of four. When I tried to establish how real the "black chiffon things" were, Sandra stated it was more as though she could see them "out of the corner" of her eye. She also reported that, as a child, she "saw" the various objects of the room assume strange shapes and "move." By the time she entered treatment, her perception of time and space had become wholly unreliable, walls threatened to "close in," she experienced periodic sensations of a "loss of contact" and of "glass walls," and her vision registered "vibrations" where none existed. Whether these physical sensations served only a defensive psychological function or whether they also represented the body's response to an excess of terror, we cannot say. With the reduction of Sandra's terror and the emergence into awareness of her memories of her parents' murderous violence and her experiencing of her own murderous response, they disappeared.

By all these means the psyche sought to defend itself against the fear of infanticide in order to survive. Nothing challenged more forcibly the concept that the devaluation of the self was merely a reflection of the parents' attitudes, or a way of pleasing them by fulfilling their expectations, than what happened when the fantasy failed and exposed the self-deception. The hope of eventually being loved appeared to break down and suicidal thoughts and wishes and even, in some cases, suicidal acts followed. Although all the suicidal patients cited here had known some degree of love, they were also victims of the violence of a parent or an older sibling or of what was experienced as "society." There is also evidence that some chose suicide in order to avoid killing.

When Ellie's defenses began to give way under the barrage of her father's growing violence and her mother's deepening

depression, her fantasies became increasingly suicidal and culminated in her declaration at the age of four: "I'm dead and
I'm at the bottom of a well." Danny came into treatment in a
suicidal state at the age of five, and it took two years before
his terror was sufficiently diminished and his rage liberated
for it to be resolved.

Although it is difficult to pinpoint the beginnings of Norma's
suicidal fantasies, she was aware of them at the age of sixteen
and reported that they were a regular part of her dream life
following her divorce. The protective character of her fantasy
— that her worthlessness had caused her mother's hatred and
that she would be loved as soon as she changed — was demonstrated whenever unbearable criticism threatened to establish her worthlessness beyond any doubt and thus to erase all
hope of ever becoming worthy enough to be loved. It was at
those times that the sudden pressure to act on her suicidal
impulses brought her into analysis. As with all the other suicidal patients discussed here, violent abuse had been a dominant element in her life. Although she had experienced it
mainly in relation to her brother, her mother's failure to protect her convinced her that he was simply carrying out her
wishes. We also cannot ignore the possibility that her preoccupation with suicide may have been a means of defending
her against the mounting intensity of her rage and the homicidal impulses elicited by those critical attacks.

With Donald, who actually attempted to kill himself, the
importance of the investment in securing love as a defense
against violence and against the fear of both being killed and
killing emerges even more clearly. Because the violence he
experienced was administered directly by his father, it is possible that he was also confronted more directly by the question
that preoccupied Norma: Do I deserve to live? The factors that
had allowed her to continue to debate the issue and to come
into analysis whenever it appeared to be approaching a negative resolution were not present to the same degree in Donald's situation. The joy of being loved by her father, which
ended by the age of six, became an ever-present resource on
which Norma drew throughout the ensuing years. When she
examined the actual emptiness of her life during her analysis,

she referred to the protective fantasy that had helped sustain her as "walking around in a mist of being loved that had no concrete basis in reality." Although there is little evidence that Donald had enjoyed a similar experience, the collapse of his hope of securing love that followed his father's particularly abusive assault and led to his attempt at suicide suggests by his very preoccupation with winning love that he had experienced loving feelings.

The degree of violence and of love appeared to be decisive in determining, not only whether suicide was confined to the level of fantasy or acted out, but whether a child was preoccupied with suicidal or homicidal impulses. The children who were dominated by a wish or an impulse to kill had been the victims of violence in an environment where there was little evidence of love, and they inhibited all fantasy out of a fear of losing control and killing. The importance of loving feelings becomes apparent as soon as we look more closely at the differences in the familial environments of the suicidal and the homicidal patients. A comparison of the parents of Donald with those of the abused children who were preoccupied with homicidal impulses reveals the decisive role played by the parents in each instance.

Despite their emotional problems, Donald's parents were devoted to their children. Although Donald's father projected onto his son the hatred he felt toward his older brother, it must have been clear to Donald that his father was an honest, well-intentioned man and also had good feelings. His mother also, despite her withdrawal and the undoubted hostility that hid behind her self-effacing façade, wanted the best for her children and demonstrated it in her less than effectual but nonetheless single-minded dedication to their needs. Nevertheless, her failure to communicate sufficient love to persuade Donald that he was worthy enough to live left him with almost no hope when his father's violence convinced him that he would never love him. Since Donald's suicide attempt did not succeed, however, we can suspect that he had not given up all hope of being loved, and that being found in time may have been an unconscious part of his plan and represented a desperate, last-ditch effort to win love — and, as it turned out, a very effective one. His parents were profoundly shocked, brought him into treatment, and examined, with a view to changing, their way of relating to Donald that could have precipitated his action.

The parents of the abused children who were preoccupied with controlling homicidal impulses, on the other hand, had very different qualities and resembled in two respects the parents of the people who had actually committed murder. Not only did one parent physically abuse the child, but in all instances the other parent was either withdrawn or seemingly cold, indifferent, self-involved, or not present. In no case did the child feel loved by either parent. Unlike Norma, who saw her mother as "noble," and Donald, who obviously felt his father's love was desirable if only he could win it, with these children the abusive and hating parent seemed to be unworthy of respect, and in some instances "didn't deserve to live," and the other parent seemed at best passive and neutral. The response to the parents' violence on the part of these children was suggested by the comment of six-and-a-half-year-old Alan, who stated following one of his mother's brutal attacks: "My mother is trying to make me a murderer."

In that connection, an interesting issue arises in relation to Donald. When I had succeeded in helping him release and reverse the direction of his aggressive feelings, he proceeded to verbalize and attempt to act out his wish to kill me, also asserting that I "didn't deserve to live." There is no question that he was transferring to me his accumulated rage at his father and expressed in relation to me exactly the same feelings that Louis had verbalized about his mother. The reversal of the direction of Donald's aggression suggests the possibility that his suicidal impulse, like Norma's, may have been a defense against his impulse to kill, in this instance, his father.

With other patients, I have encountered a similar phenomenon. Two adult patients reported that following enraging contacts with their mothers, which apparently evoked in them a wish to kill, they became suicidal. After listening to another adult patient's veiled attack on her parents, I suggested at the end of the session that she was a very angry woman and would like to commit murder, only to find during her next session that she expressed her complete agreement with my statement and proceeded to speak of "selbst-mord" and to enlarge on what she assumed I had said — that she was suicidal.

In the case of Jonny, who reported fourteen failed suicide attempts in a brief period when his wife's rejection of him had reactivated his early response to his mother's abandonment, there may also have been a reversal of the direction of his rage. "It is hard to believe," he wrote, "that I can hate myself so much and still know that I am not a bad person. It all reverts to lack of love. The child saying that maybe the reason for me not being loved is because I do not deserve it, that 'I' am no good." Although that had become his explanation for his mother's forsaking him at birth, the early experience of feeling loved by his first foster parents was his frame of reference and supplied the fabric of the fantasy that sustained him until analytic treatment helped him to resolve it. Like the strengthening influence of Norma's recollection of her father's love during her first six years, Jonny's vivid memory of having been loved by his first foster parents as well as his adoptive parents' care and concern may also account for both his repeated failure to kill himself and for the fact that he made himself the object of his aggression.

It would be difficult to overestimate the importance of the difference in the choice of a target for their aggressive feelings expressed, on the one hand, by Jonny and Donald and the other suicidal patients, and, on the other, by Louis. The operation of a system of self-deception based on fantasy, which defends the child against his fear of infanticide by ascribing the parents' hostile feelings to his own worthlessness, was still functioning with the former and implies that their hope of eventually being loved was still alive and may therefore have been a decisive factor in their unconscious decision to turn their aggression against themselves. Unlike them, Louis, abused and unloved by either parent, appeared to have abandoned all hope that his mother would ever love him. He made no secret of his hatred of her and rationalized his wish to kill her as a way of improving the world.

Despite appearances, however, there is some reason to believe that the hope of eventually being loved is never entirely extinguished. With the children who inhibited all fantasy and even committed murder, we cannot rule out the possibility that there was still a remnant of a fantasy of a depreciated self-image with its hidden objective — to win love. Even in extreme cases, where there was no memory of being loved, it is possible that the infantile experience of being cared for still functioned as a sustaining force that helped keep the patient alive. It is a very rare individual who does not have this resource to draw upon. We can assume that it is this early experience that usually enables the psychoanalytic process to operate so effectively despite the incidence of later traumas and the exposure to violent and essentially unloving environments.

Just how effectively, we can learn from Janet's experience, which may provide a fitting end to this presentation of the terror of infanticide with which these patients lived and of their valiant struggles to defend themselves by maintaining a hope of being loved through a complex system of self-deception and fantasy. Like all the patients discussed here, she blamed herself for her parents' feelings and dealt with their rejection and the violence that was part of daily living by conceiving of herself as "nonhuman," "a mistake . . . a great growing octopus that's unwanted and hateful and hating." It is a tribute to both the psyche's strength and the therapeutic help provided by psychoanalytic treatment that she was able to triumph over such formidable odds and confront her depreciated self-image and write: "I'm discovering to my infinite relief that I *am* a person . . . And also I am alive . . . and I feel things and I'm getting an idea of what it *means* to be human, which is what I am, so it's good to know all about it."

Chapter 14

Toward a Mature Society

WHEN WE CONSIDER the self-deception and the fantasies with which the children presented here defended themselves against their fear of infanticide and preserved their hope of eventually being loved, we cannot help noting the similarity of the dynamics in all instances. Whether they resorted to depression, psychosis, schizophrenia, or homosexuality, they were all involved in the same struggle; only the dimensions varied. The nomenclature that is generally applied is relevant only insofar as it indicates the severity of the threat to which the child felt exposed and the range of the symptomatology that he therefore required. Whatever constitutional or hereditary factors may also have operated, the child responded to the hating and loving elements in his familial environment by creating a psychological framework for himself that increased his feeling of safety.

From what we could gather about the parents of these children, the pain of their own childhoods appeared to have been later translated into the pain of parenthood. Society had offered them very little that might have enabled them to arrive at a sufficient understanding of their own feelings or a sufficient alleviation of their own emotional problems to make it possible for them to relate to their children's difficulties. The violent and aggressive feelings with which they emerged from their childhoods, whether repressed or acted out, frequently found their targets in their children. Although the knowledge that can break the chain of psychological trauma transmitted from one generation to the next has existed for some time, it has not been available to most people.

The reasons for that are somewhat more complex than the

usual explanations for the lag between knowledge and application. Not too long ago, the stigma attached to psychoanalysis exposed patients to suspicions of insanity and abnormality and often gave rise to conspiratorial secrecy about any such involvement. As its effectiveness began to be established, its prohibitive cost automatically restricted it to the very few. Social agencies then attempted to make psychoanalytic counseling available to poorer people and a considerably diluted version of its principles filtered down into the schools in the form of child guidance. During this period, for the most part, only those in dire distress were thought to require help. Even now, in most school situations, it is the children whose emotional problems have severely affected their ability to learn or to function in harmony with the school environment who are even considered candidates for whatever help is available. For the rest of the school population, very little is provided.

It is only recently that large numbers of observers, without defining what has become increasingly apparent — that most forms of emotional "illness" are simply manifestations of psychic functioning under varying degrees of stress — have accepted the possibility that psychoanalytic treatment may have universal applicability. When we contemplate the complexities of psychic development — the magical thinking with which the child emerges from infancy, the resulting feelings of omnipotence and the assumption of responsibility for all traumatic events, the fear of infanticide and the system of self-deception that requires that he idealize the parental image and devalue his own — the concept that everyone may need assistance in establishing his true identity is scarcely arguable.

It is possible that the time may be approaching when the difficulty no longer consists of recognizing the need but of finding the means to accommodate it. The problem appears to be two-pronged. One aspect involves the values of our society and its readiness to acknowledge the importance of emotional health; the other, the actual mechanics of providing psychoanalytic help on a mass scale. Of the two, the latter is by far the simpler. It is becoming increasingly evident that the classroom may be the place where a child may gain the emotional understanding he requires in order to become a mature and effective human being with a capacity to enjoy the important relationships of his life, including parenthood. Whether teachers are trained to perform that role or whether professional therapists conduct group therapy sessions as a regular part of the school curriculum, the school appears to be the natural center for what has come to be known as "emotional education." When we consider that the original concept of education as "book learning" has been expanded to include kindergarten and nursery school, physical education, the arts, and Dewey's theory of "learning through doing," it is not too farfetched to envision a time when emotional education may be an integral part of the school experience.

The more serious obstacle lies elsewhere. At a time of mounting tensions, the budget for minimal programs of child guidance in a school system as beset by problems as New York City's has been reduced to the point of tokenism. The first major breakthrough in the official recognition of the importance of meeting the emotional needs of preschool children, the federally funded Head Start program, was tragically scuttled before it was able to demonstrate to the general public its overriding necessity. The cost of this neglect must inevitably lead to a change in priorities, to the public demand that funds earmarked for the destruction of human beings be diverted for their growth instead. We may then look forward to a society where children need no longer waste themselves in self-depreciation but may enjoy their true identities, with all the benefits to mankind that would automatically accrue from such a maturing of society.

REFERENCES

INTRODUCTION
Fantasy and the Child's Fear of Infanticide (pages 1–14)

1. Sigmund Freud, "The Relation of the Poet to Day-Dreaming," in *Collected Papers*, vol. 4 (London: Hogarth Press, 1925).
2. Melanie Klein, "The Early Development of Conscience in the Child" (1933), in *Contributions to Psychoanalysis, 1921–1945* (New York: McGraw-Hill, 1964).

CHAPTER 1
"I Don't Like to Think of Myself as a Giraffe": The Fantasy of a Three-Year-Old Girl (pages 17–41)

1. Sigmund Freud, *Letters to Wilhelm Fliess* (New York: Basic Books, 1954), p. 204.

CHAPTER 3
Four Children Who Insisted They Belonged to the Opposite Sex (pages 50–70)

1. Sigmund Freud, "Further Recommendations in the Technique of Psychoanalysis" (1914), in *Collected Papers* (London: Hogarth Press, 1950), vol. 2, p. 370.

CHAPTER 5
The Fantasy of "A Dog That Didn't Deserve to Be a Child" (pages 92–107)

1. Anna Freud, *The Ego and the Mechanisms of Defense* (New York: International Universities Press, 1946).

CHAPTER 6
The Inhibition of Fantasy and the Predisposition to Kill (pages 108–125)

1. Anthony Storr, *Human Aggression* (New York: Atheneum, 1968; Bantam Books, 1970).
2. J. D. McCarthy and F. J. Ebling, eds., *The Natural History of Aggression,* Institute of Biology Symposia #13 (New York: Academic Press, 1964).
3. Paul Schilder, "The Attitude of Murderers Toward Death," *Abnormal and Social Psychology* 31 (1936), no. 3, p. 348.
4. Manfred S. Guttmacher, *The Mind of the Murderer* (New York: Farrar, Straus & Cudahy, 1960).
5. G. M. Duncan, S. H. Frazier, E. M. Litin, A. M. Johnson, and A. J. Barron, "Etiological Factors in First Degree Murder," *Journal of the American Medical Association* 168, no. 13 (November 1958).
6. W. Lindsay Neustatter, *The Mind of the Murderer* (London: Christopher Johnson, 1957).
7. W. Lindsay Neustatter, "The State of Mind in Murder," *Lancet* 1 (April 17, 1965), pp. 861–863.
8. Lucy Freeman, *Before I Kill More* (New York: Crown, 1955).
9. J. Altman and Marvin Ziporyn, *Born to Raise Hell: The Untold Story of Richard Speck* (New York: Grove Press, 1967).
10. Guttmacher, *Mind of the Murderer,* p. 13.
11. Duncan et al., "Etiological Factors," p. 1756.
12. Stuart Palmer, *A Study of Murder* (New York: Thomas Y. Crowell, 1960).
13. Gerald Frank, *The Boston Strangler* (New York: New American Library, 1966).
14. Neustatter, *Mind of the Murderer.*
15. Guttmacher, *Mind of the Murderer.*
16. Lucy Freeman and Wilfred C. Hulse, *Children Who Kill* (New York: Berkley Medallion Books, 1962).
17. Freeman, *Before I Kill More,* p. 133.
18. Edwin I. Megargee, "Undercontrolled and Overcontrolled Personality Types in Extreme Antisocial Aggression," *Psychological Monographs* 80, no. 3, whole no. 611, 1966.
19. Neustatter, *Mind of the Murderer,* p. 37.

CHAPTER 7
The Inhibition of Fantasy: A Case of Infantile Autism (pages 126-137)

1. F. J. Kallmann, "Genetics in Relation to Mental Disorder," *Journal of Mental Science* 94 (1948).
2. L. A. Bender, "Twenty Years of Clinical Research on Schizophrenic Children with Special Reference to Those under Six Years of Age," in *Emotional Problems of Early Childhood,* ed. G. Caplan (New York: Basic Books, 1955).
3. M. S. Mahler, "On Child Psychosis and Schizophrenia in Autistic Symbiotic Infantile Psychosis," in *Psychoanalytic Study of the Child,* vol. 7 (New York: International Universities Press, 1952).
4. L. A. Kanner, "Early Infantile Autism," *American Journal of Orthopsychiatry* 19 (1949).
5. Beata Rank, "Intensive Study and Treatment of Pre-school Children Who Show Marked Personality Deviation, or 'Atypical Development,' and Their Parents," in *Emotional Problems of Early Childhood,* ed. G. Caplan (New York: Basic Books, 1955).
6. L. Despert, "Thinking and Motility Disorder in a Schizophrenic Child," *Psychoanalytic Quarterly* 15 (1941).
7. Sigmund Freud, "Beyond the Pleasure Principle," in *Standard Edition of the Complete Psychological Works of Sigmund Freud* (London: The Hogarth Press and the Institute of Psychoanalysis), vol. 18.
8. P. Bergmann and E. Escalona, "Unusual Sensitivities in Very Young Children," *Psychoanalysis and the Psychoanalytic Review* 49, no. 3 (1962).
9. Hyman Spotnitz, "The Need for Insulation in the Schizophrenic Personality," *Psychoanalysis and the Psychoanalytic Review* 49, no. 3 (1962).
10. Hyman Spotnitz, "The Toxoid Response," *Psychoanalytic Review* 50, no. 4 (1963-64).

CHAPTER 8
A Worthless Child and a Noble Parent (pages 141-161)

1. Sigmund Freud, "The Economic Problem in Masochism," in *Collected Papers,* vol. 2 (London: Hogarth Press, 1950).
2. Theodore Reik, *Masochism in Modern Man* (New York: Farrar, Straus, 1941).

3. Sigmund Freud, *The Ego and the Id* (London: Hogarth Press, 1927).

CHAPTER 13
The Fear, the Fantasy, and the Hope of Being Loved (pages 229–239)

1. Lucy Freeman, *Before I Kill More* (New York: Crown, 1955).